REGULATORY
HACKING

REGULATORY HACKING

A Playbook for Startups

EVAN BURFIELD
with J.D. HARRISON

PORTFOLIO / PENGUIN

Portfolio/Penguin
An imprint of Penguin Random House LLC
375 Hudson Street
New York, New York 10014

Most Portfolio books are available at a discount when purchased in quantity for sales promotions or corporate use. Special editions, which include personalized covers, excerpts, and corporate imprints, can be created when purchased in large quantities. For more information, please call (212) 572-2232 or email specialmarkets@penguinrandomhouse.com. Your local bookstore can also assist with discounted bulk purchases using the Penguin Random House corporate Business-to-Business program. For assistance in locating a participating retailer, email B2B@penguinrandomhouse.com.

Library of Congress Cataloging in Publication Data

Names: Burfield, Evan, author.
Title: Regulatory hacking : a playbook for startups / Evan Burfield,
   J. D. Harrison.
Description: New York : Portfolio, 2018.
Identifiers: LCCN 2018012895 | ISBN 9780525533207 (hardback) |
   ISBN 9780525533214 (epub)
Subjects: LCSH: New business enterprises—United States. | New business
   enterprises—Law and legislation—United States. | BISAC: BUSINESS &
   ECONOMICS / Entrepreneurship. | BUSINESS & ECONOMICS / Commercial Policy.
   | BUSINESS & ECONOMICS / Government & Business.
Classification: LCC HD62.5 .B8367 2018 | DDC 658.1/2—dc23
LC record available at https://lccn.loc.gov/2018012895

Printed in the United States of America
10 9 8 7 6 5 4 3 2 1

Book design by Laura K. Corless

While the author has made every effort to provide accurate telephone numbers, internet addresses, and other contact information at the time of publication, neither the publisher nor the author assumes any responsibility for errors, or for changes that occur after publication. Further, the publisher does not have any control over and does not assume any responsibility for author or third-party websites or their content.

This book is dedicated to the founders you will meet in these pages. It has been a privilege and joy to learn from them.

Contents

THE REGULATORY ERA

"Alexa, please play 'Five Little Monkeys' by the Kiboomers," Endeavour, my two-year-old daughter, asks from the backseat. Nothing happens, so she asks again more urgently, before I explain to her that Alexa isn't in our car.

"*Yet*," I think to myself.

Netscape went public the year I graduated from high school, twenty-three years ago. I still remember the anticipation and frustration of watching web pages render line by line through my AOL dial-up connection. Forget about asking an AI voice-enabled assistant to play me music—if I wanted a song I had to dig through my stack of CDs. I met my wife standing in line for a bagel, long before you could swipe right for love.

Today, I have limitless information and entertainment available in my pocket, constant connection to my social and professional networks, and I'm never more than a tap on my iPhone away from dinner, diapers, or a driver arriving at my door. Wherever I am traveling away from home, I sing Endeavour her good-night songs through FaceTime. In the two decades since the digital revolution burst forth promising to change everything, our lives have in fact changed in unbelievable ways.

Except where they haven't.

When I voted in my last election, I stood in line to fill in circles with a pen on a ballot. If I walk into an emergency room tomorrow, I'll fill out paper forms. When I next go to the DMV, I'll need a stack of papers to confirm my identity. When Endeavour starts school in a few years, teachers will present material to her in much the same way that they did to me when I was her age. In some of the most important parts of our lives, *little has changed*.

Every day, in our cities and neighborhoods, we step into not-so-hidden time machines. They're our city halls, our hospitals, our schools. Like a bureaucratic dystopia, they've been lost to time, seemingly untouched by the digital revolution. And what's even scarier is how essential these tech vacuums are to life, liberty, and the pursuit of happiness.

Our lives as consumers have gone digital. Our lives as *citizens* remain stubbornly analog.

The Regulatory Era

This is a book about improving our lives as citizens—in America, and around the world—by building and growing startups in complex, regulated markets that are intertwined with government. Why is this book needed *now*?

We're witnessing the collision of five trends that will cause the next twenty years of the digital revolution to look very different than the last twenty years—in good and important ways.

First, tech startups are diversifying beyond Silicon Valley, both in terms of geography and strengths.

Startup founders tend to solve the problems they know and understand.

For a twenty-five-year-old programmer in Silicon Valley, think about how much life has improved. Goods and services, from toothbrushes to massages, flow to him almost automatically. News and information are at his fingertips. A car is always waiting just around the corner. A hot date could be just a swipe or two away.

Now, think about a lower-middle-class single mom working multiple jobs to make ends meet. Her daily struggles include how to affordably get across town from one worksite to the other, how to pick up her children from school on time, how to put healthy but affordable food on the table, and how to obtain new skills that will help her find a better-paying job. Those twenty-five-year-old programmers in Silicon Valley haven't done nearly as much to help her tackle her problems.

The Valley has been *the* place to build digital startups for most of the past twenty-three years, soaking up more than 25 percent of global venture capital in 2016.[1] Given its dominance, the Valley has driven many of the assumptions about *who* should build startups, *how* they should build them, and *what* they should focus on. The Valley can be a magical place, but it's also far removed from the lives of the other 99.9 percent of the people in the world.

But the world of digital startups is rapidly diversifying. Silicon Valley isn't on the decline—far from it—but the rest of the world is catching up quickly, having systematically studied the Valley model and slowly learned to apply it to their own contexts. This is true across America, and around the world.

Investment Growth by Country, 2010–2016

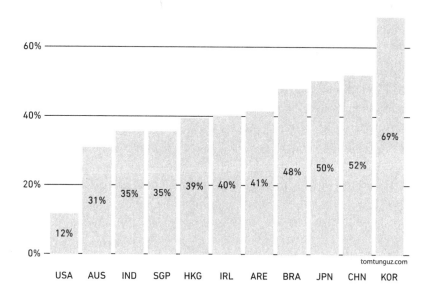

Tomasz Tunguz, a Silicon Valley venture capitalist with Redpoint, produced the chart above,[2] showing the growth rate of venture investment in the ten fastest-growing venture markets, plus the United States, from 2010 to 2016. Venture capital in America is growing at 12 percent per year, but that growth is dwarfed by economies such as India, Ireland, and Korea.

And venture capital is a *trailing* indicator of the growth of startup ecosystems. Communities are receiving increasingly sophisticated support from initiatives such as the Rise of the Rest and the Global Entrepreneurship Network, and the results are starting to show.

Over the past several years, I've worked with startups on the ground in more than fifty cities, across America and spanning six continents, every one of which now has a vibrant startup ecosystem.

Each of these ecosystems has its own culture, economic assets, and talent. Boise and Lincoln aren't going to produce the next Facebook, but their communities understand the gritty details of agricultural production a lot better than the Valley does. Houston and Baltimore might not create the next Netflix, but they have world-class talent in healthcare. This holds true for cities all around the world, most of which have historical strengths in industries that matter more to our lives as citizens than our lives as consumers.

As these startup ecosystems expand, they continue to learn from Silicon Valley in near real time, and in that sense Silicon Valley is more than a place, but a culture that has become pervasive globally. In an even more important way, however, these ecosystems are learning to play to their *own* strengths, not the Valley's. This is creating healthy space for new ideas about *what* problems people should focus on, but also *who* can build those startups and *how* they should go about building them.

Second, the easy problems in tech have been solved.

Marc Andreessen said that "software is eating the world."

That's true, but for the past twenty years, most startups have used their software to eat the low-hanging fruit first, gravitating toward problems they could solve through sheer force of technical or design wizardry. If you can become a billionaire by giving consumers dating apps or subscription cat food services, why not?

But today, most of that low-hanging fruit has been eaten. If you want to figure out a better way than Instagram to share photographs, you're going to have to go through Facebook. If you want to build a service that connects people to their favorite music, get in the ring with Spotify, Tidal, Amazon, and Google.

As Steve Case explores in his 2016 book *The Third Wave*, founders who want to solve new problems are increasingly looking to industries that are still in the infancy of their digital transformations, and most of those industries are intertwined with government.

Third, we're seeing a backlash against big tech.

As a twenty-five-year-old, Mark Zuckerberg famously declared that "privacy is no longer a social norm." Eight years later, when issuing his "personal challenge" for 2018, he pledged to address sharp criticism of Facebook: "The world feels anxious and divided, and Facebook has a lot of work to do— whether it's protecting our community from abuse and hate, defending against interference by nation-states, or making sure that time spent on Facebook is time well spent."

Those are the words of a leader trying to get out in front of calls to more strictly regulate his business. Not only have our lives as citizens lagged behind our lives as consumers, but it feels like the digital revolution may actually be *undermining* our lives as citizens. At a minimum, it's increasingly hard to argue that Facebook, Amazon, Google, or Apple have made our lives *better* as citizens, in terms of our health, our privacy, our security, or our democracy.

As people come to this disturbing realization, they're pushing back against the unchecked power of the big technology platforms, urging governments to increase their regulation of digital technologies, and forcing the world of startups to adapt to a new reality. Even Marc Benioff, founder of Salesforce.com and an icon of Silicon Valley, compared Facebook to the cigarette industry in arguing that technology needs to become more regulated.

"We're the same as any other industry," Benioff said. Like "financial services, consumer product goods, food—in technology, the government's going to have to be involved. There is some regulation but there probably will have to be more."[3]

This process is already well under way in Europe and will continue to build in America and other parts of the world.

Fourth, startups are solving urgent problems that would previously have been left to government or nonprofits.

The United Nations Sustainable Development Goals provide a quick reference to the challenges facing many parts of our world: poverty, hunger, health and well-being, education, gender equality, clean water and sanitation, affordable and clean energy, decent work and economic growth, infrastructure, inequality, sustainable cities and communities, responsible consumption and production, climate change, healthy oceans, endangered species, and justice and the rule of law.

In a previous generation, we might have looked to government or nonprofits to solve these problems. Today, governments and nonprofits are increasingly looking to startups.

The Sustainable Development Goals represent a staggering $12 trillion market opportunity.[4] The Global e-Sustainability Initiative finds that solving these problems represents a $2.1 trillion opportunity for technology startups alone.

You know what's sexier than a billion dollars? A trillion.

And finally, the technologies of science fiction are becoming reality.

My wife and I named our son after R. Daneel Olivaw, the android hero of the Isaac Asimov universe, which should give you a sense of how much science fiction we both read growing up.

Today, I routinely have the priviledge of meeting startups who are making real the fictional worlds that Asimov wrote about, whether through artificial intelligence, self-driving cars, robots, brain-computer interfaces, synthetic biology, or distributed ledgers and cryptocurrencies, many of which you'll read about on the pages of this book. What unifies these technologies is that each takes some part of our lives that was previously analog and brings it into the realm of the digital.

These emerging technologies have the mind-bending potential to solve previously intractable challenges, such as many of the Sustainable Development Goals, but the immense potential for all these technologies lies smack in the middle of complex markets, thick with regulation. As William Gibson put it, the future is already here—it's just not evenly distributed.

Taken together, these five trends are driving a collision between the worlds of startups and government—not just in America, but in every corner of the planet.

And this is a *good* thing.

In every country in the world—capitalist, communist, or plutocratic—governments regulate those things that are important to their citizens and societies. Every government in the world has a heavy hand in determining the source of their citizens' food supply, how children receive an education, and how citizens receive healthcare. No functioning government has decided to skip traffic laws or building codes.

As startups begin to tackle more *important* problems, where failure can be far more consequential than a humorous chat with Siri or shoes that don't fit showing up on your doorstep, they're going to run into governments charged with protecting their citizens through regulation. Love it or hate it, we're entering the next era of the digital revolution: *the Regulatory Era.*

The potential for improving lives in this era is profound. From a capitalist perspective, the opportunity for wealth creation is also immense. Amazon, Apple, Facebook, Google, and Microsoft—and all the startups that they have spawned and acquired—have deeply mined a narrow slice of the global economy by changing the way we entertain and inform ourselves, communicate, and purchase. Sectors like healthcare, education, energy, transportation, agriculture and food, financial services, and security represent the other 80 percent of the global economy, and have been largely untouched by the digital revolution—until now. The digital transformation of these markets is where the massive fortunes of the next twenty years will be made—both for founders and investors.

Regulatory Hacking

To win in this Regulatory Era, you will need to understand how to *hack* markets dominated by government. To those not well versed in the lingo of tech, *hacking* can have crude, violent connotations. So "regulatory hacking" might sound like shorthand for "cutting through red tape," or worse, "breaking the law," when in reality, it's about finding a much more nuanced and strategic approach to navigating complex markets. That's why this book's jacket isn't an image of cutting red tape, but rather stretching and bending it to make room for progress.

Hacker culture was born in the 1960s among a set of hobbyists floating around MIT. In this idealistic sense, *hacking* is the art and science of creatively making software systems do things they previously could not. A *hack* is something a hacker discovers that enables software to do something new and beautiful and meaningful. Within hacker culture, as soon as you discover a hack, you share it, at least among those who understand how to use it. The hackers who discover the best hacks and share them with others earn the most credibility and esteem.

Hacker culture, hacking, and hacks remain at the inspiring core of the Valley ethos to this day. But while it originated as hobbyists jamming with software systems, the Valley has taken hacker culture, added money, blown it up to the scale of societies and economies, and turned it into a set of formal methods and tools, codified in Steve Blank's *The Startup Owner's Manual*, Eric Ries's *The Lean Startup*, and the blogs of Paul Graham.

This Silicon Valley playbook should be familiar to anyone interested in building a startup: Understand your customer, develop and push out a minimum viable product, gather customer feedback, analyze, iterate, repeat, repeat, repeat. This works great for building photo-sharing apps and getting people to click on ads, but only provides a partial answer when applied to transforming clinical workflows within a hospital or reimagining how customs could work on a distributed ledger.

As the worlds of startups and government smash together, founders still need to *hack*, but they have to understand how to hack not just technology or design or even psychology, but how to hack markets dominated by government regulation.

Regulatory hacking is the application of hacker culture to complex markets that are deeply intertwined with government because they meaningfully impact the public interest. Regulatory hacking—when done thoughtfully and with the right motivations—is *hacking in the public interest*.

Who This Book Is For

This book is first and foremost for startup founders who are intentionally hacking in the public interest. I hope that by demystifying the path to success in complex markets, this book will inspire more founders to avoid the lure of the trivial and jump into solving these problems.

Next, this book should be helpful to those founders who have unintentionally stumbled into a regulatory minefield. As governments around the world take a closer look at the consequences and risks to society of digital technologies, many startups will find to their surprise that they urgently need to broaden their perspective. This book should serve as a reference guide for solving those challenges.

If you're a founder building and growing in a market complicated by regulation, then I refer to you in this book as a *regulatory hacker*.

This book is also for the *investors* who support regulatory hackers. As with founders, I hope that by lifting the fog on regulatory hacking, this book will inspire more investors to seek strong returns on capital from improving our lives as citizens.

Finally, this book is for the many *stakeholders* involved in complex markets, whether *executives* within institutions, associations, unions, advocacy groups, foundations, and research organizations, or *policymakers* within governments.

As a reader, I assume you're familiar with the Silicon Valley playbook. I do not, however, assume you're as familiar with how to get things done when working with government.

One final note for readers: Although many of the stories I share in this book involve American startups, and much of the language and many of the examples relate to American forms of government, regulatory hacking is as applicable to startups in Dubai, Singapore, Nairobi, Bogota, or Tallinn as it is to startups in Silicon Valley or Washington, D.C. To make that point, I've made an effort to sprinkle in examples of startups from around the world, where applicable.

Who I Am

Why am *I* writing a book on regulatory hacking?

Because I have had the opportunity to learn from incredible startup founders as well as from leading policymakers, institutional leaders, and experts on navigating government.

Through 1776, the Washington, D.C.–based startup incubator and venture capital firm that Donna Harris and I cofounded in 2013 with the help of Brandon Pollak and Brittany Heyd, I worked with and invested in startups tackling some of the thorniest, most deeply entrenched problems faced by citizens. I was able to learn from hundreds of startups that have successfully overcome resistance from governments and industry incumbents to produce win-win outcomes, from HopSkipDrive making ride-sharing for kids safe and secure to SeamlessDocs making interacting with your government friendly, even beautiful.

In the five years since we launched, 1776 has incubated more than a thousand startups that have collectively raised more than $650 million, all focused on regulated markets such as healthcare, education, energy, cities, food, security, and financial services. Our global Challenge Cup competition has visited more than seventy-five cities around the world, with thousands of startups competing over four years. Our seed fund has invested in thirty-four incredible companies around the world.

In addition, through our work at 1776, we realized how powerful the five trends I mentioned above would be, and yet how hard it was for founders, investors, institutional leaders, and policymakers around the world to stay abreast of the latest insights in complex and rapidly changing markets, and to make the global connections necessary to act on those insights. In 2016, we launched Union, an online community of innovators from around the world, to address this need. At the end of 2017, we spun Union out as its own startup, which I lead as CEO. Today, Union powers incubators and accelerators on six

continents, supporting more than seven thousand startups and enabling institutional leaders and policymakers to set challenges for startups to solve.

In short, 1776 and Union have given me a lot of startup case studies to learn
from. But they've also given me the opportunity to learn from leaders from the
worlds of startups and government. Over the years, we've hosted Barack
Obama and Queen Rania of Jordan, David Cameron and Marc Andreesen,
Penny Pritzker and Jeff Bezos. Many of the experts I quote in this book on how
to deal with government I met through 1776. I even helped found an angel
group for experts in navigating government, appropriately named K Street
Capital. Union, in turn, has given me the chance to learn from startup ecosystem leaders from Austin to Nairobi.

As Donna, Brandon, Brittany, and I evolved our program at 1776, and then
started to scale it globally with Union, we came to realize the insight that
forms the premise of this book: that the Silicon Valley playbook is crucial to
building a startup, but inadequate to the challenge of building and growing in
a market thick with regulation. Through trial and error, a new approach
evolved, which this book formalizes.

Along the way, I met J.D. Harrison, then a young journalist covering the
intersection of public policy and startups at *The Washington Post*, right across
the street from us at 1776. When I decided to write this book, I asked him to
help me bring to life the incredible stories of the startups and founders you'll
find in the pages that follow.

As you read this book, you'll learn a few things about my personal phi-
losophy, forged through my experiences helping our startups learn to succeed
through regulatory hacking.

First, *regulation is and will be*. Stop lamenting it and start learning how to
hack it.

I remember picking up the November 2016 issue of *Fortune* magazine, the
cover splashed in red with the headline: "The Red Tape Conundrum."[5] The
cover story made a number of thoughtful points, but one has always stuck with
me: Regulation has increased in America every four years, *regardless of who is
in power.*

There's a simple reason why regulation proliferates. Our societies and economies continuously become more complex, driven in part by technology. Regulation is how policymakers deal with that complexity, regardless of the
ideologies they might publicly espouse. Regulation has existed since the dawn

of history and will continue to exist as long as organized human societies persist.

Second, *it's not a bad thing that startups are becoming regulated.*

I'm an optimist by nature, but when it comes down to it I'm neither utopian nor dystopian about what technological progress will mean for our children and grandchildren. Rather, I have come to believe that as a society *we have a choice* about how we want technology to evolve and shape our lives. Ultimately, and as messy as it can be, government is *how* we make tough choices as a society.

Third, *the best outcomes for society come from collaboration.* I love startups, but the startup world doesn't have a monopoly on important insights into building a better future. The world I hope Endeavour and Daneel see will come as a result of startups, institutions, and policymakers coming together, each bringing their best insights to help each other. There are times when a fight is unavoidable—and this book arms founders to win those—but this book starts from a premise that collaboration usually produces the best outcomes for everyone involved.

One final note as you read this book: Many of the people that you'll meet in this book are my friends, colleagues, partners, and mentors, whereas others are people that I sought out specifically for this book. When I know someone personally, I generally use their first name. When this book is my primary connection to them, I refer to them by their last name.

How This Book Works

This book is not merely an explainer or a how-to on government regulation; it also recounts and draws lessons from the stories of startups that navigated and thrived in complex, regulated markets. I certainly find these stories fascinating. But after you've put it down, I hope it sits near your desk for a long time, serving as a reference guide as you build great businesses.

This book has four sections, each of which addresses a different element of regulatory hacking.

Section 1: Hacking in the Public Interest establishes a framework for how to understand and approach complex markets as a startup, from mapping the power dynamics within your market and finding groups willing to bet on you, to unlocking the right business model to grow in that market.

Section 2: The Foundations of Regulatory Hacking explains three things every regulatory hacker must continuously develop: a strong narrative, data to provide evidence to support your claims, and influence within your complex market.

Section 3: Business Models explains three types of business models that are unique to regulatory hacking: selling to government, selling to citizens and private institutions in regulated markets, and selling social impact.

Section 4: The Regulatory Hacker's Toolkit details four important public affairs tools that regulatory hackers can use: the media, engaging citizens, engaging elites, and formally lobbying to change the rules of the game.

The conclusion to this book provides a history of Elon Musk as *the ultimate regulatory hacker*. Each one of his startups is solving a problem in a complex market. Each is deeply intertwined with government and regulation. One of the reasons that Musk is revered to such an extent is precisely because he had the courage to tackle important, complex challenges during an era when too much of Silicon Valley was focused on getting you to click on more ads.

SECTION 1

Hacking in the Public Interest

Chapter 1

REGULATORY HACKING

Uber: The Iconic (Wrong) Example

The first time Uber entered my consciousness was in late October 2011, which just so happened to be the same week that Donna Harris and I first met. Rachel Holt, Uber's then general manager for the D.C. region (and now head of North America), had reached out, offering free ride credits to me and other tech CEOs, lobbyists, and media personalities in D.C. I received $50 in credits and was encouraged to pass the same offer on to any of my "influential" friends. Keep in mind, at the time, Uber was a scrappy, relatively unknown startup.

On the evening of November 18, 2011, Rachel flipped a switch and Uber began quietly testing their luxury-sedan-hailing service on the streets of Washington, D.C. Armed with an app-powered, car-summoning technology and already operating in a handful of cities, the company seemed to know almost immediately that it was in for a bumpy ride in the nation's capital.

While Uber had run into some minor regulatory and licensing speed bumps in places like San Francisco, New York, and Chicago, D.C. presented the first major regulatory resistance. Not two months after Uber started operations in D.C., Ron Linton, the chairman of the D.C. Taxicab Commission, declared that Uber was operating illegally. The following morning, Linton hailed an Uber and routed the driver, Ridha Ben-Amara, to D.C.'s Mayflower Hotel. When they pulled up in front of the hotel, Taxicab Commission enforcement officials were already there waiting to impound Ben-Amara's Lincoln Town Car and slap him with $1,650 in fines for, among other charges, not holding a chauffeur license, operating an unlicensed taxi, and charging an improper fare.[1]

Which is how I found myself, shortly before Christmas, in the living room of the DuPont Circle row house cum startup office of iStrategyLabs, a digital agency in D.C. owned by Peter Corbett, a tireless advocate for the D.C. tech scene and a founder of the D.C. Tech Meetup. With Uber in dire straits in D.C., Rachel had reached out to Peter, who had quickly convened a war council of leaders in the D.C. tech community. The room crackled with the feeling that this was a pivotal moment for everything we'd been working toward. If D.C. were the first city to shut down Uber, then our burgeoning credibility as a city where people could innovate would be ruined. This wasn't about Uber; this was about protecting this scrappy upstart from Big Taxi. We made plans, determining who could reach which city councilmembers or the mayor, how we could circulate petitions, who could engage what reporters. It was, in a word, a *movement*. It was more about *us* and what we believed than about Uber, and we were *organizing*.

I had a strong relationship with Mayor Vincent Gray, who was an advocate for the startup community in D.C. I emailed my friends in his office and stressed that if Uber were shut down, it would irreparably damage our shared vision for the D.C. startup community. Other people reached out to Mary Cheh, David Catania, Jack Evans, and David Grosso, all councilmembers with some sympathy to the tech community.

In parallel, Travis Kalanick sent a note to Uber's small but already fanatical customer base in D.C., most of whom, by dint of Uber's launch strategy, were influential people. His note encouraged everyone to write to their councilmember and made it one-click easy to do so. Travis and Rachel gave interviews with local and national reporters, strongly emphasizing the theme of Big Taxi trying to squash an innovative upstart offering better service at a reasonable price.

Before Uber, getting around the nation's capital via taxi was at best an outmoded hassle and at worst a headache-inducing nightmare. I can remember spending hours trapped on the congested Washington Beltway on sticky, hundred-degree July afternoons, accompanied by a driver who refused to flip on even the lowest setting of air conditioning; or standing on the curb in freezing January temperatures on K Street, arm outstretched, and after finally catching a driver's attention, learning that he's only commissioned to pick up and drop off in the District of Columbia and legally unable to take me ten minutes across the bridge into Virginia. Taxis in D.C. were also notorious for refusing to go into the historically black neighborhoods in D.C. or pick up people who didn't look "safe." Mayor after mayor had promised to reform the D.C. taxis—at a minimum to get them to start accepting credit cards—but had been thwarted by the entrenched and powerful D.C. Taxicab Commission.

The citizens of D.C. were ready to hear a story about someone taking the fight to the taxis.

That week in December 2011 marked the start of a long and grueling fight between Uber and the D.C. Taxicab Commission. It's a fight that would continue for years, round after round, but it's a fight the company would eventually win resoundingly. In D.C. and elsewhere, these triumphs have been widely attributed to a taxi-commission-crippling combination of vocal citizen armies (composed of riders and drivers), latent but intense resentment at the poor service provided by traditional taxis, sheer persistence, and of course boatloads of capital (at the time, Uber had already stacked up $50 million of the $16 billion it has raised so far).[2]

Understanding the Uber Playbook—and Its Limitations

Uber's success gave birth to a new playbook in the Valley for startups where inconvenient regulation might pose an obstacle to growth. It went something like this: Develop a disruptive product or service, launch quickly without asking permission and before anyone knows what you're doing, use early success to stack up an obscene amount of capital, use that capital to blitz your way into new markets and quickly develop a massive army of loyal users, and use those armies to topple the walls of regulators, monopolies, and special interests.

It's true that Uber—particularly in their first few years—represents a perfect case study in regulatory hacking.

The problem is, much of Silicon Valley learned all the wrong lessons, simplifying the Uber story down to "if you stack up enough capital, you can steamroll government."

Not only is that a trite and offensive reduction, it's also wrong. While Uber did have the advantage of capital, they also adroitly applied many of the concepts and tools of regulatory hacking, which you'll read about in later chapters, to achieve incredible growth in the face of obvious regulatory obstacles.

Bradley Tusk, a political consultant and early Uber investor, puts it well: "From working with [Kalanick], I found that he is tough and he can be a pain, but in terms of what I saw firsthand for several years . . . he's the smartest client I've ever worked with in terms of understanding political dynamics."[3]

Uber understood the nature of the entrenched power they were facing. They studied the power dynamics within the taxi industry and understood that they were a direct and unequivocal threat to major economic interests who had secured political protection in almost every city in America, since taxicab companies are invariably one of the top donors to local politicians. Given the iron triangles* that had formed between taxi operators, taxi commissions, and city councils, it was always going to be nearly impossible to compromise with an industry built on the monopolistic restriction of supply by local governments. Uber had to fight. You'll learn about assessing the power dynamics in your market in Chapter 2: Power.

Facing this power dynamic, Uber rapidly and systematically tested various tactics for countering the inevitable blowback to their entry into a new market, first in Washington, D.C., and then in other markets. Uber was able to refine their playbook much faster than flat-footed taxi operators were able to develop a counterresponse. This makes sense when you understand that taxi operators are inherently local. They understand their market incredibly well but are not well organized nationally or internationally. Each time Uber entered a new city, they could test and strengthen their playbook; whereas each individual taxi commission was encountering the Uber threat for the first time. Uber doubled down on this advantage by recognizing that they needed to move with astonishing speed globally before the taxi commissions and operators could get their feet beneath them. In Chapter 3: Business Models and Chapter 4: Growth, you'll learn about finding a business model that will work and developing a growth plan for complex markets.

It's ironic, given how toxic the Uber brand has become over time, but it's hard to overstate how effective Uber was in their early days at creating a positive narrative. The Uber story could easily have been about an arrogant Silicon Valley startup coming into a new town and flagrantly violating laws—many of which were designed to protect consumers from legitimate risks—while undermining existing small business owners. Instead, Uber spoon-fed the media an endearing story about a scrappy upstart, with a service people loved, being squashed by "Big Taxi." They intuitively understood that most people in most cities ranked taxis on par with airlines, mobile carriers, and cable operators as industries they loved to hate, and played that to their advantage. You'll learn

---

*A term I'll explain shortly.

about storytelling in Chapter 6: Narrative and how to get that story out there in Chapter 12: The Media.

Uber's use of influential people to launch in a new city was effective at quickly getting to critical mass and had the added benefit of turning those influential people into fanatical advocates for their service. In other words, they were able to quickly gather real power within a new city, which they could cash in as soon as the taxi commissions tried to shut them down. You'll learn about how to systematically grow and use influence in Chapter 8: Influence and then how to apply it effectively in Chapter 14: The Grasstops.

Uber understood the rule book they were violating, so they knew how to present their influential advocates and the media with plausible explanations for how Uber was not in fact violating those rules (although that became much harder when Uber eventually expanded from limousines to regular cars with their UberX service, which clearly competed with taxi services). They also understood exactly how the rules needed to be changed to allow their business model to work legally so they could quickly suggest compromises to city councils inundated with calls and emails from their influential supporters. You'll learn about navigating policy incentives and barriers in Chapter 10: Selling to Citizens and Private Institutions.

Uber employed all the tactics of a grassroots campaign, creating a movement that turned their influential advocates into community organizers, and arming their addicted users, and even drivers, with the tools to pressure policymakers on their behalf. You'll learn about engaging citizens to help you fight your battles and grow in Chapter 13: Grassroots.

Finally, it goes without saying that Uber directly lobbied city governments for changes in laws and regulations, which you'll learn about in Chapter 15: Lobbying.

Why Uber Is an Imperfect Example

I've linked nearly every chapter in this book to something out of Uber's playbook. And yet, in many ways the Uber story represents an extreme outlier rather than a typical story of regulatory hacking.

How so? For one, people genuinely loathed taxis in most cities and had for years. Second, Uber provides a service that's easy for the average citizen to understand and try quickly—and citizens are willing to pay for it. Third, the taxi regulations that Uber was attacking are abstract in many cases and downright archaic in other, even if the motivations behind them were often legitimate. (I actually *do* want someone who drives people around full-time to have a more robust driver's license, vehicle inspection scheme, and level of insurance!) Fourth, taxi commissions are localized and fragmented whereas Uber was able to act globally.

Most regulatory hackers won't find themselves facing similarly favorable scenarios or power dynamics. For example, consider startups like Josephine that are trying to chip away at food safety regulations so that you can order dinner from a neighbor's kitchen, or 23andMe providing genetic testing without the involvement of a doctor. For many reasons, convincing regulators to rethink those kinds of regulations to make way for innovation is a far taller task than trying to snuff out local rules that require drivers to issue paper fare receipts, not digital ones. And even if citizens understand the issue, it's less clear that they will definitely side with innovation.

The bottom line is this: During those early years, Uber executed their strategy nearly flawlessly—but it was a strategy that was tailored to their company, their challenges, and their unique circumstances, not one that ought to be blindly applied to any other startup that's aiming to transform a complex market.

In fact, it's not even a strategy that worked for Uber beyond a point, starting long before the Travis Kalanick meltdown of 2017.

Over time, Uber lost control of their narrative. Part of this was inevitable as Uber ceased to be the scrappy upstart and almost overnight became a global colossus, which meant the Big Taxi versus Little Innovator narrative no longer worked. Part of it was numerous unforced errors on Uber's part, with Kalanick appearing arrogant and tone-deaf on one issue after another. When you're regulatory hacking, the public has to see you as operating in their interest, which Uber seemed to forget as their success grew. And some of the regulations that taxi operators faced really were in place for good reasons.

At the same time, the taxi commissions eventually developed their own playbooks and deployed more effective strategies to combat (or at least slow) the Uber takeover. And Uber kept pushing for greater advantage until local politicians eventually learned that, at the end of the day, voters may send a passionate email about Uber but don't actually donate or vote based on a candidate's record on the "Uber issue." Citizens cared but they didn't care *that much*. Uber's overreach caused them to be seen as having more bark than bite.

Uber won many battles, but it's much less clear whether they'll win the war they started with government. In 2015, Travis Kalanick could confidently proclaim that Uber had in fact used their boatloads of capital to steamroll governments around the world. But governments move at a different pace than startups. Declarations of victory by Travis Kalanick in 2015 probably feel decidedly premature to Dara Khosrowshahi in 2018.

This is all to say that Uber isn't so much the *wrong* example for those startups looking to learn the ins and outs of complex markets. It's merely a *dangerous* example, because it's one that has been lauded as the de facto playbook despite being grossly oversimplified, taking place amid extraordinarily unique circumstances, and with the ultimate outcome still in doubt.

As you'll see, taking the wrong lessons from Uber can be the difference between success and failure.

Uber for Kids

On an unseasonably warm afternoon in October 2013, Joanna McFarland, a mother of two, stood chatting with a group of women at a child's birthday party on the outskirts of Los Angeles. As so many conversations among parents do, the discussion revolved around their children. Soon, they began commiserating about an all-too-common headache, particularly for working parents like Joanna: the logistical acrobatics required to ferry multiple kids to and from an ever-expanding list of daily activities.

Joanna cut in with what was meant to be a joke: "We need to buy a van and hire the moms and the babysitters in the neighborhood to drive our kids around," she said.

Most laughed. Not Janelle McGlothlin.

Janelle, owner of a boutique marketing firm by day and mother of three by always, immediately recognized that her longtime friend Joanna was on to something. The two continued their conversation privately and began meeting weekly to discuss potential solutions.

A few months later, they were introduced to a local attorney named Carolyn Yashari Becher, who also had three children and had been working on the same idea. Together, the trio launched HopSkipDrive in late 2014 and set out to bring the convenience of ride-sharing to busy families by matching vetted childcare specialists on wheels with parents needing transportation for their kids.

But they weren't the only ones, or even the first ones, to land on that idea.

Less than four hundred miles north, Nick Allen had jumped out to a head start in the "Uber for kids" arena. His San Francisco–based startup, Shuddle, had just raised $2.6 million from three premier venture capital firms in Silicon Valley and was starting to scale a strikingly similar service that had been rolled out earlier that year in the Bay Area. On the heels of that hefty seed round, Shuddle was already starting to garner glowing press and expand their customer and driver bases.

While HopSkipDrive's and Shuddle's business models were similar, the entrepreneurs behind them couldn't have been more different. A stark foil to HopSkipDrive's three working mothers, Allen was the quintessential Valley startup bro. After two years as a stock analyst and three as partner at a venture capital group, Allen cofounded Sidecar, an early Uber competitor in the on-demand ride-sharing space. A bachelor with no children, Allen hatched the idea for Shuddle after hearing and reading about accounts of parents using Sidecar to transport their children around town, even though the company (and rivals like Uber and Lyft) expressly prohibit it.

At Sidecar, Allen had a front row seat to Uber's conquest, watching as the market leader systematically steamrolled the competition (including Sidecar) by raising more capital and expanding more aggressively into new markets. Along the way, he watched as—to his own company's demise—Uber perfected and repeatedly deployed what he simplistically understood as their "break the rules now, deal with the regulators later" strategy, seeming to never stop to ask permission or work constructively with local governments as it barreled headlong and unapologetically into new cities.

That experience significantly influenced the way Allen approached Shuddle.

And it may very well have contributed to the company's downfall.

Right from the start, Allen mimicked the Uber approach. Shuddle launched exclusively in San Francisco in early 2014, but the company immediately went on a national press blitz, with Allen discussing his expansion plans on the *Today Show* as early as February. During that first year, more than four hundred stories were written about Shuddle, and by the following spring, the company had raised more than $12 million from esteemed Silicon Valley investors. Allen used the capital to quickly staff up and expand throughout the greater San Francisco area. During those early months, the company was reportedly burning through cash at an ever accelerating clip, but Allen's strategy—grow at all costs—never wavered. After all, that's what Uber did.

Shuddle employees would later say that Allen deliberately set out to turn Shuddle into an "Uber clone" and that he embodied the "growth-at-all-costs mind-set."[4,5]

Allen also mirrored what he perceived as Uber's strategy as it pertained to rules and regulations.

Started in 1987, TrustLine was (and remains) California's official screening program and database registry for childcare workers and in-home caregivers, including nannies, tutors, and daycare workers. By the time HopSkipDrive and Shuddle were hatched a quarter century later, California regulators and businesses had come to view the program as the gold standard for vetting childcare providers, many lauding the fact that the service went beyond standard background checks and that the certification process included fingerprint scans to ensure applicants have no disqualifying criminal convictions or substantiated child abuse complaints against them.

Those same fingerprinting procedures that positioned TrustLine as the gold standard in the eyes of parents, companies, and regulators rendered it a problem in the eyes of Allen.

For a startup laser-focused on growing at all costs, Shuddle couldn't afford to slow down to fingerprint every potential new driver, nor could it afford to wait the three weeks it sometimes took TrustLine to run their series of checks. Despite persistent warnings from Allen's cofounder, Rodrigo Prudencio, who had an elementary-school-aged daughter and urged the team to conduct identify verification checks on drivers, Allen decided to forgo the TrustLine process when vetting drivers and developed Shuddle's own certification process—one that he maintained was "safer and faster" than TrustLine's process but did not include fingerprinting.[6]

Where Shuddle saw an obstacle, HopSkipDrive saw an opportunity. I met Joanna and her team in August 2015 when they pitched the 1776 seed fund for investment. They were closing a seed round and Upfront Ventures, their lead investor, reached out to Donna and invited us to join the round. They recognized that regulation was going to be important to HopSkipDrive and they thought our focus on regulatory hacking could be useful. As Donna and I heard Joanna's pitch and got to know the HopSkipDrive team, what jumped out at us was the trio's natural empathy for their customers and how thoughtful and methodical they were about crafting their approach to regulation.

Joanna, Janelle, and Carolyn—who have eight children between them—approached HopSkipDrive not as technologists capitalizing on a gap in the market but as busy moms looking for a solution to challenges their families faced on a daily basis. By extension, they were left with a rather simple litmus test: If it wasn't a solution that they would feel comfortable using with their own children, it wasn't a viable solution at all.

Consequently, there was never any question about building TrustLine into their vetting procedure and spending the added time and resources to require fingerprint checks for all new drivers. After all, that's not a step they would be willing to forgo as parents, so it wasn't a step they were willing to forgo as founders.

But this wasn't the only reason they embraced TrustLine.

"We're dealing with the most vulnerable population in society: young children," Carolyn explains. "When you're doing that, you have to live and breathe trust and safety, and not just in your actions, but in every interaction you're having with customers, with drivers, with employees, and with regulators."

Uber's strategy and subsequent record of success early on wasn't lost on the HopSkipDrive founders. While they were building their own startup, they watched as the Silicon Valley darling bulldozed their way into one city after another with seemingly little regard for existing regulations, all in the name of disruptive innovation and a better experience for citizens.

"For us to adopt that same model and go into the California Public Utilities Commission like a bull in a china shop and say, 'We realize you don't have rules yet for ride-sharing companies and the transportation of unaccompanied minors, so guess what, we're just gonna do whatever the hell we want' . . . that wouldn't have been the attitude that showed we were all about the same things they are all about, which are trust and safety," Carolyn said.

We invested into that HopSkipDrive seed round, then doubled down with more capital into their $10 million Series A in early 2016 and then again in 2017. Shuddle crashed and burned in April 2016 and HopSkipDrive absorbed their assets to accelerate their expansion from their home market in Los Angeles into San Francisco. Since its launch, HopSkipDrive has provided parents with hundreds of thousands of rides and is now larger in San Francisco than Shuddle ever was.

Nick Allen applied the Uber playbook to a different segment of the ride-sharing marketplace, focusing on the similarities rather than understanding the differences. As we will learn at many points in this book, Joanna, Carolyn, and Janelle instinctively understood that ride-sharing *for kids* wasn't simply a minor tweak to ride-sharing *for adults*. They approached their complex market as *hackers*, methodically experimenting and refining their own playbook based on trust and collaboration.

If there is one insight above all others that I hope you take from this book, it is that regulatory hacking is a *process*, not a one-size-fits-all strategy. A brilliant hack for one regulated startup might be a disaster for another in a slightly different context. Uber became incredibly successful by learning how to win conflicts with local governments, but they have more recently come to understand they will need to collaborate to survive. For most regulatory hackers, in fact, solving important problems for citizens will involve *collaborating* with government far more often than open conflict.

The Language of Regulatory Hacking

Throughout this book, I'll use many terms familiar to you from the world of startups, but I'll also use terms to explain concepts in ways important to regulatory hacking.

First, I refer to *citizens* where you might normally see the word *consumer*. This is intentional. Regulatory hackers ultimately serve citizens. Citizens are more than mere consumers to be engaged, advertised to, and activated, and they have certain rights and responsibilities that matter regardless of how much money they have available to spend. Citizens exist within the context of societies, and the health of those societies matters to the health of individual citizens.

The aggregate interest of the citizens within a community is the *public interest*. Anyone who took freshman economics is probably familiar with the concept of public versus private interest. If a consumer doesn't use a dating app, he may live a lonely life but it's not clear how this impacts *other* people. If on the other hand a citizen doesn't consume preventative healthcare and develops a chronic condition, then sooner or later it will cost society money to keep that person alive and healthy.

The public interest is what makes the potential impact of the digital revolution in these markets so great. If Elon Musk makes electric vehicles and hyperloops viable as forms of mass transportation, it improves the lives of the untold number of citizens that would directly use those cars and pods, but it would also reduce society's carbon footprint and help keep the planet livable for our children and grandchildren. Elon Musk's creations are so compelling precisely because they impact *all* of us as much as they benefit the specific buyers and users of his products.

The public interest, however, also drives market distortions. These distortions create *complex markets*. When I refer to complex markets in this book, I mean that in a particular sense. E-commerce or advertising are no doubt complicated industries. But healthcare is complex in a way those industries are not.

Healthcare is complex in the sense that it is highly regulated in many dimensions. To take one simple example of the complexity inherent in healthcare, almost every society on the planet believes that citizens have a right to some level of healthcare. In Europe, that is generally through universal payment and provision. In America, it is, at the least, through a belief that nobody with an acute condition should be turned away from an emergency room. Because of this, it is often difficult or impossible to sell even important healthcare solutions directly to citizens because they have been conditioned to expect that healthcare should be provided and paid for by someone else.

Or consider what it takes to market a new drug or medical device. It would be prohibitively expensive for each of us as individual citizens to do the research to verify that the pill our doctor prescribed us is safe and necessary. There is a public interest in ensuring that any drug on the market has been rigorously tested. As a result, in the United States, the FDA enforces a lot of rules on anyone selling a drug or medical device to citizens. The world of drugs and medical devices is *complex* in a way that the market for smartphones isn't. Before going to market, Apple doesn't need to prove that iPhones actually make our lives sufficiently better to offset the costs and any side effects. It just needs to convince us they're cool.

Of course, a market can become complex over time as the impacts to the public interest are better understood. While many people sensed that the emergence of massive, global, pervasive social media platforms was having a profound impact on many of our lives, it didn't present a clear and present threat to the public interest until it became obvious how addictive these platforms could be or how easily nefarious actors could anonymously use these platforms to undermine social cohesion and democratic norms in democratic societies. As soon as these platforms became a specific threat to the public interest, governments moved to start regulating them. Social media is becoming complex in a way it never was before—for example, through a simple regulation that Facebook and Twitter *know* who is actually advertising on their platforms.

It's not just social media. As policymakers begin to grasp how profoundly many new technologies are affecting societies, you will start to see other lightly regulated markets become more complex sooner rather than later.

If you are launching a startup in a complex market, I refer to your startup in this book as a *regulated startup*. The term is not meant to imply that every startup operating within a complex market is directly regulated by governments. It's merely shorthand for "startups operating within complex markets with lots of regulation."

If you're the founder or a prime mover behind a regulated startup, I refer to you as a *regulatory hacker*. If you're an investor in a regulated startup, then almost every insight that applies to the founder of a regulated startup applies to you as well. While an investor rarely understands a business as well as the founder building it, a strong investor *should* understand the patterns behind regulated startups well.

Regulatory hackers use *regulatory hacks* to validate and scale their ideas and technologies within complex markets. Regulatory hacks are simply creative tools that allow you to get things done within a complex market faster or cheaper than you might otherwise. As with growth hacks, once you understand the hack, it becomes obvious in hindsight. But after advising hundreds

Summary of Key Terms in This Book	
Term	*Definition*
citizens	Individuals as they exist within the context of societies. The health of those societies matters to the health of individual citizens, and vice versa.
the public interest	The collective interest of the citizens within a community.
complex markets	Markets with significant distortion from government regulation to protect or promote the public interest.
regulated startup	A startup business operating within a complex market.
regulatory hacker	A cofounder or executive of a regulated startup. A regulatory hacker is responsible for crafting and executing a strategy for success within a complex market.
regulatory hacks	Tools that allow you to get things done within a complex market faster or cheaper than you might otherwise.
the Valley	Shorthand for Silicon Valley, specifically, as well as many of the assumptions and beliefs that Silicon Valley has evangelized around the world.
the Hill	Shorthand for the government apparatus in Washington, D.C., specifically, as well as the collective culture of national, regional, and local governments across America and around the world.

of regulated startups, many of the hacks in this book were not at all obvious to them at first blush.

There are two final shorthand references that I'll use throughout this book. The first is *Silicon Valley*, or *the Valley*, which I sometimes use specifically but more often use to refer to the global startup culture defined and evangelized by Silicon Valley, with its particular assumptions about *what* problems to solve, *who* should be solving them, and *how* to do so.

The second reference is *the Hill*, which I use as an explicit cultural contrast to the Valley. I sometimes use it to refer to the U.S. federal government apparatus that surrounds Capitol Hill in Washington, D.C., but more often use it to refer to the global culture of governments at the national, regional, and municipal levels.

The Methodology: Be a Scientist, Not an Engineer

As I said before, if there's one insight above all others that I hope you take from this book, it's that regulatory hacking is a *process* rather than an out-of-the-box game plan. Regulatory hacking is not a *rejection* of the hacker culture of the Valley but rather an application and extension of those ideas to hacking in the public interest.

One of the most important tenets of hacker culture is experimentation. In fact, if there's one conversation I have had most frequently with first-time founders, it is to abandon an engineering mind-set to building a startup in favor of a scientific mind-set.

The engineering approach of identifying a problem, envisioning a solution, then developing and executing a project plan to get there is seductive because it gives you a clear indication of linear progress, but there's just one problem: Your initial vision is almost certainly wrong. In fact, no matter what kind of startup you're building, it's incredibly rare to hit the trifecta of right problem, right solution, and right business model out of the gate. The odds grow even slimmer when launching a startup in a complex market, where the power dynamics are vastly more intricate and the nuances and challenges are magnified.

This is why successful hackers think like scientists, not engineers. Scientists do their homework on the existing literature on a topic of enquiry, form testable hypotheses, and run experiments so that they can take the learnings, revise their understanding of the world as necessary, form new hypotheses, conduct new experiments, and continue getting closer to whatever important truth they seek.

This scientific approach to building startups has famously been enshrined in the Lean Startup Methodology, as developed by Steve Blank and popularized by Eric Ries in *The Lean Startup*. The Lean Startup Methodology calls on startup founders to trade gut feelings for testable business hypotheses, long-term planning for rapid-fire experiments, and blind intuition for an unwavering skepticism. The mantra of the Lean Startup Methodology is "build-measure-learn," meaning to quickly put something out in the real world, rigorously assess the response, and then apply those learnings.

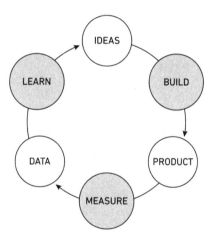

As much as this hacker wisdom on build-measure-learn has served simpler startups well, it especially holds true for regulated startups. Tackling the inefficiencies that hamstring modern healthcare systems and untangling the knots that strangle urban transportation networks involve far more players and rules and therefore a greater degree of complexity. The chances of gauging the power dynamics in your market just right from the get-go, for instance, or creating the bull's-eye-perfect solution on your first attempt, are frankly far slimmer for regulatory hackers than they are for founders solving simpler problems. Often, as you'll see in the examples throughout this book, you'll have to build-measure-learn many times until you finally discover the magic formula that works for your regulated startup.

Over the course of the rest of Section 1: Hacking in the Public Interest, you'll learn how you can find viable business models for complex markets, how you can iterate and refine your methods to grow in those markets, and how you can leverage regulatory arbitrage to find early adopters, first movers, and strategic funders. But before all that, the first step you need to take as a regulatory hacker is to identify the power players in your world and understand how that power flows so you can harness it to your advantage. You'll learn how in the next chapter.

Chapter 2

POWER

It was in the wee hours of the morning in February 2007 when I woke up in a fog to my iPhone ringing. I had twenty missed calls from a number I didn't recognize. I answered to an urgent voice on the other end asking, "Evan, are you at home?"

Strangely groggy, I answered that I was.

"Where's Vera?"

Vera, my wife, was away visiting her family in her native Russia at the time, which I told the voice on the other end of the line.

"Then who is in your garage? The fire department is about to break down the door."

I threw on some clothes and stumbled downstairs and out my front door. There were flashing lights everywhere. As I approached the driveway, firemen with axes were in fact preparing to chop down my garage door. I stopped them, quickly punched in the code to open the door, then jumped back as a wave of smoke billowed out.

My car had been running for hours.

In startup fashion and with my wife out of town, I had pulled two straight all-nighters on an important project. Having finally finished it shortly before midnight, I had driven home, pulled into my garage, grabbed my keys, gone into my house, and immediately collapsed into bed, forgetting to turn my car off with its fancy keyless entry system. The car engine kept running. Carbon monoxide started building up in the garage and seeping into my and my neighbor's homes. We were all asleep and if one of our carbon monoxide alarms hadn't sounded (my neighbor's happened to go off first), it's likely that none of us would have ever woken up again.

The fact that nearly all homes in America have inexpensive, reliable carbon monoxide alarms saved our lives.

Have you ever wondered *how* it came to be that homes are now equipped with carbon monoxide alarms?

It's because a venerable company, not a startup, got creative about regulatory hacking.

Kidde's history dates back a full century to Walter Kidde, who started the Walter Kidde Company in New York in 1917. One year later, his company introduced the first smoke-detection and carbon dioxide–based extinguisher system for use onboard a ship. Six years after that, Kidde's innovative company introduced the market's first portable carbon dioxide fire extinguisher.[1]

Jump forward nearly ninety years, and the company was still innovating, now developing the first home alarm system that could detect both smoke and carbon monoxide, all in one ceiling-mounted device. At the time, deaths from carbon monoxide poisoning, especially among children, were a growing, but still under-the-radar, health concern, and there were no laws or regulations requiring such devices to be installed in homes, as there were for smoke detectors.

That presented a challenge for a company trying to sell an innovative, potentially lifesaving new device. Kidde's leadership needed to create demand and build a market. But how?

Kidde first turned to various building code regulators and associations involved in the formation of building codes, that complex labyrinth of rules that specify the compliance standards for building homes and commercial buildings. Kidde's plan: Convince those regulators and associations that requiring carbon monoxide alarms would, for a small added cost, make buildings safer and save tons of lives. Who could oppose that idea?

As it turned out, fierce opposition came from the building code associations, which held huge sway with regulators. Kidde discovered that those associations were beholden to powerful industry players, like construction groups, building owners, and large real estate developers, none of whom wanted to see additional rules and mandates added unless they were absolutely necessary. At the time, the problem of carbon monoxide poisoning hadn't risen to a high enough level of public concern. Kidde's attempts to seed new requirements by working through the building code process went nowhere.

Kidde went back to the drawing board, taking a wider view of the challenge they were facing. While the motivations of the building code associations didn't align with the company's interests, surely someone had to be motivated to see homes become safer for children. That's when the team learned about a recent study conducted by the National Association of Pediatric Nurse Practitioners that showed that carbon monoxide poisoning was now one of the leading causes of death in children in American households.

They had been looking at the problem the wrong way. This wasn't a building code issue, the team realized. This was a public health issue—and Kidde had the solution.

The team began building a coalition of pediatric nursing groups, pediatric physician groups, children's health organizations, and other influential groups whose mission included promoting the health and safety of children.

However, the company didn't simply cast a wide net across the country in building their coalition, at least not at first. Instead, Kidde dug into the data to identify the states that had reported the most child deaths attributed to carbon monoxide in recent years—states like Massachusetts, New Jersey, and New York, where carbon monoxide poisoning often results from faulty heating systems in cold weather.

The company launched its early efforts exclusively in those states, where it could tell the most compelling narrative about an urgent and growing public health problem. It's powerful to start a conversation by asking, "More kids die each year in *your* state from carbon monoxide poisoning than anywhere else in America, so what can we do about this?"

Working in close coordination with its children's health coalition in those states, the company launched outreach campaigns designed to educate the public about the magnitude of the problem and pressure state lawmakers to pass legislation requiring the installation of carbon monoxide alarms. Through media stories, calls and letters to lawmakers, events hosted by nursing groups or local fire stations, and other activities, Kidde and their partners began to see bills introduced and eventually passed in state after state, requiring builders, homeowners, and apartment building owners to buy and install the alarms.

The results were immediate and eye-popping. Not long after legislation was approved in New York, Kidde's market shot up nearly 500 percent. With every new bill that was signed into law around the country, the company's market opportunities continued to grow rapidly. Once the company had created a process for building those coalitions, it began to replicate the same process in states across the country.

Today, more than thirty states have enacted laws requiring carbon monoxide detectors to be installed in residential dwellings, and another dozen or so have issued regulations requiring or encouraging their installation, according to the National Conference of State Legislatures. More than a dozen states now require the alarms to be installed in hotels and motels, and as of 2017, California, Connecticut, Illinois, Maine, and Maryland mandate that schools use carbon monoxide alarms.[2]

Kidde struggled at first because they made the simplest assumption about the power dynamics impacting their market, which is that their product involved homes, and therefore building codes. It wasn't until they widened their aperture and really understood all the potential players and policies impacting their market that they were able to craft a winning regulatory hack, one in fact based on the health and safety of those most affected by carbon monoxide deaths. And through that regulatory hack they created a market from thin air now worth hundreds of millions of dollars and helped save countless lives.

Including mine.

The Power Map

Complex markets involve many different individuals and organizations, each striving to further their interests, all within a thicket of existing and emerging laws, regulations, and norms. You cannot win as a regulatory hacker until you understand the game you are actually playing. And that requires mapping out the power within your market.

When you're done reading this chapter, you should be able to build a power map for your startup and begin testing hypotheses to improve that power map over time. To help you create a comprehensive power map, this chapter starts by laying out the types of players you are likely to find on your map as well as the types of rules likely to govern it.

This is a long chapter but an important one. Your power map will be the foundation for everything else you do in regulatory hacking. Attempting to validate and scale a startup in a complex market without a comprehensive understanding of the players, rules, and power dynamics within your market would be like sitting down to pick up a game of chess halfway through but not knowing the size of the board, the position of the pieces, or even the rules of the game.

A power map is first and foremost about *power*. Power can be formal, such as the ability to approve or deny a building permit, or it can be more informal, taking the form of financial resources, communications reach, influence, or credibility. Until you understand the different dimensions of power within your complex market, you'll be missing potential obstacles to your strategy as well as opportunities for regulatory hacks that could be the difference between success and failure.

Like any game, the shifting networks of power that define your complex market have two dimensions: the players and the rules. Each *player* will have different motivations and capabilities. You need to map out *all* the players that might have power relevant to your regulated startup, and understand their interests and capabilities. In a complex market, the rules of the game are *policies*. Sometimes these are *laws* passed by legislatures or municipal councils— or issued by edict. Often they are *regulations* created by regulators and enforced by bureaucrats, or even administrative policies within public or private organizations. Additionally, *norms* of behavior within complex markets can be as binding as any formal regulation.

The idea of players and rules will become clearer once we unpack a simple hypothetical example.

Understanding Your Power Map

Let's say you want to sell a new education app to American teachers. You've identified a pain point for most middle school math teachers: Kids become bored by math. You have an idea to develop an app that could help teachers get through to kids by having them apply mathematical concepts to compete in a video game–like environment. To identify the various players on your power map, start by asking a simple question: Who is going to benefit from your app?

The answer is easy: middle school math teachers and the kids in their classes.

Unfortunately, in complex markets, there is often a disconnect between who benefits from a solution, who uses it, who provides it, and who your actual customer is. So rephrase the question: To whom are you going to sell?

In this case, teachers and students, or even their parents, tend to have limited willingness to spend personal funds to improve learning outcomes in the classroom, as they expect the school to provide that. Individual schools are unlikely to be your customers, either. Most buying decisions in American schools are made by school districts, so you will likely wind up selling to districts.

Once you've thought through your potential customers, you need to think about who *influences* that buyer—in this case, school districts.

Well, teachers and school administrators within that district will likely advocate for the tools they prefer. Parents, both individually and collectively, in the form of PTAs, are also likely to influence school districts. Meanwhile, local government leaders, including mayors, city councilmembers, and school board members have plenty to say about the decisions being made in their school districts (and as politicians, those players are likely to be influenced by their citizens, including parents and teachers). Then you will have local education regulators who may have rules in place that either make it easier or harder to sell your wares into districts.

You should also ask: Who is currently *making money* from your complex industry?

You will likely find incumbent corporations like Pearson, McGraw-Hill, and Kaplan, who rake in billions every single year by selling content and services to school districts, including textbooks and software for middle school math teachers.

Next, widen your aperture and ask: What are the *layers* within your complex market? In America, you will find state-level boards of education and regulatory agencies that are setting education policy statewide, not to mention the U.S. Department of Education, which is a source not only of rules but also funding for school districts, particularly ones trying to experiment with new approaches to education. You'll also run into trade associations, from state-level PTAs that fold up into a national PTA, associations of school principals, associations of district superintendents, and so on, in addition to powerful local, state, and national teachers unions.

You can then start to *segment* your complex market and think about different special interests within it. You'll find numerous advocacy organizations

Power Map

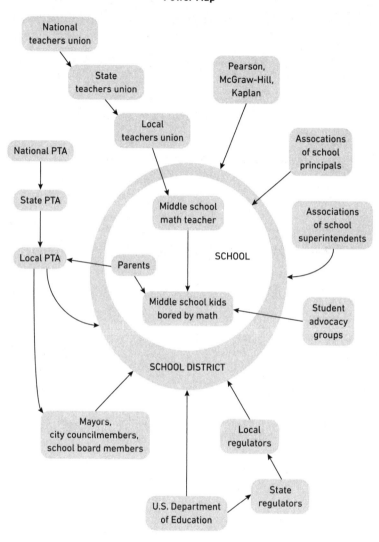

representing the needs of underprivileged students, special needs students, immigrant students, and more.

Finally, who are *thought leaders* that influence your market's thinking? In this case, any number of universities and think tanks and nonprofits across the country conduct research on what works and what doesn't work when it comes to educating our children, which may influence everyone else on your power map.

In terms of the rules of the game, you may have to comply with federal data privacy laws related to minors. Different school districts may have different regulations about the use of computers or tablets in the classroom, or how they can go about procuring apps. You may also have to confront norms within the math teacher community that associate anything that feels like a game as an unserious or trivial way to teach.

So, without diving into their motivations and who influences whom in what ways at what times, or the merit of any of the rules, you already have a basic power map if you want to sell a game-based math learning tool to American middle school teachers to help them educate their students.

Drilling down and segmenting certain players can expand your power map and reveal some potential regulatory hacks. For example, does the data show that certain populations of children have particular difficulties with learning math? Is there an advocacy group that represents them? Could they get the Department of Education to fund a pilot to explore whether your app can help that population improve outcomes? Could you take the results to a leading university to do a blue ribbon study on whether game-based learning apps like yours can improve math scores at lower cost to taxpayer than traditional approaches? Or perhaps you could receive certification from a national association representing math teachers who could help you offer pilots to math teachers across the country?

Now that you have seen a quick example of power mapping, let's break down each of the constituent elements of a power map.

The Players

While the power map for each particular startup is unique, there are common features to most power maps. As you ask the key questions above, make sure you keep referencing back to these different types of players to ensure you're not missing anything.

As a starting point, there tend to be four different types of players you'll find on your power map: governments, institutions, citizens, and influencers. Within each of these buckets, you will find players with what may be vastly

Power Player Taxonomy

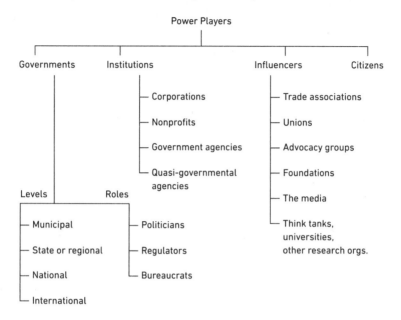

different objectives and motivations, and it's critical for the success of your startup that you understand the intricacies.

Governments

When you think of government, your first thought is probably the president or Congress. But keep in mind that government operates on many levels, such as municipal, regional, or state governments, federal government, and international governing bodies. In different countries, you'll encounter different types of government, whether they be federations, republics, or oligarchies. In each, the power dynamics, the incentive structures, and the relationships between different government bodies will vary tremendously.

Most people within governing bodies fill one of three roles: politicians, regulators, and bureaucrats.

Politicians depend on the goodwill of the governed to maintain power. They include city councilmembers and school board officials all the way up to federal lawmakers and presidents. In democratic governments, politicians are directly responsive to voters, but also to donors, institutions, the media, and other influencers, who can help them reach those voters when they're up for reelection. Depending on how often they are up for reelection, their appetite for short-term wins or long-term investments may vary. Their political party affiliation is likely to impose some ideological restraints as well, although ideology tends to matter far less for regulatory hacking than most people assume. Even in nondemocratic governments, political rulers are likely to be responsive to the mood of their people while at the same time needing access to money to provide services to those people.

Beyond politicians, governments have *regulators*, who often work closely with but have different objectives than politicians. Regulators are persons or governing bodies that supervise a particular industry or business activity. Regulators include taxi commissioners all the way up to the chairman of the Federal Reserve. Regulators are less explicitly responsive to voters and institutions, as they tend to have more independent standing within a government.

Depending on the role and the nature of the government, regulators may suffer from more or less *regulatory capture*. Regulatory capture refers to regulators becoming more responsive to the needs and the wants of the industry that they regulate than they are to the public interest. For example, taxi operators have traditionally been strong donors to mayors and city councilmembers, and therefore taxi operators might be in the majority on a taxi commission. Or the chairman of the Federal Reserve might come from a lucrative job on Wall Street and reasonably expect to return to Wall Street when their term expires, which could cause them to sympathize with Wall Street over Main Street when setting monetary policy and regulating the financial system.

Unlike politicians and regulators, *bureaucrats* tend to have long-term careers in the same governing body (sometimes in the same role) while politicians and regulators come and go. In many cases, these bureaucrats are public sector workers who simply want to be promoted and gain a little more power. Unlike in the private sector, however, public sector workers often have asymmetric incentives that make them rationally risk-averse. In other words, if they take a risk and win, they are unlikely to make a financial windfall given civil service regulations. If they take a risk and lose, however, they could stand to lose their jobs and reputations.

Zac Bookman, the cofounder of OpenGov*, stresses this point: "The risk for these folks is really high, because they don't really get rewarded if it goes

---

*You'll learn more about OpenGov in Chapter 5: Arbitrage.

well. Maybe they get a little pat on the back. If it doesn't go well, it's a black mark for everyone."

With this in mind, you can start to see why your city's mayor is going to respond to a different set of incentives than your city's top public health regulator, who's going to respond differently than a career bureaucrat who has been working inside a women's health clinic for fifteen years. It's important to understand these different roles because while government can feel like a faceless monolith, it's actually a collection of individuals, each with different motivations and constraints.

As Carolyn from HopSkipDrive says of their experience:

"We made it easy for the government to get behind us. The one thing that aligns us with government, that I think most people miss, is that safety is our highest priority. Theoretically, the purpose of these regulatory agencies is public safety. That's why these rules are in place. It's not because they're trying to actively squash innovation. Whether innovation is squashed is an unintended consequence."

Carolyn simply googled numbers for the California Public Utilities Commission and started calling up lawyers there. "You'd be surprised how willing people are to speak with you, because again, these are people who see themselves as public servants," she says. "Generally speaking, especially at the higher levels, they went into this field because they actually want to work with people like us.

"In government and politics, relationships are critical. Understanding every role was key to our success. We had outside counsel who gave us great insight into the organization—the difference between the enforcement division and the licensing division, who runs which division, and with whom we needed to speak.

"In all of our conversations, we tried to connect around our shared interests. From a safety standpoint, in the event of an incident while using a rideshare, no one is distinguishing between companies. It negatively impacts the perception of the industry as a whole. So, like the regulators, it's important to us that kids all over the state are in safe hands."

Perhaps, paradoxically, one dimension of power within the government sphere that I won't talk much about in this book is that of partisanship and *political parties*. We've hosted hundreds of government leaders at 1776 over the years—and our startups have had numerous opportunities to engage with them on their issues. It's startling at first how little an individual policymaker's stance on issues involving digital disruption are colored by their party affiliation, particularly within municipal or regional governments. Nothing about Uber's early hurdles in American cities had to do with Republicans and Democrats. Nothing that HopSkipDrive dealt with in trying to solicit a permit was about ideology. Nothing that's happening right now around drone regulations, agricultural reform, healthcare innovation, or artificial intelligence has much, if anything, to do with which party holds control of state or federal legislatures. This is about defenders versus attackers, incumbents versus disrupters, not red versus blue. While that isn't true everywhere in the world, it's more consistently true than you'd imagine. Although you might need to take ideology into consideration more when you're looking to form coalitions* or gather endorsements, by definition, the disruptive technologies driving the rise of the Regulatory Era don't fit easily into predefined ideologies.

Institutions

After governments, you'll have institutions on your power map. For our purposes, *institutions* are operating entities that provide a service to citizens. These could be corporations, nonprofits, government agencies, or even quasi-governmental agencies, any of which could have a meaningful financial stake in the market or markets that your startup is disrupting.

Corporations are private, for-profit businesses. They can be anywhere in size, from small businesses all the way up to massive multinational corporations like Walmart or Airbus. Nonprofits by contrast are private businesses that are not required to pay taxes, generally because they are doing something formally deemed to be in the public interest. Like corporations, they can range in size from small local community colleges all the way to massive multinational nongovernmental organizations like the International Red Cross.

To make things even more confusing, certain institutions can be agencies that provide services to citizens and are directly part of government. In the United Kingdom, hospitals are government agencies operating within the National Health Service. School districts in America behave much like nonprofits, but are actually agencies within municipal governments.

There are also quasi-governmental agencies, such as the Washington Metropolitan Transit Authority, or "Metro," which operates the subway system for

---

*We'll discuss coalition building more in Chapter 8: Influence.

the Washington metropolitan area. The Metro isn't part of the federal government, nor any regional or municipal government in the Washington area. It has a board of directors and a chief executive. It charges riders fees to use its service. Yet it's a government agency chartered by a consortium of governments and subject to various laws, regulations, and norms in common with other government agencies.

For-profits, nonprofits, government agencies, and quasi-governmental agencies will all tend to have different rules, incentives, constraints, and cultures, and it's important to understand these. For regulatory hackers, though, what is common across these institutions is often more important than what's different. They all represent bureaucracies that generate revenue by providing products and services to citizens. They must all operate within a constrained budget, whether constrained by shareholders, trustees, taxpayers, or some combination, which means they have stronger or weaker incentives to operate efficiently. They all face competitive threats, some more immediate and tangible than others. And they must all grapple with what the digital revolution will ultimately mean for their institution and therefore for their livelihoods.

Take the Metro example I used above. A subway is a natural monopoly. It doesn't make sense to have competing subway operators within a given area. So in theory the Metro could charge whatever price optimizes their revenue. Unfortunately, in most cases, if subways charge ticket prices that actually cover their costs, then they can't induce enough people to ride instead of taking cars. There is, however, a *public interest* in mass transit, namely that it's an extremely efficient way to move people around, thereby reducing congestion on roads and reducing greenhouse gas emissions. For these reasons, numerous governments around the world subsidize both the capital costs and the operating costs of subway systems. Metro is no different. They generate revenue from fees paid by riders as well as subsidies from governments. This guarantees, though, that they are constantly budget-constrained and looking for efficiencies, which new technologies can provide.

Despite being the only mass transit option in the region, Metro does face competitive threats. It has seen a significant reduction in ridership over the past few years[3] as new services such as Uber Pool have made it cheaper to ride door-to-door than take mass transit. Metro also needs to watch out for long-term technological disruption, such as autonomous vehicles—both passenger vehicles and buses—and even hyperloops and flying taxis.

For many regulatory hackers, it is almost impossible to get much done in complex markets without working with or through institutions. They may be your customers, partners, funders, competitors, or all of the above. In this sense again, the Uber case study remains an exception rather than the rule for regulatory hackers. Kidde needed to work with homebuilders. Even HopSkip-Drive has found that unlocking much of their market has required partnering with schools and government agencies.

Citizens

Governments and institutions work together in complex markets to provide services to the benefit of citizens. If you are a regulatory hacker, then your product or service should also benefit citizens. In some cases, individual citizens may be your users or even your customers, as in the case of Uber or 23andMe. In many other cases your regulated startup may serve the public interest, even if no individual citizens are your direct users, such as with services that help transit systems optimize bus routes. On an individual level, the vast majority of citizens certainly hold less power than any governments or institutions. And yet citizens may at some time be the most important player on your power map,* as collectively they hold tremendous influence over government and therefore over the institutions operating within complex markets.

Citizens aren't homogeneous, though. In the same way you would segment user populations into personas, you should think about how demographic and psychographic dimensions will impact how citizens will react to what you're doing. Who benefits? Who sees what you're doing as a threat? Who is passionate enough to take action to help you, or even organize other citizens to take action?

Influencers

Governments, institutions, and citizens are the obvious players for most regulatory hackers when putting together their power maps. The best regulatory hackers, however, have a nuanced understanding of the role of *influencers*. These are also the players, though, most often ignored by unsophisticated

---

*You'll learn about hacks to engage citizens in Chapter 13: Grassroots.

regulatory hackers, to their detriment, when thinking about power dynamics within their complex market.

Influencers are any individual or group (or institution) that seeks to sway the decisions and actions of governments, institutions, citizens, or some combination thereof. Influencers can be individual people, such as a particularly trusted adviser to a political leader, but may also include trade associations, unions, advocacy groups, foundations, the media, think tanks, and other research organizations, including universities. Often, influencers are composed of or funded by collections of institutions, though you will also encounter influencer groups comprising governments, such as the United States Conference of Mayors, for instance, or the National Association of School Superintendents, or associations of citizens, such as the Sierra Club.

Trade associations represent institutions or professionals. They range from massive and influential groups such as the U.S. Chamber of Commerce to niche groups such as the American Association of Political Consultants. There are more than *ten thousand* associations headquartered in the Washington, D.C., region *alone*. Associations vary as widely as you would expect, but by definition they tend to bring assets within their area of specialty, such as expertise, credibility, reach, influence, and financial resources. Associations generate revenue from dues and sponsorships paid by their members. Because of this, they are constantly striving to demonstrate their relevance and value to their membership, which creates an opening for potential regulatory hacks.

Unions are associations for workers. Like trade associations, unions range from massive and influential, such as the AFL-CIO, to niche groups. And as with trade associations, unions generate their revenue from dues and need to show relevance to their members, opening up potential hacks.

Advocacy groups are associations formed around an issue rather than an industry, profession, or group of workers. Obvious examples are patient advocacy groups such as the American Cancer Society or environmental groups such as Defenders of Wildlife. While some advocacy groups have amassed significant endowments, most generate their revenue from some combination of donations, memberships, and sponsorships.

Foundations are private organizations established from donated funds for the purpose of donating those funds to others in the form of grants. Foundations may also make investments from their endowments and support certain forms of advocacy. Foundations are influential because they have money that they have to spend promoting issues in the public interest.*

The media is also an important influencer within complex markets.** For the purpose of your power map, you need to understand what media those key players you've identified are reading, as well as any perspectives those publications bring. To provide a clichéd example, the Valley cares a lot about *The Information* and Dan Primack's newsletter in *Axios*, whereas the Hill cares about *Politico* and Mike Allen's newsletter in *Axios*. Each complex market has its own key voices that help to shape opinion.

Finally, think tanks, universities, and other research organizations can command significant influence within certain complex markets. An obvious example would be healthcare. If Harvard Medical School publishes a peer-reviewed article in the *New England Journal of Medicine* that validates the impact of your healthcare app, it will probably help you to unlock your market. But there are many other ways in which credible, third-party validation can help regulated startups. If the New America Foundation provides a rigorous analysis of the work your education startup is doing with Arizona State University, then it will help you to open up conversations with other universities. Understanding the thought leaders within your complex market is important.

As with governments and institutions, so for influencer groups: How you see the world depends on where you stand. If you are the American Petroleum Institute (API), representing the interests of the major oil and gas producers, then you will probably take a different view on renewable energy than the Sierra Club. That doesn't necessarily mean that API will seek to destroy your renewable energy startup—or even that a productive partnership isn't possible. But API will have a different lens on the same issues than the Sierra Club. In the same way, the National Education Association—one of the major teachers unions—will probably have different views on certain aspects of innovation in education than the National Alliance for Public Charter Schools.

---

*You'll learn more about business models and hacks involving foundations in Chapter 11: Selling with Social Impact.

**You'll learn more about regulatory hacks involving the media in Chapter 12: The Media.

The Rules of the Game

As you begin to understand the players on your power map, you also need to understand the rules of the game. In a complex market, these rules are policies. Policies can take several forms, but all policies exist to regulate the behavior of individuals or organizations—either to cause or prevent people from doing things. Policies fall into three broad buckets: laws, regulations, and norms.

Laws are rules enacted by political leaders—ranging from a municipal city council to a national legislature. In almost every country, there are complex procedures that govern the creation and modification of laws, which makes them hard to enact but also hard to change once in place. In the American political system, at least at the national level, modern laws often provide high-level rules while leaving many of the details to various regulatory bodies.

Regulations are rules enacted by regulators or bureaucrats, often in consultation with players in the market. Many regulations come from government, often to fill in the details of laws enacted by politicians. Other regulations, however, come from private industry bodies or organizations. For example, if you've ever wondered who sets the regulatory standards for motor oil, such as "10w40," it's not anybody within the Departments of Energy or Commerce, and certainly not within the United Nations. Rather, API defines those regulations for the global petroleum industry and for the manufacturers and retailers that depend on them. In a similar way, Facebook determines what constitutes inappropriate content on their platform, which is a form of regulation with far-reaching consequences for free speech, democracy, and community decency standards. But it's not set by any governmental body formally accountable to citizens or the public interest.

Part of what sets regulations apart from laws is that they are generally easier to change in response to changing marketing conditions or new technologies. In the American system, Congress passes major legislation, such as the Affordable Care Act, but the Centers for Medicare and Medicaid Services have wide latitude to change the regulations around what doctors and hospitals can and cannot bill to Medicare and Medicaid. While it's not simple to change those regulations, they're still far easier to change than the Affordable Care Act. Different bodies have different procedures for changing regulations, but in general it's quicker and easier to make changes for more esoteric issues at more local levels of government.

As a simple example from 1776, after we launched our seed fund in 2014, we discovered that the D.C. government had problematic regulations governing the management of venture funds. If it was a smaller fund, which ours was, then Donna and I would both have to go through a lengthy process to become registered investment advisers. These onerous regulations were one reason why many venture funds in the area were based just across the border from D.C., as Maryland and Virginia had much simpler regulations. We didn't think it was reasonable for the government to expect us to become registered investment advisers for a private venture fund, and we didn't really want to leave D.C., so we reached out to the mayor's office to raise our concerns. We explained the situation and they reached out to the appropriate regulatory body within D.C. They were unaware that this regulation was causing venture funds to avoid D.C. and agreed it didn't clearly serve the public interest. After a few emails with our attorneys, they were able to change the regulation to clarify that it didn't apply to venture funds. The entire process took a few weeks. Of course, if it were a federal regulation, it would probably have taken a few years.

In addition to laws and regulations, many complex markets are governed by various norms. Norms are rules that are not formally enforceable but are often observed by many or most players in a complex market. An example you may be familiar with is the Hippocratic Oath, which in popular mythology requires doctors to "first do no harm" and other commandments. Most people assume that the Hippocratic Oath has actual regulatory power, but in fact most doctors—at least in the United States—do not take the Oath upon graduation from medical school, and even for those who do, it does not have any binding enforceability. Regardless, the tenets of the Oath do matter, as they set norms of behavior that are important to many doctors. If significant groups of doctors believe that home genetic testing can cause harm to patients unable to properly interpret the results, it won't matter that the Oath isn't technically a law or regulation. Home genetic testing startups will encounter resistance regardless.

When thinking about the laws, regulations, and norms that govern your complex market, it's important to keep two things in mind. First, why do these policies exist at all? And second, how can you achieve the same objective as the existing regulation in a different way?

The Valley loves to argue that regulations get in the way of innovation, often with the explicit assertion that problematic regulations are the result of regulatory capture and at the behest of "dinosaur" economic interests to protect their rent-seeking behavior. (Of course, they also advocate passionately for "good" regulations that favor their economic interests, such as net neutrality.) There is truth to the idea that existing regulations tend to favor incumbents. But you should also recognize that most regulations were at least originally created with the public interest in mind.

Sophisticated regulatory hackers don't simply attack regulations because they're inconvenient to what they want to do. They first endeavor to understand the underlying objective the regulation is seeking to achieve. For example, it was inconvenient to Uber that many cities required taxi drivers to hold special driver's licenses. But that doesn't make these regulations *unreasonable*. In fact, I would argue that they make an awful lot of sense. Particularly in their early days, Uber lumped all these regulations together into their assault on "Big Taxi." Another approach, though, could have been to show how the Uber platform achieved the same underlying goal—public safety—in a different way. Of course, if the Uber platform did *not* do so, then this should have been a product development priority, perhaps by integrating real-time vehicle monitoring technology into their app, something that HopSkipDrive did early on.

How to Build Your Power Map

Building your power map follows the same build-measure-learn process as customer discovery in the Lean Startup Methodology, except in a complex market you don't just have to understand your customer, but often also your user or beneficiary, your regulators, and a variety of other stakeholders that can block or unlock your access to your market.

The first step in building your power map is to do preliminary research to form hypotheses about the players and rules of your power map. You should start by running through the following questions:

- Who is going to *directly benefit* from my product or service?
- Who is going to *use* it? Is that the beneficiary or a provider to the beneficiary?
- Who is my *customer* going to be? That is, who will pay for it?

Power Map Template

Power Map				
Player	Relationships	Interests & Motivations	Capabilities	Constraints

- Who *influences* those users and customers?
- Who is currently *making money* from my complex market?
- What are the *layers* within my complex market?
- How can I *segment* my complex market?

As you form your hypotheses about the players who might be relevant on your power map, you should also be forming hypotheses about how those players might relate to each other and your regulated startup.

- What are each player's relationships to other players?
- What are each player's interests and motivations?
- What are their capabilities to block or unlock?
- What laws, regulations, or norms are they subject to?

Once you have built your hypotheses about your power map, you need to measure and learn. As with customer discovery for a startup in a simpler market, you do this by leaving your office and talking with people.

If you think that your user is going to be American obstetricians, then it goes without saying that you need to be talking with obstetricians. But you should also be having direct conversations with pregnant women, obstetric nurses, hospitals, insurance companies, the Centers for Medicaid and Medicare Services (since around half of births in America are paid for by Medicaid), the American Congress of Obstetricians and Gynecologists, and a host of others. In Chapter 8: Influence and Chapter 14: The Grasstops, you'll learn hacks to get access to leaders within these players. In Chapter 5: Arbitrage, you'll learn the motivations that might cause certain institutions or governments to take a risk on you as an early adopter or first mover.

Each time you engage with a player, you should learn something new that refines your power map. It may strengthen or weaken your confidence in a hypothesis. It may help you to uncover a new player you need to explore, a new capability or motivation for an existing player, or a new policy that could impact you.

This process of build-measure-learn should continue as long as you are building your regulated startup. There's no point at which your power map is *done*; rather, you will be continually refining your understanding of power dynamics and watching how they change over time.

As you go through this iterative process of build-measure-learn there are a few things to keep in mind:

1. Keep Your Aperture Wide

First, regularly check your aperture to make sure you're not getting tunnel vision around your power map. The players whose interests are aligned with yours may be further afield than you assume. In the case of Kidde, the company had to widen their aperture beyond the players involved in setting building codes to include pediatric doctors and nurses, who had a different set of incentives that more closely aligned with Kidde's. With that understanding, they were able to forge partnerships that paved the way to their success. If you limit your power map to only those players who are most obviously in your lane, you risk missing potentially breakthrough regulatory hacks.

Similarly, players who consider you a threat to be squashed may come from outside your immediate market. Be sure to think about your power map from many angles and trace the ripple effects as far and wide as they may lead, lest you be blindsided by a threat that you never saw coming.

2. All Players Are Either Attackers or Defenders

The second thing to keep in mind is that players on your power map will likely have strongly differing perspectives on what is in the public interest and how best to promote it. There are always legitimate disagreements about how to improve the world, and it's rarely obvious a priori what policies or technologies will work or not, and when. However, many of the disagreements you will encounter will go beyond intellectual debate and instead be primarily driven by how the public interest aligns with a player's personal or institutional interest. You're unlikely to find a player willing to make great sacrifices for the public interest, so it's crucial for you to evaluate whether a given player is fundamentally an attacker or a defender.

This is true whether the player is a corporation, nonprofit, government agency, or quasi-governmental agency. As discussed above, what institutions have in common is a desire to protect the institution and therefore the livelihoods of those within the institution.

If a player is the dominant incumbent in a market, their mind-set will usually be one of a defender. They will tend to view anything that disrupts the status quo with concern—whether new technologies or entrants with new business models. On the other hand, anyone other than the dominant incumbent will have more of an attacker mind-set. If they are an established but not the dominant player, they may not want to see new technologies that completely flip over the existing game board, but will be looking for any edge that can allow them to leapfrog the dominant competitor. If the player is an also-ran, they may be very open to radical experiments in technology or policy, given that they have little to lose and potentially lots to gain from flipping over the board and seeing where the pieces fall. As a regulatory hacker, you need to consider whether your solution will help entrench the dominance of the defender or give an edge to attackers, and approach them accordingly.

3. Skepticism and Empathy

The final thing to keep in mind is to avoid facile assumptions but rather test hypotheses through direct engagement. Don't assume you know where a local policymaker will fall on specific regulations or how a trade association will respond to your entry into the market. Develop a hypothesis, but measure the strength of that hypothesis through engagement. When doing so, approach your complex market with a healthy blend of empathy and skepticism—but not cynicism. It's easy to look at trillion-dollar industries like healthcare and education and assume that nobody with any power under the current system wants to see that system changed. It's easy to assume that you're the first person to ever recognize the maddening inefficiencies involved in a visit to a doctor. It's easy to assume that you understand the potential of a new technology like blockchain better than anybody in the stodgy energy industry does. Almost all of these assumptions are probably wrong. The people within these complex markets are, by and large, motivated by a powerful sense of mission and understand where their own inefficiencies lie. They can see the potential of new technologies and are probably trying to figure out how to apply them on their own.

The reason that the changes to our lives as citizens from the digital revolution have lagged those in our lives as consumers isn't because the Valley is more virtuous or talented or "in the know" than the Hill. Or at least it's dangerous to assume that you'll win as a disruptive new entrant because of these reasons. Rather it is because these markets are *complex*. It's not an immutable law of the universe that doctors' offices must be frustrating and inefficient. But it's also not because doctors just don't care or are dumb. If you're going to be the regulatory hacker to impact the public interest in a big way, then make sure it's because you use your fresh set of eyes to understand the complexity of a market *better* than anyone else, rather than staying naive and arrogant about how hard change will be.

Chapter 3

BUSINESS MODELS

It was in the U.S. Army that Blake Hall mastered the art of the pivot.

A third-generation soldier, Blake was a sophomore in Vanderbilt University's ROTC program on September 11, 2001. Upon graduation, he earned his commission as an infantry officer. After completing the U.S. Army's Airborne and Ranger Schools, he reported to his unit. Within five months of taking over his first platoon, his battalion commander selected him to lead the battalion reconnaissance platoon, including three elite scout teams and a section of highly trained snipers.

Reconnaissance platoons are the eyes and ears of the battalion, trained to provide surveillance and take on information-gathering missions, rather than engage directly with the enemy. "Our job was to see and not be seen," Blake says. "That's what we all trained for over the better part of a year before deploying to Iraq."

Then came the curveball: Just weeks into what would be a fifteen-month deployment from mid-2006 to late 2007, while finishing their training on a base in Kuwait before moving into combat zones in Iraq, senior officers pulled Blake and his platoon into an unexpected briefing. "Forget everything you guys have trained for as scouts," they told his platoon. "You're now going to be a direct-action force hunting high-value targets." In the days that followed, his platoon received new equipment and intelligence attachments and were told, in his words, to just "figure this shit out."

With barely two weeks to prepare for their first mission in Iraq, Blake's platoon didn't get off to a great start. During the first couple of months, they succeeded on only about one out of every five missions—that is, eliminating or capturing an identified high-value target—which was about half the 40 percent average success rate for similar platoons in the region.

But they kept learning, and by month three, the platoon caught up to the theater average and tallied some high-profile captures, including several senior al-Qaeda leaders. The next month, his team was punching above average, and their success rate continued to climb from that point forward, month after month, until eventually his unit was knocking out 90 percent of their targets, sometimes with unprecedented speed.

Soon, his brigade commander selected Blake's platoon as his go-to high-value-target force for all of northern Iraq. Along the way, Blake and his unit developed new tactics for daylight operations that were taught throughout the special forces and other platoons pursuing similar missions.

Then, in December 2006, Blake's unit moved down to Baghdad to support General Petraeus's surge strategy. Dubbed the "surge strike force," the unit's pace of operations picked up dramatically, with missions assigned from Fallujah to Baghdad. Blake's platoon continued to learn and adapt—improving their success rate each month. The platoon's success caught the attention of operators from the British Special Air Service (SAS) who were targeting a vehicle bomb network in south Baghdad. They were having difficulty targeting the network at night, so they asked Blake's platoon to target the network during daylight hours. Over the next two weeks, Blake's platoon eliminated nine of the network's top ten targets and eliminated the next layer of the hierarchy that reported to them.

U.S. intelligence officers told Blake it was the fastest they had ever seen a cell like that destroyed.

Those eighteen months, he says, were his "introduction to entrepreneurship."

"If you think about that, you're given a random problem, you have a team, and you just go out and figure out how to solve it, sometimes with limited time and resources, but you figure it out," Blake says. "I started to think, if I can lead a team to that level of proficiency under those conditions, maybe I can do something similar in business and really solve a meaningful challenge."

Blake enrolled in Harvard Business School after returning home, and as part of a school project during his second year, began working on TroopSwap. Hailing from a military family, Blake knew how much U.S. soldiers, veterans, and their families depended on Craigslist to buy and sell goods over the internet. He also was highly aware of the website's shortcomings. Craigslist was very basic, it was impossible to know for sure whether you were buying and selling to fellow military members, and it didn't have certain categories for markets home to major military bases.

Blake and three classmates set out to build a more trusted and universally available Craigslist-like website exclusively for the military community.

They built a beta version and ran the concept past USAA and Military.com, whom they viewed as essential distribution partners, and the initial response was overwhelmingly positive. As the team sped up work on the project, Blake was able to convince USAA to give TroopSwap access to an API for a large subset of their members who were military and had already been screened against government databases. This allowed Blake and his company to build in code that could instantly verify that an individual's identity was tied to a service record.

And then . . . there was silence. A week passed, then another, then another, with no headway beyond the initial enthusiasm from both groups. When Blake asked them what the normal timeframe was for them to move on a project like this, "They told us, 'Well, normal for us is two to three years, but if we're moving really fast, eighteen months.' There was no way we were going to sit around and wait that long."

So Blake did what he had learned to do so well in the military—he and his team changed course and embarked on a slightly revised mission.

"At the time, the Daily Deals space happened to be hot, and we had a few conversations with some marketing managers from companies who we knew wanted to reach that military audience," he says. Still using the USAA API as their military status verification tool, he "decided to try instead to build a daily deals site exclusively for members of the military."

Blake and his team raised about $500,000 in seed money, and in April 2011 they launched their military-only daily deals site under the TroopSwap brand. But it didn't take long to realize the business model simply wasn't sustainable.

"I started to look at the churn data," he says. "It just didn't make any sense. We were churning out close to 10 percent of our membership every month. It wasn't going to work, and unfortunately, I knew we were going to need to change again."

Around that same time, Blake had a series of illuminating conversations with potential partners, including one with the marketing lead for a Microsoft program that offered free e-learning vouchers to members of the military. Blake learned that veterans had to physically bring their military separation

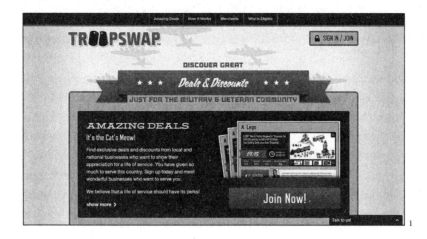

papers from the Department of Defense into a brick-and-mortar Department of Labor office to obtain the vouchers.

Blake was vexed. Didn't this redemption process defeat the entire point of e-learning, in that it's supposed to be remote and convenient and accessible? The program's marketing manager told him, "Yes, we know it sucks, but we have no way to verify if someone on our website is really a member of the military community, and without a way to verify identity on our website, we have no way to protect ourselves from fraud and abuse, and thus we have to confine the distribution of this program to brick-and-mortar outlets where we can actually check ID."

Blake continued to hear feedback from other companies along the lines of, in his words: "You know, we don't really love your idea of a gated garden, but we do think that your ability to verify identity in real time is impressive. If you would actually build this verification technology into an API that we can integrate into our own properties, that would be valuable."

His team went back to the drawing board. "We started to realize that what we had been trying to tackle was really a symptom of a bigger problem, and that simply proving who you are when you are online is really difficult," he says. "We wondered, what if we built a PayPal for identity?" Instead of attaching credit or debit cards to a single-sign-on, you could attach verified ID cards that confirm that you're a teacher or a first responder or a student or a veteran, and once you verify it on any site, you could then bring your identity with you to other sites, too."

Again, Blake and his team pivoted, quickly repositioning the company to focus on distributed infrastructure rather than a gated garden for military community members. Not long after, in November 2012, Under Armour became the first major brand to deploy Blake's technology into their online checkout process, allowing the retail giant to quickly verify military identity and make special offers to veterans.

He realized his company was really onto something this time around.

"It's not just military that has this challenge around identity and trust," Blake says. "It's students, it's AARP, it's AAA, it's every employer that a company wants to have an employee discount program for." Soon, the company—newly rebranded as ID.me—was working with the likes of Under Armour, Bed Bath and Beyond, Microsoft, and the Department of Veterans Affairs to deploy their identity verification technology. Within forty-five days, ID.me had signed up nearly fifty thousand military users.

2

"We were like, 'Okay, awesome, that's product-market fit right there,'" he says. "Now we can really run."

Blake and I had been friends since he moved to D.C. from Cambridge in 2011, so I had a front-row seat as he searched for a business model that could scale. What was powerful to watch was his obsession with what the data was really telling him. He wanted leading indicators of whether a model would work, rather than waiting to watch a failing model run to its bitter end. He also had a knack for always pivoting into a larger potential market.

TroopSwap was a neat idea that might have worked, but creating what was effectively a digital driver's license had vastly greater potential for impact and financial return. Like many regulatory hackers, Blake needed patience and creativity to find a business model that could scale into a massive opportunity in a complex market.

Today, ID.me has raised more than $32 million in capital, including a $19 million Series B in March 2017. More than six million citizens have created accounts, with ten thousand more signing up each day, and AARP recently chose ID.me as the single-sign-on solution for their thirty-eight million members. ID.me customers include eight federal agencies, three states, a major city, and over two hundred national retailers and brands.

Business Models

Like Blake Hall, as you explore your power map, you'll simultaneously be searching for a business model that can scale. The two are inexorably linked: If your power map changes, chances are you will need to revise your business model. Your power map is the chessboard and your business model is your plan for winning the game.

Before you learn about the nuances of business models for regulated start-ups, or *regulated business models*, it's useful to start with a primer on startup business models in general. Every startup is different, and yet these business model patterns appear over and over again. Startups with similar business models will likely encounter common challenges, so it's important to study what has worked and what hasn't for startups like yours.

Although there are always exceptions, your business model will almost certainly fall into one or more of the following three types:

> *Direct*
> B2C (business-to-consumer)
> B2B (business-to-business)
>
> *Indirect*
> B2B2C (business-to-business-to-consumer)
>
> *Multisided Business Models*
> Marketplaces
> Ad-supported

Direct Business Models: B2C and B2B

Direct business models are the most obvious and intuitive. You provide a product or service to a consumer or a business and they pay you for it.

If you're selling to an individual consumer, you will often use digital channels to reach them, optimized for selling items at smaller price point with higher velocity. Fitbit sells their smartwatch directly to consumers via their website. In this way, FitBit is a B2C startup. In general, B2C startups need to have efficient costs of customer acquisition, as they will face correspondingly lower lifetime customer values. To build a big startup, you will also need a market with a large pool of consumers facing the problem that you're solving.

If you're selling to a business, then you may have a wider range of channels available to you. If you're selling a small-ticket item, you may still be using digital channels that look a lot like those you would use to reach consumers. Many SaaS* startups—such as an email marketing tool like MailChimp—at least start by using consumer marketing techniques to reach their customers. But if you're selling to businesses, you may also be able to take advantage of inside sales or direct sales to reach your customer. Palantir sells relationship analysis software to businesses that costs hundreds of thousands of dollars, or even millions of dollars, per year; Palantir can afford to hire sales executives who build personal relationships with prospective customers.

Whether consumers or businesses, the key to these business models is that you cultivate and maintain a direct relationship with your customers. You find them, you keep them, you grow them, and you convince them to refer their friends and colleagues to you.

Indirect Business Models: B2B2C

Indirect business models have always existed but have become more nuanced with the rise of digital distribution channels. If you do not have a direct relationship with your customer, then you are using an indirect business model. One obvious form of indirect relationship is distribution via a retailer. When FitBit sells their smartwatches via Amazon, they have at least a somewhat in-

---

*Software-as-a-service, or software that you use online through a subscription rather than licensing and installing on your own servers.

direct relationship with their customer, in that Amazon maintains control of many aspects of getting customers, keeping customers, growing customers, and driving referrals. Think about it: If you buy a FitBit on FitBit.com, then FitBit's almost certainly going to use that experience to upsell you to FitBit accessories. If you buy a FitBit on Amazon.com, then Amazon will instead use that experience to upsell you to whatever people tend to buy along with FitBits, which may or may not be FitBit accessories.

You also employ indirect business models when your customer and user are different people. Many SaaS business models have this dynamic. When MailChimp sells their solution directly to an individual who needs to do some email marketing in their personal or professional lives, then it is acting like a B2C business, using digital channels to directly reach consumers. When MailChimp sells to a business that makes the service available to their employees, things get trickier. Twenty years ago, businesses tended to have much more direct control over what tools their employees used. Today, a business can purchase MailChimp only to find that most of their employees prefer to use HubSpot. When MailChimp sells to a business, it then has an indirect relationship with their end-user. In many cases, these companies go to great lengths to build direct relationships with their end-users and treat them like customers, even if they have actually sold to the business rather than to the individual.

The key to indirect business models is understanding that you really have to cultivate and maintain two different customer relationships: one with the intermediary and one with the end-user. If you're FitBit, then you have an important relationship with Amazon (or with Best Buy, or perhaps a bulk purchase agreement with United Healthcare to give FitBits to everyone they insure). But in order to ensure customer satisfaction and build brand loyalty, you also have to maintain a relationship with the individual who is the intended user of your product.

Multisided Business Models: Marketplaces and Ads

Multisided business models have existed since the dawn of time, but the digital revolution has turbocharged these models and helped create some of the most valuable businesses in the world. The essence of multisided business models is that you have to add value to at least two different user groups, one or more of which may be your actual customer. These business models tend to require sufficient scale for network effects to take hold before they become viable.

The most obvious form of multisided business model is a marketplace. Since traders first started congregating in convenient locations in the Fertile Crescent, brokers have made money by connecting buyers and sellers. Uber and Airbnb have simply taken marketplace models to mind-bending scale by using the internet and mobile phones. Uber and Airbnb don't actually provide you with rides or rooms. Individuals with their own cars and homes do so. Uber and Airbnb also don't capture most of the value in the transaction. Again, the individual providing the service does. What Uber and Airbnb do is provide sufficient convenience and trust to make it viable to press a button on your phone in nearly any city in the world and find a ride or a room that fits your needs in a few minutes.

Another popular form of multisided business models are advertising-supported models. These have also existed for eons. When I was a kid, I had a paper route delivering newspaper to subscribers who paid a small sum to receive a paper every morning. Those subscribers were customers, but they weren't the newspaper's most lucrative customers by any stretch. The most lucrative customers were advertisers who paid significant sums to get their message in front of the paper's subscribers.

Taking these models to the extreme has made Google and Facebook vastly more valuable than any newspaper ever. Facebook and Google provide powerful tools to users for free. Users pay for these tools not with money but by trusting Facebook and Google with incredibly detailed data about their interests, urges, obsessions, likenesses, and physical whereabouts. In turn, Facebook and Google generate revenues by selling what they know about you to brands via precisely targeted ads. For Facebook and Google, you aren't the *customer*—you're the *product*.

Network effects are the double-edged sword of multisided business models. For marketplaces, if you don't have enough sellers, then there is no reason for buyers to come to your market. And if you don't have enough buyers, then why should sellers bother to come? Once you can get the marketplace dynamic started within a given community, though, the benefits of network effects can become explosive. As frustrated as many people might get with Uber's behavior, it continues to grow, largely because network effects continue to lock drivers and riders into their platform in cities all around the world.

Network effects also drive a similar dynamic for ad-supported business models. Advertisers generally won't spend significant money on a platform until it has a sufficient density of audience. Startups have to build great tools and acquire millions of users before they can start to monetize through advertising. Once that virtuous cycle has started to work, though, it can be extremely difficult to compete against a free tool backed by vast ad revenues.

Regulated Business Models

All of the insights above about direct, indirect, and multisided business models apply to startups in simpler markets as well as more complex ones. What make *regulated* business models unique are the significant regulatory distor-

Regulated Business Model Taxonomy

How Does the Citizen Benefit?

Directly / Indirectly

Is the citizen the customer?   Who provides benefit?

Yes

Institution   Government

Will the citizen pay full cost?   No

B2B(+R)   B2G

Yes   No

Dorsata   SpaceX

Government subsidy   Social impact

B2C(+R)   B2C(+SR)

Tesla   Mamotest

B2C(+R)   Regulated marketplace   Is it delivered via the public or private sector?

23andMe   Uber   Private / Public

Will the institution pay full cost?   B2G2C

SeamlessDocs

Yes / No

B2B2C(+R)   B2B2C(+SI)

TransitScreen   EverFi

tions that come from government efforts to promote and protect the public interest.

As a regulatory hacker aiming to benefit the public interest with your product or service, the key question for you to explore is the extent to which a citizen is actually your user and is willing to pay for the benefit to that citizen.

Healthcare is a canonical example. Nearly every product or service involved in healthcare should exist to ultimately benefit patients, whether it's aimed at doctors, hospital administrators, or insurers. But only a small fraction of those products and services are intended *for use* by patients. And in most countries in the world, patients pay directly for an even smaller fraction of the products or services involved in healthcare. As a result, if you're seeking to hack healthcare, you may have difficulty selling a solution to the citizen who most directly benefits from it, even if that citizen is also the user.

This distinction between who benefits from your product, who uses it, who provides it, and who pays for it is the tension to explore when building your power map and searching for your regulated business model. You'll have to deeply understand these relationships to find a regulated business model that can scale.

If the Citizen Is Your User

If the citizen is your user, the next question to explore is whether they'll pay enough for your business model to scale.

If the citizen is your user *and* will pay enough for your solution, then you'll likely be able to develop one of two business models: "business to citizen (with regulation)" or "regulated marketplaces."

An example of a B2C(+R) business model is 23andMe. This company sells its home genetics tests directly to citizens who have demonstrated a willingness to pay, but it operates with a high degree of regulation, given the significant public health issues inherent in their service.

Examples of regulated marketplaces are Uber and Airbnb. Both are marketplaces in which buyers have demonstrated a willingness to pay for the service, but they operate with significant regulation that governs their relationships with both their buyers and their sellers.

If the citizen is your user but is *not* willing to pay enough for the benefit that your solution provides, then you should ask yourself whether there is an entity willing to subsidize your solution or otherwise provide incentives for citizens to use it.

If governments are willing to do so, then in many ways you're still a B2C(+R) startup. An example of a B2C(+R) startup that benefits from government subsidies is Tesla. At least for a little while longer, if you buy a Tesla, the United States government will give you a $7,500 tax credit.[3]

Interestingly, governments aren't the only players willing to provide subsidies or incentives for solutions that benefit citizens. Other institutions may be willing to do so, like a corporation or foundation. In this case, you may be able to develop a "business to citizen with social impact," or B2C(+SI), business model. Social impact is the willingness of certain institutions to pay for services that benefit citizens. When foundations or nonprofit organizations do so, it is often directly aligned with their mission. When corporations do so, it is often to generate positive brand recognition with citizens or policymakers and is referred to as "corporate social responsibility." B2C(+SI) models can be thought of as a special case of an ad-supported business model, except the audience that matters to the advertiser isn't necessarily the user base, but rather citizens or policymakers more broadly.

An example of a B2C+SI startup is Mamotest (which you'll meet later), where corporations subsidize mammograms for Latin American women.

If You Serve the Citizen Through an Institution

If *government* pays to provide your solution to citizens, then you have a "business to government to citizen," or B2G2C, business model, which, given the complexity of government procurement rules, is a special case of a B2B2C business model. An example of a B2G2C business model is SeamlessDocs, where government bureaucrats use SeamlessDocs to create interactive web and mobile forms that citizens use to seamlessly interact with government. SeamlessDocs has had to become adroit at selling to municipal governments to make their business model work.

If an *institution*, such as a corporation or hospital or utility, provides the solution to the citizen and is willing to pay you for your product or service, then your business model is "business to business to citizen (with regulation)," or B2B2C(+R). An example of a B2B2C(+R) business models would be TransitScreen. TransitScreen sells their real-time information display solution to property owners who put their digital screens in the lobbies of their buildings so that citizens can more easily choose among transportation services. The beneficiaries and users of the digital screens are citizens, but the provider and payer are property owners.

You will also find business models in complex markets in which institutions provide solutions to citizens, but the provider is paid by other institutions looking to demonstrate their social impact. If an institution is paying you to provide a product or service to another institution that will then provide it to citizens, then your business model is "business to business to citizen (with social impact)," or B2B2C(+SI).

An example of a startup with a B2B2C(+SI) business model is EverFi. EverFi provides digital learning solutions to schools, which use them to teach important topics to students. Neither the student nor the school pays EverFi, though. Rather, EverFi finds third-party payers such as corporations or foundations willing to pay to make sure students receive EverFi's supplemental digital learning.

If You Serve the Citizen by Serving an Institution

Finally, if citizens benefit from your product or service, but only in the abstract sense of the public interest, then you have either a B2G or a B2B(+R) business model.

Is government willing to pay for your solution to further the public interest without any direct engagement from citizens? Then your business model is "business to government," or B2G. An example of a B2G startup is SpaceX. Citizens don't directly use the launch services that SpaceX provides to NASA or the Air Force, but they do benefit collectively in the long-term, abstract sense from cheaper launch services.

Is an institution willing to pay for your solution to further the public interest? Then your business model is "business to business (with regulation)," or B2B(+R). An example of a B2B(+R) startup is Dorsata. Dorsata provides tools that make it easier for clinicians within OB-GYN practices to follow best practices when treating women. The patients do not use the Dorsata service. They might not even know that their OB-GYN is using Dorsata. But Dorsata helps improve the quality of care while reducing costs. And healthcare providers and insurance companies are willing to pay for Dorsata's services for these reasons.

The Crux of Your Business Model

You can group regulated business models into three buckets, based on the core challenge unique to each of them.

If you sell directly to government, either B2G2C or a B2G, you have to understand the unique challenges and benefits of government procurement. You'll learn about these types of business models in depth in Chapter 9: Selling to Government.

If you sell to citizens or private institutions, whether B2C(+R), B2B2C(+R), B2B(+R), or a regulated marketplace, you have to understand how to navigate policy incentives and barriers. You'll learn about these types of business models in depth in Chapter 10: Selling to Citizens and Private Institutions.

Finally, if you're leveraging social impact, either B2C(+SI) or B2B2C(+SI), then you need to understand the world of social impact and how to use it to your advantage. You'll learn about these types of business models in Chapter 11: Selling with Social Impact.

Combining Regulated Business Models

In many cases, you'll find that your regulated startup may have multiple viable business models. Perhaps you could sell to government, or you could sell to a private institution with a third party paying, due to social impact. You shouldn't assume that the first or most obvious business model you discover is necessarily the right one for your business. Instead, you need to be a scientist and search for the optimal business model, or combination of business models, that will enable your business to scale.

This kind of creativity in mixing and matching regulated business models is helping One App get people off the street and into homes in Portland, Oregon. Tyrone Poole, the founder of OneApp, has one of the most extraordinary journeys to product-marker fit you'll ever hear.

"It was the rock-bottom moment in my life," Tyrone says about the first night he found himself sleeping in a homeless shelter, nearly twelve years ago. What stands out most vividly, he says, was the smell of the vomit on the front of his shirt. Everything Tyrone still owned was stuffed into two duffel bags underneath the broken cot on which he lay awake in the dark—a cot that a shelter volunteer had begrudgingly wheeled out after a police officer had dropped Tyrone at their doorstep a little after midnight.

By that point, Tyrone had been homeless and couch surfing for months, his young daughter spending some nights with him and others with her mother, his parents, or other relatives. Earlier that evening, a cold one in Portland in late 2006, Tyrone's latest host had politely but firmly shown him the door. At the time, Poole was still recovering from a severe leg injury and relegated to crutches, so he dragged his belongings and his body thirty blocks on one good leg to the nearest rail station, only to collapse and vomit from the pain and exhaustion when he got there. The cop who found him—once Tyrone had a chance to explain his situation—offered to take him anywhere he needed.

"But I had nowhere left to go," he says. "There was no one left to call."

Lying on the cot at the homeless shelter, Tyrone eventually turned the vomit-stained shirt backwards to avoid the stench. He hoped it would help him sleep, but it was no use. "I didn't sleep a wink that night," he says. "Not a wink."

It was a shocking and heartbreaking turn of fortune for a man whose life held nothing but promise just a year earlier. At the time, Tyrone was training to become a firefighter at Portland Community College, and by 2005, he had earned a fire science degree and emergency medical technician certification. His career and his life were pointed squarely in the right direction.

That changed suddenly that December, when Tyrone fell during a training exercise, tearing a muscle and shredding the lymph node in his left leg. The injury ended his firefighting career and placed Poole in and out of the hospital for the next nine months. Without a paycheck, he couldn't afford rent, and because he had been injured in training and not on the job, there was no workers' compensation to fall back on. He wasn't physically able to work, either, so he didn't qualify for unemployment benefits, nor had he yet been injured for more than a year, so he couldn't apply for federal disability assistance.

As his injured leg needed to be elevated at least sixteen hours a day, Tyrone was left floundering with no way to earn an income and was soon evicted from his apartment. He moved most of his belongings into a storage unit, but when he fell behind on the payments a few months later, the unit's contents were auctioned off. It didn't take long before his car was repossessed, too.

"I was winning at life not that long ago," he says. "Suddenly, here I was in a shelter."

It was at that shelter that Tyrone learned about one benefit he did qualify for—what's known as a low-income housing voucher, which would essentially pay for him to live in an apartment in the city for one year with his rent paid by the government. His spirits were lifted momentarily, only to be dashed again when he learned he would still need to be approved by an apartment management company. With his credit ruined over the previous year, the application rejections started trickling in one by one. Worse, each application came with a price tag: $35 here, turned away; $50 there, turned away again. Not only was the process disheartening, it was becoming prohibitively expensive for someone with no steady income and no savings whatsoever.

"I'm sitting here with a letter in my hand telling me someone will pay for me to live somewhere, and yet I'm still sleeping in a shelter because I can't find somewhere that will take me," he said.

Luckily, Tyrone was approved for an apartment just days before his voucher was scheduled to expire, which would have landed him on the street. He soon started volunteering and then working at a local YWCA, helping other homeless individuals and families navigate the very same process to find affordable housing opportunities. That led to a job with the Housing Authority of Portland, where he eventually wrote a "dissertation" for policymakers on the inefficiencies in matching supply and demand for low-income housing, complete with painful data on the percentage of people who were awarded housing vouchers that lapsed before they were able to find housing for which they qualified.

His personal and professional journey opened his eyes to a market opportunity that he believed would help homeless individuals in need of housing and property managers alike—and the seed of an entrepreneurial idea was born.

On December 12, 2017, almost eleven years to the day since Tyrone found himself sleeping in that shelter, he launched OneApp, an online housing platform that screens prospective tenants against the exact application criteria for hundreds of different rental properties. The tool allows home seekers to fill out a single application and instantly see all of the units in the area for which they are approved.

Over the next month, more than a thousand renters created OneApp accounts while more than ninety of the roughly hundred and twenty-five property management firms in the Portland area signed up to list their properties on the for-profit startup's platform. During that period—one of the quietest times of the year for apartment rental activity—five hundred applications were submitted through the platform.

OneApp generates revenue from multiple sources in multiple ways. "We earn revenue from the renters, the property management companies, the government, and eventually, from the data, too," Tyrone explains.

That is, renters pay a small fee—about $35—to use OneApp's platform. Meanwhile, property managers can sign up to list their units for free, but some of the portal's signature perks are reserved for premium accounts. For instance, if a unit goes unrented on the platform for more than thirty days, the listing manager automatically receives a notice like the following: "This unit has been vacant for more than thirty days. Did you know there are fifty renters looking for housing in your area who we know would qualify to live there? Click here to see who they are."

The next screen on the platform shows the property manager fifty grayed-out renter faces—and a sign-up button to upgrade their account for $199 per month if they would like to contact them.

"Right now, the only alternatives are putting a banner outside or going through one of a few rental websites to find leads," Tyrone says. "Then you just have to sit by the phone and hope, and even if you do get inquiries, you don't know that they will meet your application criteria."

With a premium account on OneApp, he said, property managers can reach out directly to preapproved home seekers, invite them to an open house, or provide some other incentive to entice them to consider their property. They can also pay to boost their listing in search results on the renters' side of the platform.

The OneApp marketplace benefits from a clever twist, though: Government helped launch his marketplace.

Tyrone helped develop and then won a $275,000 contract with the state of Oregon to build a new low-cost housing-finder website using OneApp's technology. Not only is OneApp earning revenue from the technology contract, but by using OneApp's portal, Tyrone's startup now has exclusive access to list and process applications for some four hundred fifty publicly owned affordable housing units throughout the city, bringing in nearly another $1 million in expected annual revenue. Having exclusive access to those units also increases the supply of homes on his platform, making it all the more attractive to home hunters—which in turn makes it more attractive to private property managers, too.

OneApp's platform provides a more streamlined and friendly experience for citizens, so the government has been willing to pay to use the technology. At the same time, the technology provides a more cost-effective, one-application-fits-all experience for apartment seekers, so they, too, are willing to pay to use the technology. And of course, property managers want to list their properties where prospective tenants are looking, and they are willing to pay extra to be able to segment and target only those renters who would be eligible to move in.

Sequencing Regulated Business Models

Tyrone Poole is helping get the homeless into homes by combining elements of different regulated business models.

Dr. Nora Khaldi is, in turn, hoping to cure diabetes by thoughtfully staging different regulated business models over time as her company, Nuritas, matures.

More than four hundred million people around the world suffer from diabetes, which the World Health Organization has declared a global epidemic. Every single day, more than four thousand people die from the disease, the vast majority of them sufferers of type 2 diabetes, according to the organization, which projects that diabetes deaths will increase by two-thirds between 2012 and 2030.

I first met Nora when she won the Challenge Cup Dublin in 2015, the same year Tyrone won the Challenge Cup Portland. Nora is an Irish mathematician with a PhD in molecular evolution whose Dublin-based startup is combining artificial intelligence and genomics to disrupt the way that scientists discover and develop drugs and other healthcare products. Nuritas leverages their AI engine to select and extract peptides—basically, amino acid chains that exist naturally in animal and plant material, including food and food by-products. The extracted peptides can be used to develop new health supplements as well as medicines for diseases ranging from inflammatory conditions to type 2 diabetes.

"Pharma's approach to finding new active molecules is close to random, it's like searching the ocean for a treasure chest without a map. It usually takes years and millions of dollars," Nora said. "What we do is provide the map."

Nora started to develop the processes and technologies to identify and extract these potentially game-changing compounds while conducting research at University College Dublin and the University of California Davis. And while she knew she could cut down the exploration-to-discovery-to-production process time considerably over industry norms, when it came time to launch the company, she realized that it would still be years before Nuritas would have regulator-approved, market-ready peptides to sell or license to other companies.

"We were small, but I wanted to start earning revenue right away, because I wanted to pay our staff and show some proof of concept to investors," Nora says. "Our initial goal was to get as many clients signed up as possible."

Rather than waiting around to see lucrative but long-term returns on investment from peptide patents, Nora layered in some short-term cash-generating activities while Nuritas was getting off the ground. Notably, she immediately began consulting for large food companies to help them identify valuable molecular compounds hidden inside their by-products—that is, the material they would otherwise discard.

"These companies all have any number of by-products that they don't know what to do with, and those by-products, if you break them down and run them through the right computer program, can be transformed into something superbly valuable by identifying and extracting the one or two compounds within that by-product that may be commercially viable."

Nora designed Nuritas's contracts with the food companies to include a onetime discovery fee as well as royalties derived from the future sales of material they had been discarding, thus ensuring some money would start flowing into the company immediately but also giving Nuritas a stream of revenue that could fuel the company's growth while it continued to build its own portfolio of valuable, IP-protected peptides and eventually pursue private investment.

"The minute we got investment, we stopped that model to focus on what we had aimed to do all along," Nora says. "But that provided very important support for us in the beginning."

Barely a year later, Nuritas announced that it had made a scientific breakthrough that was subsequently hailed as a potential game-changer in the fight to prevent type 2 diabetes. One year after that, in December 2017, Nora and company raised a $20 million Series A round led by Cultivian Sandbox, a venture capital firm specializing in agtech, which added to previous funding from VisVires New Protein, Marc Benioff, Ali Partovi, and U2 band members Bono and The Edge.

Sometimes, as Blake learned with ID.me, you need to pivot from one business model to another to unlock the next phase of growth or the next larger market. Or, as Nora understood, the right long-term business model won't solve your short-term challenges. As a regulatory hacker, you should never stop exploring ways to improve your business model, even if that means evolving it over time or taking a short-term detour that gets you to the right place in the long-run.

Finding a Regulated Business Model

The process of finding a regulated business model is a process of experimentation. You need to think about all the players on your power map: your beneficiary, your user, your provider, your payers, your regulators, and your influencers. Finding a business model that scales for a regulated startup isn't simply about the customer, their problem, and your solution. It requires finding a business model that unlocks value across the entire spectrum of stakeholders—and avoids those opposed to your solution from using gatekeepers to block you from the market. If your solution doesn't fit for any one of your stakeholders, or you cannot check those opposed to you, your regulated business model is unlikely to work.

Regulated Business Model Canvas

Power Players • Beneficiaries • Users • Providers • Customers • Influencers • Regulators	Problem	Solution	Unique Value Proposition
		Key Activities	
	Cost Structure	Revenue	
	Rules		

Finding a regulated business model is about simultaneously solving both a math problem and a political problem. Your regulated business model requires you to think about your product or service; your value proposition to each stakeholder; the channels necessary to reach your user, your provider, and your payer; the nature of the ongoing relationships that you will have with each; how other players across your power map will react to your moves; your revenue model; and your cost structure. If you solve the political problem but fail the math test, then your business model won't be profitable enough to scale rapidly. If you solve the math problem but fail the political test, then you are likely to be a comet that shines brightly for a moment before burning up—or getting shot out of the sky.

While building your power map, you should be exploring regulated business models in parallel by forming hypotheses about each of these dimensions. From here, you will go through as many iterations of build-measure-learn as necessary to validate your regulated business model. Most of your learnings will in fact invalidate key hypotheses across your business model. Each time you invalidate one, you have to work back through the math *and* political calculus of your business model to understand the implications to every other hypothesis. In a sense, building a regulated business model is like solving a multidimensional Rubik's Cube. Each time you build-measure-learn, what you learn may remove a variety of other possible business model solutions—or it might unlock ones you hadn't imagined before.

This is one of the biggest challenges of hacking in the public interest: the patience to figure it out. The problems to solve are obvious. The inefficiencies are great. The markets are huge. But complex markets have many more dimensions than simpler markets. Building your regulated business models will therefore likely require many more build-measure-learn cycles than simpler ones.

Chapter 4

GROWTH

Dan Yates and Alex Laskey always took the Civic, not the 4Runner.

And that's where the conversation started.

Dan—a Harvard graduate and computer whiz in his late twenties who had already started, scaled, and sold an edtech startup—owned a gas-guzzling Toyota 4Runner SUV. Alex, one of Dan's closest friends and a political polling guru, owned a relatively old, gas-sipping Honda Civic sedan.

As Alex recalls, "That 4Runner was really fun to drive, we both loved that thing, and yet, whenever we were together, even if we were going out with both our then girlfriends, now wives, we would always take my Civic. It was far more cramped, far less comfortable, and yet, we took the Civic everywhere. We even drove it to go camping one year, which seems ridiculous now."

Why? "We did it because we were environmentalists, and we knew that the Civic got better mileage and was better for the environment, so we were willing to sacrifice comfort," Alex says. "That led to this 'aha' moment, where we realized we were going to absurd lengths and making ourselves uncomfortable to save a little bit of gas, and yet neither of us had any idea how energy efficient our homes were or whether we were being environmentally friendly there."

"We agreed that there should be some consumer transparency there," he added.

So Alex and Dan set out to create and market, as Alex describes it, "a better energy bill." More specifically, the duo embarked on a startup journey to leverage cutting-edge behavioral science research to motivate homeowners to save

energy and be more thoughtful about how they use electricity. They envisioned
a utility bill generation software that would show consumers how much energy
their homes used in the past month in comparison to their neighbors and to
other homes like theirs, and Opower was born.

The business model question quickly emerged, as it so often does for regulatory hackers trying to solve a problem in the public interest: Who would be
the buyer?

Right away, Alex and Dan ruled out citizens as their customer. On average,
an American family spends only about 2 percent of its income on electricity,
so shaving off, say, 10 percent of that wasn't likely to incentivize an individual
homeowner to pay extra to receive a special energy report or a better version
of their existing utility bill.[1]

Source[2]

Then, the question became whether a revamped, more insightful energy
bill was something utilities would pay Opower to produce for their customers,
or whether it was something a local or state government might be willing to
pay to produce as a public service in the interest of energy conservation. Over
time, it became clear to Alex and Dan that the most logical buyer for their
software platform would be the entities that were already sending out electric
bills in the first place—the utilities.

Except, they soon realized that selling to utilities meant they would still
need to sell—in a way—to government, too.

"Once it became clear that the market for us was utilities, it also became clear that one reason utilities might buy from us would be if regulators encouraged or at least authorized them to use our platform," Alex said. "On the other hand, one of the obstacles to selling to them might be their hesitance about whether or not regulators were going to approve us."

He added: "Right away, it was obvious that we were going to sit right at that seam between regulators and utilities."

With that in mind, Opower's growth engine became two separate, but aligned, sales forces—one charged with selling regulators on the idea that the company's software should be approved, or better yet, incentivized or mandated, for use by utility companies, and a second team charged with actually selling the software to those utilities. In a way, the first team was helping create market demand for the company's product while the second actually sold that product.

That growth engine proved more powerful than Dan or Alex could have imagined when camping in Dan's Honda Civic. Since Opower was founded in 2007, Opower has helped reduce electricity consumption so much that it's the equivalent to taking multiple nuclear power plants off the grid. The model proved to be a windfall for their investors as well, with Opower going public less than seven years after founding, before being acquired by Oracle in 2016.

You'll Need a Growth Engine, Too

Building a power map and finding a business model that can scale are table stakes for a successful regulatory hacker. If you want to succeed at the scale of economies and societies, then you'll need to grow exceptionally fast for a sustained period of time. As Paul Graham succinctly puts it: "A startup is a company designed to grow fast."

As you'll learn in this chapter, growth isn't simply about marketing, nor is it something that you explore only *after* you've found a business model that can scale. Rather, developing a growth model is an extension of the same iterative process of build-measure-learn that you should be using throughout your startup journey.

Growth Hacking

Before we explore how to grow your regulated startup, let's review the basics of how startups should think about growth: growth hacking.

Growth Hacking

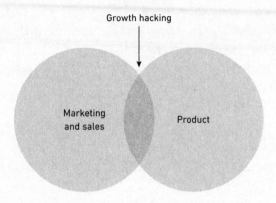

Growth hacking is the hacker ethos applied to the challenge of rapid growth. Specifically, growth hacking is a process of rapid experimentation across marketing and product development to identify the most efficient ways to grow a business. Whereas traditional businesses think of product development as a separate and distinct function from marketing and sales, growth hacking sits at the *junction* of product development and marketing. Some growth hacks are simply using digital channels in creative new ways. But many of the most powerful growth hacks are about building features into the core product that accelerate growth.

Great startup teams spend every waking moment thinking about how to accelerate their *growth flywheel*. The growth flywheel starts with *getting* a customer for your product, then *keeping* that customer by surprising and delight-

Growth Flywheel

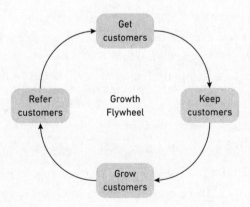

ing them, *growing* your relationship with that customer by offering them new things they can do with you, and finally getting that customer to *refer* new customers to you. Once you get the growth flywheel turning, it can create powerful momentum toward faster and faster growth—which Paul Graham pegs at an ideal of 5 to 7 percent *per week*.[3] Growth hacking uses the interplay of digital channels and the product itself to spin the growth flywheel faster and faster.

Consider how Dropbox became a utility nearly as pervasive as email or a web browser. This is surprising since Dropbox is essentially just online file storage, which wasn't especially novel when Drew Houston and Arash Ferdowsi founded the company in 2007. What made Dropbox unique was a supersimple user experience that made it as seamless to store files in the cloud as it was on your local drive. Dropbox also employed two growth hacks in their early days to incredible effect. First, their website was nearly as spartan as the Google homepage, without much information about Dropbox's features or pricing plans. Instead it urged visitors to do just one thing: try Dropbox. A free trial immediately got you a few hundred megabytes of free storage, so you could start putting your most used files in the cloud with Dropbox immediately. They reduced any and all friction to *getting* customers.

The second growth hack complemented the first by offering you more free storage for each friend you referred to Dropbox, who in turn would receive free storage as well. Five or six referrals would probably get you enough free storage to move all your important files onto Dropbox.

This dynamic accelerated Dropbox's growth flywheel by artificially creat-

ing network effects using the currency of free storage. Of course, free storage costs Dropbox real money. They could have spent that money on other forms of marketing, such as Facebook ads, but by using free storage as a currency to get people to *refer* new customers, they were also *keeping* and *growing* existing customers.

The key insight is that these growth hacks involved both the product itself and the channels to reach more customers for the product.

Growth Hacking Meets Public Affairs

Regulatory hackers need to be growth hackers, too. The ever-increasing sophistication in how to grow a startup via growth hacks is important for all startups. But because of the unique challenges regulated startups face, growth hacks alone won't prove sufficient.

Growth hacking offered Uber no insights into how to handle taxi commissions wanting to shut them down, or how to turn those fights into media spectacles that would actually drive more riders to their service. Growth hacking couldn't teach HopSkipDrive to handle compliance with TrustLine or help Opower create the regulatory nudge to get utilities to buy their service.

Once government becomes a stakeholder in the problem you want to

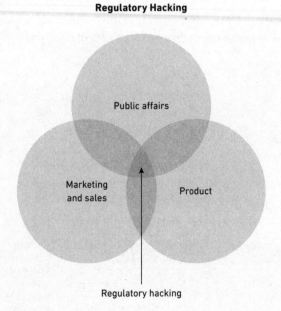

Regulatory Hacking

Public affairs

Marketing and sales

Product

Regulatory hacking

solve—once you're a regulatory hacker—growth hacking can only be a partial solution to growing your startup. You also need to employ the skills of public affairs, or the art and science of managing public stakeholders.

If growth hacking is the fusing of product with marketing, regulatory hacking is the fusing of product and marketing with public affairs.

Beg Forgiveness or Ask Permission?

Much of the rest of this book, and in particular Section 4: The Regulatory Hacker's Toolkit, will explore various regulatory hacks and the tools you use to craft new hacks for your regulated startups. Many of these regulatory hacks will fall into one of two broad strategic categories. Either you're begging forgiveness or you're asking permission. Uber begged forgiveness (or at least Dara Khosrowshahi eventually has). HopSkipDrive asked permission. Like Uber, 23andMe begged forgiveness. Opower asked permission.

Your answer to this question should flow from a cold, pragmatic reading of your power map and an understanding of the imperatives of your regulated business model. But whichever answer you pursue, it will drive many of your subsequent decisions.

The Iron Triangle: When to Beg Forgiveness

When the Valley thinks about regulation standing in the way of innovation, they tend to think about the quintessential example of regulatory capture: the *iron triangle*.

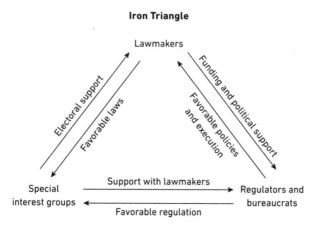

Common at all levels of government, in most every part of the world, iron triangles refer to trilateral, mutually beneficial, and self-reinforcing relationships that develop between lawmakers, regulators, and special-interest groups (the latter generally representing large, powerful incumbent institutions). Like most examples of regulatory capture, iron triangles tend to subordinate the broad public interest to the narrower benefits of powerful private institutions or special interests.

By teaming up, this often-small group of "*insiders*" can maintain a stranglehold on all policymaking decisions in their area of concern, presenting a united front against encroaching "*outsiders*" who may try to tinker with rules that these three groups have spent years or even decades locking into place.

Here's how a typical "you-scratch-my-back" iron triangle scheme works. Regulators and bureaucrats who run government agencies (the rule interpreters and enforcers) count on their friends in the legislature (the rule makers) to block any attempts to change rules that are important to them or, inversely, that would scale back their agency's power. Lawmakers, meanwhile, depend on those agency officials to maintain certain contracts and interpret laws in ways that benefit their constituents and their donors, including private institutions and special interests. In exchange, those private institutions provide support (financial or otherwise) to those lawmakers and help drum up support for the work of the regulators and bureaucrats, helping them advance their respective agendas and gain more power. When the time comes, those private-sector groups then expect to be consulted and appeased when new rules affecting their interests come up for discussion.

These kinds of relationships are designed to not only accomplish a policy objective in the short term but also to lock in for the long term the inherent value buried within these lucrative markets.

How do you know whether your regulated startup needs to prepare to take on an iron triangle? The question to ask is this: Does someone lose power or make less money because of your solution, and is that someone, be it a private institution or industry consortium, relatively monolithic, well-organized, and powerful? Said another way, do you find yourself in a zero-sum game in which, in order for your regulated startup to win, someone else must necessarily lose?

If so, you're in an iron triangle scenario, and you need a strategy to breach those walls.

Iron triangles tend to create big, juicy, obvious opportunities for regulatory hackers because they force inefficiencies and technological stagnation to build up over time, layer upon layer. To grow quickly in a complex market dominated by an iron triangle, it may be less about the growth, per se, and more about hacking the iron triangle. Put a big-enough crack in the dam, and the water will do the rest for you.

The first step in hacking an iron triangle is understanding who's currently benefiting from the triangle and who's losing. Naturally, the three constituencies that comprise the iron triangle tend to benefit from its existence, or else they wouldn't be holding up their respective parts of the bargain. On the other hand, there's almost always someone (besides you) who gets a raw deal. Most often, due to the very nature of the iron triangle (a system that prioritizes special interests over broad public interests), it's going to be the public—the citizens—who get the short end of the stick.

Such was the case for Uber. Before Uber arrived on the scene, nearly every city played host to an impenetrable iron triangle that featured more or less the same three players. One player was the local taxi industry, consisting of representatives from any number of local taxi operators. The second player was the city council, the members of which establish the laws by which taxis can operate. The third player was the taxi commission, tasked with interpreting and enforcing those laws. The well-heeled taxi industry and their lobbyists helped elect (and then reelect) mayors and city councilmembers who protected the rules the local industry had worked for decades to put in place—laws that limited competition and maximized profits. Those mayors then appointed regulators to lead the taxi commissions, regulators who often came from the industry, and those city councilmembers voted accordingly on legislation that could undermine the operations or long-term success of the cab companies. The taxi commission did its part enforcing the rules that had been put in place to protect the industry. In short, all three of these parties benefited from the triangle they had locked in place. Meanwhile, citizens (in this case, taxi riders) were the ones who were losing out in the form of an inefficient, expensive, and often unpleasant experience trying to move about a given city. When Uber entered D.C., you still couldn't pay for a D.C. cab with a credit card. Uber didn't need to be great for citizens to clamor for them. They just needed to suck a bit less than the incumbent.

The next step in hacking an iron triangle is determining which of the three parts of the triangle you should start to put pressure on by organizing and leveraging the concerns of the losing party. Uber did exactly this. Which group is most directly beholden to the collective voice of citizens demanding a better way to move about their city? In this case, it's not the taxi operators (no amount of rider complaints or frustration would ever make them cede to Uber). It's not the taxi commissioners either, because as long as riders are generally kept safe, their jobs don't hang in the balance based on how pleased people are with the level of service.

It's mayors and city councilmembers who, at the end of the day, must be responsive to voters. Uber went to the grassroots and was able to mobilize, amplify, and funnel citizens' frustrations about the taxi industry's iron triangle directly to the politicians they voted into office. Over time, the pressure that Uber, by way of their vocal and influential ridership, applied to that part of the triangle was enough to weaken and eventually cripple the regulatory fortresses that had been erected over decades in city after city.

The final step is evaluating the consequences of "begging forgiveness," which is a polite way of saying you should have a sense of how aggressively you can ignore or "reinterpret" existing laws, regulations, or norms while you rally citizens to your cause. For Uber, the practical consequences of ignoring taxi commission regulations were typically vehicle impoundments and small fines, which were asymmetrically small costs compared with the spoils from successfully breaking the iron triangle in a given city. For 23andMe, however, the consequences of ignoring an FDA cease and desist order could have been dire. When the FDA finally suspended their ability to sell home genetics testing, 23andMe had to compromise.[4] In other cases, you may simply not be able to beg forgiveness, so your triangle-breaking hack may have to be something else, perhaps leveraging the media or grasstops to break the weakest part of the triangle.

Part of the consequences of "begging forgiveness" that you should assess are ethical as well as practical. Philosophers have assessed the moral implications of civil disobedience against bad laws since well before Henry David Thoreau. It's not my place to guide your moral considerations, but breaking rules, even if you believe they're not in the public interest and may be changed later, isn't something to be done lightly. When people roll their eyes at the Valley breaking laws in the name of innovation, it's often because of a sense that it was done trivially, as if startup founders believe that laws were meant for lesser people. As a regulatory hacker, you are working to further the public interest, which implies in contrast that you *do* think through your actions and their implications carefully.

To break it down, if you see an iron triangle in the middle of your power map, then growth may be more about removing the impediment of the iron triangle than anything else. The first step in hacking an iron triangle is to *really* understand your power map, knowing which stakeholders comprise the triangle, how they benefit from it, which stakeholders lose, and how the power dynamics work between those groups. Who influences whom and how? Next, you must find ways to put strain on whichever part of the triangle is most closely linked to, and may be most responsive to, those who are losing from the regulatory capture taking place. Finally, know what you can get away with, what costs you're comfortable bearing, and the moral implications of your actions.

Conquering Inertia: When to Ask for Permission

Uber *had* to beg forgiveness. There was never going to be a hack in the early days that involved taxi commissions giving them permission to operate. That does not, however, mean that iron triangles are the norm when it comes to regulatory hacking. The truth is that not every regulated startup will confront an iron triangle; in fact, most won't. Often, you'll develop a solution that's so innovative in nature that there won't be an entrenched incumbency to siphon value away from. You may have a solution in which no one really loses—and in fact, many will gain—or at least a dynamic where there's no obvious, well-organized loser in the short term.

HopSkipDrive is a great example. With HopSkipDrive in place, parents have an easier time moving their kids from one place to another, kids get to soccer practice and dance rehearsals on time, local businesses have a few more full-time working parents to draw from in the labor pool, caregivers have a new income opportunity, cities see fewer cars on the road and more jobs, and of course, HopSkipDrive profits. Looking at it another way, who loses? Maybe the traditional nanny and au pair industry. However, those groups are so fragmented and the consequences so far off they are unlikely to represent any kind of meaningful opposition to HopSkipDrive.

Startups like these, who have no known enemies, must face no regulatory resistance, right?

Not quite. In complex markets, even a status quo that is suboptimal for absolutely everyone involved is, nevertheless, the status quo. While this book will attempt to dispel many myths and misconceptions about government, regulation, and bureaucracy, the idea that governments move slowly, even when a move is obvious, is true almost across the board.

Penny Lee brings a unique perspective to this brutal truth, with experiences that stretch from the Hill to the Valley. She's served as the executive director of the Democratic Governors' Association and as a senior adviser to Senate Majority Leader Harry Reid, but was also instrumental in launching K Street Capital and scaling it to more than forty politically connected angel investors. Today, she leads strategy for 1776, where she helps regulatory hackers refine their strategies.

"I worked for the U.S. Senate where it was said, 'all good things go to die,'" Penny shares ruefully. "No senator or congressman was ever voted out of office for not being innovative enough. It's important to understand that more often they want to talk about the issue and not the solution. Innovation is not in their DNA. They can create a lot of noise and harm your business more often than they can help advance the cause."

The same often holds true at the state or municipal level.

Consequently, startups in this scenario do face a powerful enemy to growth. It's called inertia.

As discussed in Chapter 2: Power, government's innate disinclination to make changes and take risks stems from their asymmetric incentives—bureaucrats stand to gain little, but have a lot to lose, by disrupting the status quo. Politicians and regulators are no different.

The propensity to stick with what works, even if it doesn't work all that well, and the resulting aversion to change can put a vice on any regulated startup trying to do something a little differently. That holds true whether you're trying to sell your solution to a government, need a government to amend or scrap a rule that's preventing you from doing what you want to do, or need a government to help you build or scale a market by providing incentives to your potential customers.

"What we've learned is that we're not necessarily selling based on rational economics," Valor Water's Christine Boyle says.*

---

*You'll learn more about Boyle and Valor Water in Chapter 8: Influence. They provide water utilities with a product that helps the utilities find hidden revenue opportunities by analyzing the data already flowing through their pipes.

"Selling to government and selling in these markets," she continues, "especially when you're trying to establish a new category, doesn't follow the rules of enterprise sales 101. It isn't based on a straightforward, ROI-type decision equally weighing costs and benefits. Honestly, it's mostly about minimizing risk. That's the name of the game."

Or, as David Yarkin, the former deputy secretary for procurement for the state of Pennsylvania, puts it: "No one in government wants to be last, but no one in government wants to be first, either."

So how do you overcome inertia so you can grow quickly? You find a "hero mayor."

Mayors are often the perfect hero candidate because they are uniquely powerful, accessible, and responsive. With one or two good connections and even a small dose of persistence, getting a meeting with most mayors isn't a herculean task. At the same time, they have very real power to swiftly and decisively take action, unlike what you'll sometimes find at lower levels of bureaucracy or at the highest level of a federal government agency. For any regulated startup that may have a ready-made victory for government but needs to find that first brave champion to take a leap of faith, mayors are often the best place to start.

That said, a "hero mayor" is not usually a literal mayor, but any leader in government or within an institution whom you can convert into a flag-bearing, loud-and-proud champion of your startup. She must have the authority to make or at least strongly influence decisions, must passionately buy into the change you're selling, and—this is important—must see your product or solution as an opportunity for personal victory. You want to make your offering a future feather in her cap. A hero mayor could be a governor, a federal regulator, a school superintendent, or an executive within a private health system.

For Valor Water, it was a public utility director.

"What we have found is that they want to be seen as the hero," Boyle says. "You know, like, 'We figured out this thing, we found this company that solves this problem, and this is going to revolutionize how we're operating.' And they can present that to their board. They can present that to their bosses. Making someone a 'hero,' so to speak, can be a powerful strategy."

For HopSkipDrive, their heroes were the commissioners of the California Public Utilities Commission, who had been made to look like corrupt luddites by their bruising battles with Uber. HopSkipDrive presented them with an opportunity to show that they *wanted* to support innovation and *could* be creative, if presented with the right opportunity and approached in the right way.

Another way to overcome inertia? Find ways to effectively eliminate or radically reduce risk.

At Valor Water, Boyle recalls that "[e]ven though utilities were very interested in our hidden revenue concept, they still weren't convinced there was enough waste to justify spending money to try to find money," describing her early meetings with what she described as "friendly" and "forward-thinking" utility officials in the Los Angeles area. "That's just the risk environment in which they operate."

So Boyle devised a pricing strategy that would all but eliminate risk for the utilities.

"I knew based on my research that these utilities across the country were losing between 3 percent and 5 percent of their revenue because of meter problems," she explains. "So we went to them and offered performance-based contracts . . . in other words, we would tell them, you only have to pay us if we uncover, say, another 2 percent of revenue that you're missing out on."

With that clause in place, the risk effectively shifted over to Valor Water. The strategy helped Boyle land her first several clients in the L.A. region, and not once did she fail to meet or exceed the amount of revenue she promised to find. Eventually, she started using those early successes as proofs of concept and abandoned the performance-based contract model—but she says that pricing strategy was critical to helping her link those early deals, break the inertia, and build momentum.

The great thing about complex markets where inertia is the major issue with growth is that the same asymmetric incentives that make it hard to get people to try new things start to work in your favor once you have a few strong case studies.

As David Yarkin might put it, once you can get a few to go first, it's great that nobody wants to be last.

Putting Hacks Together

The iron-triangle construct and the hero-mayor construct aren't mutually exclusive. Now and then, regulated startups aiming to grow fast will find themselves grappling with the latter scenario at one level of government only to discover that an iron triangle exists at a different level of government. SeamlessDocs, for example, helps governments turn paper forms and static PDF documents into dynamic, e-signable, easy-to-fill-out electronic forms. At the municipal level, this was a totally blue-ocean space, and the challenges that founder Jonathon Ende faced were by and large the result of inertia and risk aversion. However, it was when his company tried to enter the federal marketplace, where contracts are measured in millions of dollars rather than in thousands, that the startup faced major headwinds from entrenched incumbents who had essentially constructed iron triangles to lock in all that value.

Writing Your Own Rules

Not every regulatory hacker will find themselves operating under either an iron-triangle or hero-mayor scenario. These are merely two of the most common constructs that you should be familiar with and prepared to take on as you figure out how to grow fast. Sometimes the right approach lies beyond begging forgiveness and asking permission, a strategy that Ola Doudin has pursued thoughtfully in dealing with regulations that don't exist yet.

After growing up in Jordan, Ola graduated from the University of Birmingham and joined Ernst & Young in London as a financial services consultant in 2008, one week before Lehman Brothers failed. As startup ecosystems began to take hold in pockets of the Middle East, Ola moved back to the region in 2010 to lead an entrepreneurship initiative, right before the Arab Spring exploded.

After experiencing two successive society-altering crises in five years, Ola discovered an emerging new cryptocurrency called Bitcoin while perusing Reddit. She quickly became obsessed, she says, intuiting the massive economic and societal implications of digital currencies decoupled from central banks. She learned everything should could about the cryptocurrency and the distributed ledger technology behind it over the next year. In 2014, Ola founded BitOasis, a Dubai-based startup that offers an online cryptocurrency wallet and exchange platform to markets across the Middle East, North Africa, and Asia.

Cryptocurrencies like Bitcoin remain unregulated in the UAE, without formal rules governing exchange platforms like BitOasis. But that didn't stop Ola from treating her startup as though it operated in a highly regulated industry.

"In our situation, we understood the risks that regulators would be concerned about, and we know there will eventually be regulations," she says. "We took steps early on to put in place policies and operational practices that would address those concerns. We basically self-regulated our work right from the beginning."

Ola leaned on her knowledge of the financial services industry from her time in London, and today, her legal and regulatory compliance team is as large as her technology team. The former group, she adds, is comprised of certified compliance officers who have worked in or around the financial services industry.

"Obviously we're a tech company, but we have also thought of ourselves as a financial services company all along, so we created and implemented compliance policies that are on par with what other banks have in place," she says. Building good relationships with industry regulators has been as important, she says, as the connections she has built with any other stakeholders.

"We've invested in understanding financial regulations and the regulatory environment, and that has served us well," she says, adding that BitOasis's proactive approach to compliance not only prepares the company to sustain its operations without a hitch when regulators eventually do write the rules that will govern her industry, but it has also endeared her company to those very regulators, as she has taken a cooperative rather than combative position.

"Regulators take you seriously when you've taken the time to understand existing regulations, understand where regulators are coming from, and why they are doing what they're doing," she says. "It's important that we take the time to look at our work through their eyes."

She added: "Building a culture of regulatory compliance in our company from day one has given us a competitive edge in our market."

Ola hasn't waited for permission. But she put in place a robust framework early, so she won't need to ask forgiveness either. In fact, it's more likely than not that she'll be one of the first people regulators engage when they are ready to start writing the rules. Her sophisticated approach has helped drive amazing growth. I met Ola for the first time for coffee in Dubai in April 2017. Donna and I made the easy decision to invest in BitOasis a week later. Within a few months, exchange volumes had increased by a factor of ten, and BitOasis hasn't slowed down since.

The Tools of the Trade

As you think about growing fast in a complex market, you'll want to focus on Section 2: The Foundations of Regulatory Hacking and Section 4: The Regulatory Hacker's Toolkit. You'll read lots of stories about the hacks that startups have used throughout the book, but you'll want to focus as much on the tools that underlie those hacks. When should you leverage the media versus the grassroots? When can you accomplish what you want with soft grasstops persuasion versus formal lobbying? How can you use these tools in concert?

What is important to understand is that the methodology behind finding a growth model is, again, the same as for building a power map and finding a regulated business model. Be a scientist. Do your homework. Formulate your hypotheses about what will work. Test them in the real world. Don't be afraid when your experiments fail as long as you use them to refine your approach. But more important, be a hacker in the truest sense. Use your creativity and intelligence to figure out ways to help societies and economies to do novel, clever, and important new things. Have some flair as you hack your way through your complex market!

Chapter 5

ARBITRAGE

Cars are getting insanely smart. But what about the asphalt they travel on?

That's where Shahar Bahiri, Daniel Yakovich, Gabriel Jacobson, and Michael Dan Vardi—the cofounders of Valerann—have set their sights.

Started in 2016 in Tel Aviv, Valerann has developed smart road studs that replace reflective "cats eye" lane markers and collect pinpoint-accurate data about everything from road conditions and traffic flow to the presence of major accidents and stopped vehicles. The studs can even communicate with autonomous vehicles to provide their driving systems with real-time data about what's happening around them on the road.

Developed by Bahiri while he was working for a road operator in Israel following a career in the military, Valerann's technology can provide valuable, real-time insights to governments, private road operators, and technology platforms like Waze, Google Maps, and Uber.

"We're basically turning roads into data infrastructure," Michael says.

For Valerann's cofounders, the big challenge wasn't just getting people excited about their idea, but proving the technology actually worked. That meant piloting on real roads. The cofounders needed to show not only that their sensors would work as intended under normal wear and tear, but that they could stand up to extreme scenarios, like a snow plow scraping over them repeatedly.

So how do you convince a government or private road operator to let you embed smart road studs in their roads and run a litany of tests? And who pays to do that?

You start by identifying the right candidates.

For roadway innovation, according to Michael, the global leader has long been the United Kingdom. "The UK has a reputation for pushing innovation around roads and highways," he says, noting that Britain was the "original birthplace of the road stud" and that many roadways in the country are already lined with less-sophisticated sensors.

"We knew that going to the UK would mean we didn't have to convince them to install something completely new, but rather a better version of the technology they were already accustomed to," Michael explains. "That's a much easier sell than trying to convince someone to invest in something they are unfamiliar with or haven't bought into already."

No less important, the British government in December 2016 announced a new £150 million grant program for companies with technologies that can make travel safer, quicker, and more reliable.[1]

Enticed by the environment in the UK, Valerann split their core team, sending two cofounders to Great Britain to focus on pilot programs while the other two remained in Israel to lead research and development. The UK pair would quickly begin talks with two major British road operators, Highway England and Transport for London, on a joint pilot program to deploy Valerann's sensors.

While things progressed in the UK, Valerann was looking for other test beds as well. "In most countries, finding those test sites would be very difficult. What we need are governments or road operators that have a real appetite for innovation and are aligned with our vision that roads have to be a key part of transportation information systems," Michael said.

As it happened, on the other side of the Atlantic, Transurban, a $25 billion publicly listed Australian company that develops and manages smart toll roads in Australia and North America, was launching the Transurban Smart Highways Challenge, powered by our Union platform and championed by Jennifer Aument, Transurban's president for North America.

The first thing I noticed about Jennifer was her ardent *love* of infrastructure. She talks about roads and railways and ports the way other people might discuss fine wine or exotic cars—and she's spent her career bringing innovation to infrastructure.

At Transurban, Jennifer leads a $4 billion project to build and manage HOT lanes on the I-95. HOT is infrastructure slang for "high occupancy tolls," meaning that drivers pay tolls to drive in certain lanes on I-495, I-395, and I-95 in Virginia. The tolls vary by segment to keep the traffic in those lanes free-flowing. If too many people start using a segment, then the price goes up to keep the traffic running smoothly. The proceeds from the tolls then fund future maintenance and expansion for the Beltway.

Transurban operates under a seventy-year partnership with the Virginia Department of Transportation, meaning they have to stay in front of long-term trends in transportation and technology to protect their investment. Ride-sharing? Self-driving cars? Electric vehicles? Jennifer has to be smart about how startups playing around with these technologies could impact her highways today and tomorrow. In the same way, growing her business over time depends on winning more public-private partnerships like the Beltway and I-95 HOT lanes. Transurban's mastery of cutting-edge technology is an important factor in winning those competitions. "We are always open to new partnerships," Jennifer says. "We think of our road network as a seventy-mile active transportation laboratory. Bring us technologies or strategies that will drive more customers, enhance service, or improve safety, and Transurban is game."

Union, as I mentioned in the Introduction, is an online innovation community that powers incubators and accelerators on six continents, supporting more than seven thousand startups. One way that Union helps an innovator like Jennifer is through our *challenges*. We identify an innovation challenge that's a top priority for an organization like Transurban. We open that challenge up to startups around the world via the Union community. We use the data from Union to quickly narrow the field down to the most relevant and promising startups. Then we pick a handful to go through an intensive ninety-day program with that organization to jointly develop a paid pilot, and possibly provide an equity investment, culminating in a Demo Day in front of the organization's top executives, like Jennifer.

It was at the Demo Day for the Smart Highways Challenge that Michael sealed the deal with Jennifer, when he did his best Steve Jobs impression by sharing just one more thing: A video showing how the Valerann studs can change color to alert drivers of potential hazards, flashing red, for instance, if there's an accident ahead, or blue if black ice is forming.

"A number of our startup candidates tried to pitch us on a new technology, but Valerann nailed it because they led with strategy instead," Jennifer says. "It was clear they had done the work to understand our business and could clearly articulate how their product could support our goals. With that said, the pitch matters. I understood the technology. I appreciated the alignment with our business strategy. But when Michael played the video simulation of his product literally lighting up the Beltway, I was sold. That's the future. Let's go for it."

For Valerann, the relationship with Transurban would prove invaluable.

"It was clear they could be the perfect partner and the perfect client," Michael says of Transurban. "In our first few interactions with Transurban, we were really trying to do two things: One, we spent time to understand their day-to-day operations, their motivations, their dynamics, their business, so that we could find where we could help them. And two, we wanted to make sure they viewed roads the same way we do and the value in the data."

As a result of the Smart Highways Challenge, Transurban and Valerann are forging a formal partnership to conduct a paid pilot program. "We are clearly aligned in our vision at this point, and we're on the cusp of a very special relationship," Michael says. The two are also in early talks about a potential Transurban equity investment in Valerann.

For Valerann, both Transurban and the UK government represented entities that managed major roadways that could be used to test their studs, both had demonstrated that they were willing to take risks and invest time and energy to stay on the cutting edge of transit innovation, and both were motivated to help Valerann in their own self-interests.

However, Transurban is in the *business* of making highways smart. They have to compete to win RFPs from governments on the basis of their technological and data advantages in managing highways. To protect their long-term investments, they have to stay in front of new trends. The Transurban team is acutely aware that sensors, artificial intelligence, autonomous vehicles, and other emerging technologies are going to transform their business. Unlike a government agency, they don't have the luxury of sitting back to see how things play out over time. They *have* to stay at the leading edge.

"We called it the Highway Challenge because we wanted startups to compete with each other for contract opportunities, but in the end, the startups really challenged our internal team," Jennifer emphasizes. "They weren't looking to the future of transportation, they were running toward it. It reminded our team that to keep up—or, better, lead—we can't get weighed down in our own bureaucracy or bias."

Regulatory Arbitrage

For Valerann, Transurban was the perfect partner, a company that controlled major U.S. roadways *and* had a strong incentive to deploy new technologies. For Transurban, Valerann was the perfect startup, designed to help their business model today and future-proof it tomorrow.

Arbitrage is the practice of taking advantage of a difference in perceived value between two or more markets.

For Transurban and Valerann, each represented vastly greater value to each other than either would have to generic counterparties in their complex markets—thereby creating a mutual arbitrage opportunity. These arbitrage opportunities can be critical for regulatory hackers, whether finding early-adopter customers, first-mover regulators, or strategic funders.

The Limits of "Ramen Profitable"

Why are early-adopter customers, first-mover regulators, and strategic funders so crucial to the success of regulated startups?

One reason is that regulated startups struggle to fit into the model of "ramen profitable." Paul Graham defined "ramen profitable" in a 2009 blog post[2] as "a startup that becomes profitable after 2 months, even though its revenues are only $3,000 a month, because the only employees are a couple 25 year old founders who can live on practically nothing,"[3] or at least packets of instant ramen. Although Graham's blog post was simply observing that some lightweight software or app startups had succeeded using the model of ramen profitable, this quickly turned into the norm, with mainstream venture capitalists becoming conditioned to wait until they see "traction" before they pour significant capital into a business.

While this model works great for "lean" startups that can survive on incredibly low burn rates while they iterate until they find a scalable business model that investors will fund, the Regulatory Era presents two big challenges to this state of affairs.

First, regulatory hacking requires more than the programming skills and persistence that makes ramen profitable work for startups developing simple apps or software solutions. Succeeding in complex markets takes more real-world experience and insider expertise than most twenty-five-year-olds have had time to gain. Shahar Bahiri had to apprentice with a road operator for years before he knew enough to invent intelligent road studs. The three co-founders of HopSkipDrive had to become moms before they understood what working families really need in a transportation service for their kids.

If you're a forty-year-old with the experience, credibility, and network to hack a market like energy, health, or transportation—and have a family to support—then ramen profitable may not be good enough for you.

Second, regulatory hackers often face the same challenge as Michael and Valerann: Accessing your market depends on having evidence that your technology works, which requires getting your technology into a production environment.* But nobody wants to put things into production environments without evidence that it works. This circularity creates a huge chasm for regulatory hackers to cross.

So even if your founding team were able to live the ramen-and-sofas life, the research and development necessary to build "deep" technology can be expensive. Try developing durable road studs packed with more than ten sensors capable of communicating in real time with autonomous vehicles zipping by at seventy miles an hour, while being energy-efficient enough to survive for ten years on solar panels and batteries. Now do it on a shoestring budget. Deploying in real-world environments takes time and can be expensive. Gathering outcomes data and turning that into peer-reviewed evidence burns money. Working through regulatory obstacles can be time-consuming and expensive—even with the benefit of the hacks you're learning in this book.

The market opportunities for regulatory hackers are massive, but the chasm you have to cross is deeper and wider than for simpler startups. This "chasm" problem is compounded by the aversion that many mainstream VCs have to market complexity and regulatory risk. Mainstream venture capitalists are learning to become better investors in the Regulatory Era, but your startup can die waiting for them to catch up.

For many regulatory hackers then, unable to either hum along at ramen profitability or quickly tap into mainstream venture capital, it is *critical* to find early-adopter customers, regulators, and funders. Of course, the holy grail for regulatory hackers is when you can find an early adopter like Transurban that brings all three to the table.

---

*You'll learn more about this in Chapter 7: Data.

Finding Early-Adopter Customers and Institutions

For some regulatory hackers, finding early-adopter customers is no different than for any other startup. Uber, HopSkipDrive, and Kidde all had to find early adopters in the same sense that a dating app would, and as would many B2C and regulated-marketplace startups.

ID.me, Opower, and Valerann, however, had business models that depended on finding institutions or regulators willing to take a big risk on them. Many regulated startups with B2B, B2B2C, B2G, and B2G2C business models will fall into this bucket. These institutional early adopters are critical. Early revenue is the ideal form of early funding, particularly when that revenue comes with other hard-to-find assets. As you strive to prove that your regulated startup can work, institutions can bring assets that may be almost impossible to find elsewhere, such as Transurban's ability to test Valerann's technology in a live environment or USAA's ability to provide ID.me with API access to validated datasets of military veterans.

Even when you're growing, institutional partners can bring market access and connections to regulators that you might find difficult to obtain otherwise. For example, the Washington Beltway and I-95 is only one of fifteen highway systems around the world that Transurban operates.[4] If Valerann's road studs work on the Beltway, then Transurban can quickly take them global.

What many institutions often *lack* is speed and agility. Large bureaucracies often aren't great at hacking. This is your arbitrage opportunity. You're trading your ability to hack their complex market for their irreplaceable assets. Different institutions face different competitive dynamics. Some may need to protect their status quo, whereas others might want to topple the chessboard. You have to understand your power map well enough to figure out who has the greatest need—because that's where your arbitrage opportunity lies. Success as a regulated startup often depends on finding the institutions for whom your potential value is greatest. Those will be the ones with the motivation to overcome inertia and take on risks with you.

For regulatory hackers, the winning hack can sometimes require you to carefully think through a Rubik's Cube of early adopters and favorable regulatory environments to find the optimal hack. Some industries present particularly complex opportunities for regulatory arbitrage—perhaps none more so than the medical and healthcare fields, as Matt Angle has discovered.

Angle casually describes his startup, Paradromics, as a "broadband modem for the brain," one that could help those who are blind see, those who are deaf hear, and those who use wheelchairs walk. Founded in 2015 in San Jose, California, Paradromics is developing very small brain-implanted chips "no bigger than an antacid tablet" that can create a data-rich, real-time connection between a human brain and a computer. The breakthrough has the potential to help treat lost senses like sight and touch, power robotic prosthetics with a patient's thoughts, and even understand and eventually treat more complex mental disorders.

For a next-generation medical device like what Angle's team is building, many companies—established and startup—flock to Europe, where regulatory approval from the EU's safety commissions can be easier and faster to come by. Several of Paradromic's peers in the advanced medical device arena have followed suit, pursuing the EU's green light and seeking traction across the pond rather than in the United States. That includes companies like Boston Scientific, which has multiple times secured the EU's stamp of safety approval rather than waiting to try to secure approval in the United States.[5]

"A lot of companies in our world will go to Europe first," says Angle, who has a PhD in neuroscience and specializes in nanotechnology. "We decided not to."

Angle elected instead to market his first product to university-based animal research labs. The technology system features sixty-five thousand wires that are inserted into the brain through a tiny hole in the skull and then hooked up to a recording device about the size of a Nalgene bottle, allowing researchers to take an unprecedented look into the inner workings of the brain in any number of animals and glean insights that may inform new medical breakthroughs for humans.

"These research labs are anxious to be able to use this kind of advanced technology to further their studies, and for us, it allows us to quickly build some awareness, gain acceptance, and bring in some early revenue," Angle says. "That sales component, forcing us to think like that from an early stage in our company's development, is especially valuable."

It's also an opportunity to generate earned media before ever putting one device in a human.

"When we turn our system on for the first time in an animal, we'll make the largest neural recording ever by a major magnitude, and I think that will garner positive attention," he says.

Most important, though, partnering with animal research labs will allow

Paradromics to earn modest revenue while generating preclinical data that other healthcare or medical device startups might otherwise pay inordinate amounts of money to obtain. It's ramen profitable for the Regulatory Era.

"A lot of companies pay for preclinical data, and for startups, that can be very expensive," Angle said. "They're basically paying to hold experiments just so they can get the data they need to even get to clinical trials, and here we'll be able to obtain the really robust preclinical data we need before we can get approved for human testing."

Rather than raising capital to fund clinical trials, Paradromics found a way to generate revenue and show continuous progress, an elegant arbitrage hack indeed.

Nora Khaldi took a similar approach with Nuritas.* Nuritas's AI software scans through billions and billions of genomics data points to find peptides with potentially significant health benefits. This technology is relevant for personal-care products, food supplements, and medicine. While working on a long-term breakthrough in the pharmaceutics market, with the associated long regulatory approvals, Nora generated cash in the short run by using her technology on a contract basis with food manufacturers, a significantly less-regulated market.

Finding First-Mover Regulators

Paradromics may have found success without following other advanced medical device companies to the EU, but arbitrage opportunities aren't limited to institutional partners. Governments that are willing to innovate with regulation and provide favorable regulatory environments can offer arbitrage opportunities, too.

We got an early, informal taste of this at 1776 with RideScout. Founded in Austin in 2011 by Joseph Kopster and Craig Cummings, both West Point graduates with distinguished army careers, RideScout was a mobile app that could monitor every mode of transportation in a city and instantly tell you the cheapest or fastest way to get where you were going—by bus, bike share, car share, Uber, taxi, subway, walking, driving, or whatever other way to get around a city happened to have available.

---

*You met Nora and Nuritas in Chapter 3: Business Models.

Joseph and Craig launched in Austin but had trouble getting traction. Austin didn't have a strong multimodal transportation system and at the time didn't have a mayor or department of transportation leadership who "got" RideScout and wanted to help.

D.C., however, had a great multimodal transportation system and a mayor and D.C. Department of Transportation (DDOT) director who really wanted to support and engage startups to improve the lives of the citizens of D.C. RideScout ended up moving their business operations to 1776 shortly after we opened in 2013. We helped them build a strong partnership with Mayor Gray and his administration—ranging from the mayor attending their launch party and bringing the D.C. media with him, to DDOT working to actively promote the app to citizens.

Donna and I ended up making RideScout our first investment, shortly after we launched our seed fund. Ninety days later RideScout was acquired by Daimler-Benz,[6] giving us a 1,200 percent internal rate of return on our first investment. Arbitrage can be a powerful thing!

Mayor Gray's support of RideScout was opportunistic and informal, but more and more cities, regions, and countries are making these opportunities intentional and formal.

Most governments in the world want to grow their startup sector as a way to create desirable jobs and buzz. One breakout startup success can become the economic engine of a region for a generation or more. The Washington, D.C., region is still receiving second- and third-order benefits from Steve Case building AOL into a major force in the late 1990s. Austin benefits in the same way from Dell.

Instead of competing on the basis of tax incentives or a generic claim to "ease of doing business," smart governments are learning to compete on the basis of their openness to innovation, often through flexibility around regulation. Forward-looking civic leaders are looking at the legacy assets of a region and thinking about how to craft a regulatory strategy that makes it as easy as possible to attract and retain startups in areas that align with those assets.

Financial hubs like Singapore and London have sought to double-down on their dominance in financial services by launching "fintech sandboxes" that provide expedited regulatory waivers for fintech startups that meet certain conditions. Australia has sought to lead through flexible regulations for drones, explicitly looking to take advantage of their vast open spaces and their dominance in industries such as natural resource extraction that can serve as obvious early adopters of drones. Pittsburgh has sought to build on its academic strength in robotics at Carnegie Mellon University to lead in autonomous vehicles—with a willingness to be creative on regulation a key element of Mayor Peduto's strategy.

And then there's Dubai.

Dubai: The Disney World of Innovation

Towering over the sparkling shores of the Arabian Gulf, where fewer than fifty years ago little more than a fishing village stood, Dubai is now a dense, complex, and breathtaking cocktail of steel and glass and cutting-edge technology rising from the Emirati sand. The region's population surged more than any other on the planet over the latter half of the twentieth century, and it continues to be one of the world's fastest-growing cities, with residents coming from every corner of the planet.[7]

However, that also presents an array of challenges: among them, how to provide sufficient housing, healthcare, education, infrastructure, energy, and fresh water to nearly three million people living in a dense urban metropolis in the middle of the Arabian Desert. Meanwhile, the longtime bedrock of the Dubai economy—oil—has become less financially dependable in recent years as prices have dipped. Dubai's leaders have been understandably focused on diversifying the regional economy.

As we have seen so many times for regulatory hackers, challenge begets opportunity.

Driven by bold commitments from Sheikh Mohammad bin Rashid Al Maktoum, vice president and prime minister of the UAE and the ruler of Dubai, the city has over the past few years swiftly built a reputation as an oasis for startup founders with world-shaping ideas.[8]

I remember sitting down with key members of the prime minister's office in 2015 to outline a vision for how Dubai could leapfrog to become the world's next London or Singapore for technology and innovation by becoming the single easiest, most-enticing environment on the planet for regulatory hackers. Dubai, I argued, had everything necessary to become the go-to destination for creating the future. What I didn't appreciate at the time was how quickly and comprehensively the leadership of Dubai could execute on that vision.

Among the core ingredients that render Dubai a perfect test lab for the Regulatory Era is its centralized political and economic system. That is, when

Sheikh Mohammad comes out and decrees that Dubai will be a world leader in solar energy or autonomous technologies, every part of the government, the private sector, and the social ecosystem organizes around that goal in a way that you simply don't see in the United States.

The city is also being built—both physically and with regard to laws and regulations—all around you, every day. For regulatory hackers in need of a test kitchen, there couldn't be a better one. And this isn't merely aspiration—startups, investors, and cutting-edge innovation are taking root. All told, startup investment in the UAE topped $1 billion in 2016 from near zero a few years earlier. That same year, the number of privately owned startups that received equity funding in the country grew 45 percent year over year.[9]

In other words: It's working.

As Noah Raford, chief operative officer and futurist in chief at the Dubai Future Foundation, explains it, "Dubai's major advantage is that it's used to operating at the speed of entrepreneurs. Dubai is an entrepreneurial project itself. It has incredible, long-term, hands-on leadership that's used to taking big risks. So when it comes to fundamental innovations and new technologies, it's a natural test bed for ideas of the future."

Bear in mind, the first time I met Noah he was wearing an impeccably tailored suit, hipster glasses, construction boots, and a cowboy hardhat with the words "Dr. Death" etched on the side. Dr. Death was walking around slinging bills from a giant wad of cash to various contractors, rushing to complete the Offices of the Future—the world's first fully functional 3-D–printed building, which looked like it was ripped straight out of a scene from the Jetsons.

Noah is an American expat with a PhD from MIT in urban planning. When he's not slinging cash on the construction sites of the future, he's one of the world's preeminent minds on the future of cities and urbanization. He has served as a member World Economic Forum's Global Council on Artificial Intelligence and Robotics and doubles as an author and hobbyist DJ. More important, he has been a catalyst behind the realization of Sheikh Mohammed's vision through his work with the Dubai Future Foundation.

Noah's focus has been on launching initiatives in areas where Dubai could lead, which fall into a regulatory gray zone that Noah refers to as "a prelegal space." That is, it wasn't *illegal* in Dubai to 3-D print a building, per se, but there simply weren't yet international standards or regulations in place to govern how it should work and what new safety protocols engineers would have to abide by. As a first mover in allowing 3-D printing and construction startups to come innovate, Dubai was able to learn how to establish a regulatory framework for this new technology before other cities.

Ola Doudin took advantage of this same willingness to accommodate "prelegal" innovations when she was looking at where to launch BitOasis. Dubai's reputation for innovation in regulation, she says, made it a no-brainer.

As part of Dubai's quest to become one of the most innovation-friendly hubs in the world, the city has taken bold measures to establish a foothold as the global destination for startups and innovators interested in blockchain technology. (Blockchain is the technology that underlies cryptocurrencies like Bitcoin; blockchains are distributed ledgers, or digital platforms that enable developers to create trusted tools for exchanging value of all sorts.) In the boldest step to date, the crown prince of Dubai a few years ago committed to moving all government transactions to a blockchain by 2020, making headlines around the world.[10]

It's that attitude that attracted Andrew Keys and ConsenSys, his Brooklyn-based startup founded in 2015, to create a blockchain blueprint in a city halfway across the world.

On an otherwise nondescript stretch of land spanning more than two thousand hectares outside Dubai, Keys and ConsenSys are working with Noah and the Smart Dubai Office to conduct an experiment that may fundamentally change the way we buy, sell, and lay claim to real estate and other property in the future. In collaboration with the Dubai Land Department, one of the region's biggest real estate developers, and one of Dubai's largest banks, ConsenSys has built a blockchain-based land title registry for every parcel of those two thousand hectares. Each parcel is tagged with a special blockchain-encrypted token, allowing landowners and government officials to easily and securely track the chain of custody for that parcel over time.[11]

For ConsenSys, finding an environment where both public and private sector players were willing to invest the land, time, and resources required to test how this potentially disruptive record-keeping system would work in the real world was paramount.

"There's nothing better than actually getting the requirements from a government and working with them to test what works and what doesn't," says Keys, who noted that the company is being paid to build the system. Maybe even more important, he continues, "When other countries want to do this later, we will have helped set the precedent."

And land is just the start. Keys says his company is working with the Dubai government to adapt the very same concepts to change the way supply chains work, healthcare and medical treatments are delivered, and even the way we think about and prove our individual identities.

In November 2017, I moderated a panel at the annual STEP startup-fest with Noah and Jeff Holden from Uber Elevate, Uber's flying taxi experimentation wing. The panel was interesting, but the conversation backstage revealed why Uber Elevate was committing to Dubai. As Holden put it, adding landing stations for flying taxis is easier in a city that's always half under construction anyway. And the regulatory frameworks are as dynamic as the built environment.

Startups like Consensys and Uber Elevate and cities like Dubai need one another in equal measure. Dubai simply cannot achieve its bold economic development objectives without attracting some of the world's most ambitious startups, but those same startups would find it very hard to prove their ideas at scale without a regulatory test kitchen like the ones city leaders have built in Dubai.

It's at that harmonious nexus of mutual benefit where invaluable regulatory arbitrage opportunities are born.

NYC: If You Can Build It Here, You Can Build It Anywhere

Dubai is an exceptional case that would be hard for most cities or regions to replicate, but cities of all shapes and sizes are exploring their own ways to implement this new model of economic development.

New York City is the largest city in America and a global financial hub, but it has never been more than an also-ran to Silicon Valley when it comes to startups, perpetually competing with Boston and Los Angeles for second. To grow their startup economy, New York City leaders have to find a way to channel the talents of a diverse workforce—and attract venture capital—that relies on the things that make New York unique.

Mayor de Blasio appointed Miguel Gamiño as chief technology officer of New York City in October 2016. Gamiño came to New York from a similar role in San Francisco, but before that he was the founder of multiple startups in El Paso, Texas. "As a former startup guy who converted to a public servant, I think I have a very interesting view of those two worlds, and maybe I can appreciate how they fit together better than some other people on only one side of the fence," Gamiño says.[12]

Shortly after starting in New York City, Gamiño launched the city's NYCx initiative.[13] NYCx is the world's first municipal program that transforms urban spaces into hubs for tech collaboration, research, testing, and development. New York City's diverse population, economy, and landscape offer a unique opportunity for technology companies to develop tools that can improve the lives of all New Yorkers and, potentially, the world. It can be considered in some ways a "flexible regulatory zone" for testing new technologies, smack in the middle of the gritty reality of the Big Apple.

An important part of NYCx is a focus on ideas that can improve the lives of everyday residents, help communities thrive, and be a model for other cities around the world with similar challenges.

"The most talented engineers and designers can build things that make a lot of money, or they can build things that benefit people's lives, ideally doing well by doing good things," Gamiño explains. "The story I tell is, imagine a single mother with one or more kids who works one or more hourly jobs. She qualifies for programs the city offers to help her succeed, funded by taxpayers. Most of the time, in order for her to let us know she exists and qualifies, she has to stand in line somewhere and fill out a bunch of forms. I'm not saying technology itself fixes that, but if we create an alternative for her to submit that information or engage with us wherever necessary, at her convenience, then she doesn't have to take off a day of work, or spend money for childcare unnecessarily."

NYCx offers two types of opportunities for startups. *Moonshot Challenges* encourage global entrepreneurs to think big about NYC's most ambitious problems, propose bold solutions, and deliver groundbreaking business models that improve the lives of New Yorkers. *Co-Lab Challenges* invite startups to work directly with community residents to solve neighborhood challenges while aiming to scale solutions across the five boroughs. "Moonshots are not just us trying to peek around the corner [to see the future], but actually design around the corner," Gamiño says.

NYCx allows the city to set aside areas for startups to test their solutions, including Governors Island, a popular seasonal destination for recreation, arts, and culture with acres of park space where, for example, startups participating in a *Moonshot Challenge* will test solutions to bring Wifi to the entire island and accelerate adoption of 5G connectivity across NYC. In another example, startups participating in two *Co-Lab Challenges* will test their solutions with the Brownsville neighborhood in Brooklyn, a largely underserved community where the city is looking at ways tech can help address the neighborhood's needs.

"NYCx Co-Labs is an evolution of the work we've done with community leaders to identify needs," Gamiño explains. "Co-Lab challenges allow all New Yorkers to benefit as we expand the winning solutions in neighborhoods with similar challenges across all five boroughs."

The NYCx program offers awards up to $25,000 (so far) to startups with winning proposals, but more important it presents an opportunity to test new tools and technologies that address a number of real-world challenges. NYCx challenges include accelerating electric-vehicle usage by increasing the number of fast-charging stations and increasing nighttime safety to boost small businesses in neighborhoods. All of this provides startups the unique opportunity to prove their solutions in the kind of crazy, tough environment that New York City affords.

Another core component of the program is the NYCx Technology Leadership Advisory Council, which is made up of a diverse group of community leaders tasked with helping increase engagement in the challenges. In other words, it helps regulatory hackers engage and understand the stakeholders on their power maps.

"NYCx is intended to transform and strengthen the relationship between the industry, the government, and the community, and NYCx brings together leaders in industry, government, and community who might not otherwise ever be in the same room together," underscores Gamiño. "Together, they will be instrumental in helping us shape technology for the benefit of our communities across New York City, and around the world."

Gamiño talked me through his vision for NYCx over breakfast shortly after he arrived in New York. We talked about what Dubai was doing and the opportunities New York had to chart its own path. Gamiño's turn-of-phrase has stuck with me to this day: "Dubai is really cool but not representative of our reality; however, we do share common goals in wanting technology to benefit people. New York City is real, complex, and messy—its beauty and strength. For us, it's about making technology work for people, and if you can build it here, you can build it anywhere."

Sometimes Harder Is Better

Sometimes the right arbitrage move as a regulatory hacker isn't to find the easiest regulatory environment but rather the hardest.

Nora Khaldi learned this with Nuritas. Over time, she was able to teach her

AI software the regulations for different countries and different markets. Today, her system knows to focus on peptides that will meet specific regulatory requirements to expedite the approval process. It knows, for example, the rules around potential products or ingredients for the personal-care market in China, Japan, or Europe. Or the rules for FDA approval for pharmaceuticals.

Once her artificial intelligence could do the regulatory calculus along with the genomics math, the right strategy for Nuritas was actually to focus its system on the hardest regulators, not the easiest. In pharmaceuticals, the FDA sets the bar for the rest of the world. If a drug is approved in the United States, then it will generally sail through approvals in other countries. In personal care, on the other hand, Europe, Japan, and particularly China set the highest bars. Gain approval there and you're set elsewhere. Therefore, the Nuritas team can focus the AI on finding peptides with health benefits for personal-care products that meet the Chinese standards and know that they'll be approved almost everywhere else. The same with pharmaceuticals that meet FDA standards.

As always with regulatory hacking, the right answer for your startup will come from a full understanding of your power map and the rules that govern it, sometimes on a global scale.

Finding Chasm-Crossing Capital

This isn't a book on how to raise funds from mainstream venture capital. There are many great blogs, incubators, and accelerators that can take you through the fundraising process for pre-seed, seed, Series A, and beyond. There's a formula and you should know it. Mainstream venture capitalists can bring significant assets beyond just cash, and they are increasingly interested in complex markets, with Uber, Airbnb, and 23andMe as obvious examples.

Zac Bookman has even managed to raise $80 million from some of the Valley's most renowned investors to help state and local governments make sense of their financial performance data.

Bookman's journey as a regulatory hacker started several years ago when he was running a Stanford-based nonprofit that was analyzing the long-term implications of a budget crisis that had crippled the state of California. "The state was totally upside-down financially," he says. As part of their project, Bookman and his team began talks with officials from a city in the heart of the Valley. As the discussion progressed, Bookman asked the head of the city's budget office for access to the municipality's data, offering to "help you drill through it, identify trends, and better understand your financial performance."

The response: "Wow, that sounds really useful. How do we get you our budget data?"

"What do you mean, 'How do you get us your budget data?'" said Bookman. "You're the freaking budget director!"

On closer inspection, Bookman was startled to realize the state of California was using accounting programs based on technology introduced many decades earlier. "Contrary to popular myth, the people running these governments weren't stupid, and they weren't lazy," he says. "They were just using thirty-year-old technology that wouldn't let them see where all the money goes, and that wouldn't let them share information with elected officials, and as a result, citizens were understandably losing trust in their government."

"We could solve this," said Bookman, whose remarkable career has included stints as a trial attorney, as an adviser to U.S. Army General H. R. McMaster in Afghanistan, and a Fulbright Scholar studying government corruption in Mexico. "Rather, we had to solve this."

Started in 2012, OpenGov is doing just that by providing a SaaS platform to local and state governments that helps them plan, visualize, analyze, collaborate on, and share information about how tax dollars are being allocated across public programs. The idea was to allow government agencies to streamline their budget process, track their performance, allow citizens to see and understand the process as it unfolds, and provide feedback.

"We help power more effective and accountable government, from the budget development process through performance analysis through citizen engagement," Bookman says.

Bookman's access to mainstream venture capital was helped by one major hole card: His cofounder and chairman was Joe Lonsdale, a prominent venture capitalist who made a fortune as the cofounder of Palantir, which has built a major business helping governments sift through data. Lonsdale wasn't just comfortable with complex markets, he was seeking them out.

"In business, you want to find your unfair advantages," Bookman says. "Not illegal advantages, but unfair advantages. We've obviously had success with our chairman being a very successful entrepreneur and investor and the cofounder of Palantir. I can be the charismatic, long-haired rebel leader, but I'm not delusional—none of this would have happened without having Joe and other great people around me."

While some mainstream venture capitalists like Joe Lonsdale *are* seeking out opportunities in complex markets, as a regulatory hacker, you should also be thinking about four sources of capital that are particularly important for regulated startups to understand and cultivate: strategic investors, sectoral investors, impact funds, and government grants.

Strategic Investors

Strategic investors are institutions looking to benefit from the appreciation in the value of the equity of the startups they help launch into a complex market. In my experience, strategic investors are not investing for financial returns alone, but rather to ensure that they have strategic alignment with you, to benefit themselves as they help you launch successfully, and in some cases to get an anchor position in your equity for a potential future acquisition.

Transurban is being a strategic investor when it sees the potential in smart road studs and knows how helpful they can be to Valerann. They want to be investors, not just a partner in a pilot.

It isn't necessarily a bad thing that many strategic investors will want to make an early acquisition if your technology works and you start to gain traction. As a rule of thumb, it takes at least $100 million to scale a regulated startup in a complex market. The vast majority of regulated startups will struggle to raise this for one reason or another. The next best option is to be acquired early by an institution for whom you fulfill a strategic need. These exits can create significant wealth for you and your team and ensure your idea has the balance sheet and market access necessary to reach its full potential. By securing strategic investment, you're increasing the odds of this kind of positive outcome down the road, without precluding the possibility that you will raise the $100 million or so necessary to take your regulated startup all the way to the promised land.

Sectoral Investors

The number of seed funds and venture funds around the world has exploded over the past decade. There are now many venture capitalists that focus on specific complex markets, such as edtech, healthtech, govtech, fintech, and smart cities. These sector-specific funds often have a thesis to prove and are actively looking for strong teams with new ideas that fit that niche.

If you're pitching your edtech startup to Sequoia, then you're competing against every other idea that Sequoia is seeing. If you're pitching the same edtech idea to Rethink Education or GSV Capital, two strong edtech investors, then you're presenting an opportunity to funds that *have* to move capital within the education market. With that said, you're also dealing with investors with significant expertise in your complex market, so you have to know your power map cold, have thought through your regulated business model, and have your narrative and data ready to go.*

In other cases, it's not about the sectoral expertise of a fund, but rather the expertise and experience of a particular general partner. Twiga Foods, a 1776 portfolio company, has raised the largest seed round and Series A in East African history.** Twiga uses mobile phones and data analysis to streamline supply chains for fresh fruits and vegetables sold through informal markets in sub-Saharan Africa. They have a massive market opportunity, but it's not for the faint of heart. Luckily, as a Twiga board member, I was able to help connect them with Fadi Ghandour, the founding partner of Wamda Capital and the leading venture capitalist in the Middle East. Fadi made his fortune building Aramex, the "FedEx for emerging markets." Instead of being intimidated by supply chains in Africa, Fadi understood the market potential and knew he could help the Twiga team navigate past the inevitable landmines.

In the same way, OpenGov obviously benefited from Joe Lonsdale's early interest in its space, but the same held true for their Series B, which was led by Andreesen Horowitz, one of the preeminent venture capital firms in the Valley. Zac Bookman explains that this was largely due to finding the right person: "Andreesen had a crazy partner—Balaji Srinivasan—who was very far out on the horizon in the govtech market."

Impact Funds

Sectoral funds aren't the only venture capital funds that have to find strong deal flow for a particular thesis. Impact funds focus on startups with positive social impact, which your regulated startup should, by definition, have. Impact funds vary in their theses as much as any other venture investors, but in general they're looking for startups that can generate venture class returns while also executing against social impact targets. Some have formal require-

---

*Narrative and data are both important concepts you'll learn about in Section 2: The Foundations of Regulatory Hacking.

**You'll learn more about Twiga in Chapter 8: Influence.

ments that you report social impact data to them on a regular basis. Others simply want your mission to align with their thesis, but will then let you focus on building your business.

In many cases, your optimal funding strategy may include a mix of venture capital and impact funds. Twiga is one example, combining financial investors like Wamda with impact investors interested in reducing food inflation in Africa. Another startup that has done this well is EverFi, which provides digital learning programs to schools in underserved areas.* EverFi has raised venture capital from financial investors such as Jeff Bezos, Eric Schmidt, Ev Williams, and Allen & Company. They have also raised significant capital from impact funds such as Rethink Impact, founded by Jenny Abramson, and the Rise Fund, a global impact fund managed by TPG and cofounded by Bono and Jeff Skoll.

Government Grants

A final source of capital for regulatory hackers is government grants, which have the benefit of not diluting the ownership of founders and early investors. In the United States, agencies such as the Department of Defense, National Institutes of Health, the Department of Energy, and the National Science Foundation are particularly active as grant funders for startups.

Government grants can often be useful for "deep tech" startups that require significant research and development before they can prove they have a viable technology. Paradromics is a great example. When Matt Angle was getting started, he secured an early investment through the U.S. Small Business Administration's Small Business Innovation Research, or SBIR, program. SBIR is a highly competitive program that provides government funding to support startups that are engaging in cutting-edge research and development that has clear commercialization potential. The program is part of the U.S. government's efforts to more broadly stimulate innovation and increase private-sector commercialization of new technologies stemming from U.S. government–backed research and development.[14]

"The SBIR program is a great source of early funding for startups like ours, because no one was really investing in this area of technology when we were starting out," Angle says. "Not only do you obtain the funding, but you also

---

*You'll learn more about EverFi in Chapter 11: Selling with Social Impact.

gain some credibility when you get a show of faith from that program." He later noted that he was able to use SBIR's validation to raise a small but important round of additional seed money from angel investors.

Later, in the summer of 2017, Paradromics competed for and won an $18 million investment from DARPA as part of a broader $65 million program to pursue the development of neural implants that allow the human brain to speak directly to a computer. The initiative, dubbed the Neural Engineering System Design (NESD) program, awarded similar levels of funding to five academic groups. Paradromics was the only company—startup or otherwise—accepted into the four-year program.

While the agency naturally hopes to earn a return on $18 million in taxpayer dollars, there are additional motivations at play, Angle points out.

"The U.S. government and an agency like DARPA need to stay on or ahead of the curve—said another way, they want to avoid big technological surprises," he says, noting that the program was born after the Soviet Union developed the first satellite, Sputnik, in the 1950s. "They can't afford to be behind on technologies that could affect our national interests or national security, so there's a strategic play here beyond just the financial play for the government."

These grant-funding programs can be particular useful for startups like Paradromics that know they have a lot of work to do to prove their technology before they're ready for the inevitable pressure to scale that comes with venture capital.

"One thing that I think is very important: There's an expectation in Silicon Valley that entrepreneurs should project unrestrained confidence when presenting your company or your technology—but that's incommensurate with what we're doing," Angle says. "This is highly technical and quite complicated, and in order to be successful in the long run, we need to be a little bit circumspect and constantly question what we're doing. To some degree, that's probably true for any startup, but I think it's especially important for startups in these new and complex markets. I have seen companies err on both sides—some that have failed to raise money and eventually failed because they couldn't demonstrate the level of confidence and conviction that investors need to see, while others raised a shit-ton of money but never advanced beyond vaporware because they couldn't escape from their own propaganda."

Blake Hall similarly took advantage of government grants in building ID.me, having received over $6 million in a series of grants from the National Institute of Standards and Technology (NIST). "When NIST awarded us $2.6 million as part of the President's National Strategy for Trusted Identities in Cyberspace it was a huge moment for the credibility for the company as well as for our bank account," Blake says.

Strategic investors, sectoral and impact funds, and government grants aren't mutually exclusive—nor are they incompatible with mainstream venture capital. The best regulatory hackers will figure out how to put together the right mix of funding in the right sequence. The key thing to understand about these sources of funding is that, unlike mainstream venture capital, you aren't competing against every other startup investment opportunity out there. Instead, you are finding groups that are looking for a startup like yours that meets a need they have—whether it's to explore a particular technology or support an investment thesis they've already bet on.

How to Win with Arbitrage

As you look to take advantage of regulatory arbitrage to find your early adopters, first-mover regulators, and funders, here are some key things to bear in mind.

First, the key to finding breakthrough arbitrage opportunities is to understand your power map and think about for whom you have the most potential value—whether an institution, a government, or a funder. Think about whether a player is an attacker or a defender. For Valerann, most governments don't face competitive pressure to stay on the leading edge of technology. But Transurban does!

In the same sense, San Francisco already has more startups than it can house, so it doesn't tend to be particularly flexible with regulation. New York City and Dubai, on the other hand, want to draw more startups and are motivated to get creative with you.

In the same way, NEA, a mainstream venture capital firm that has generated outstanding returns for forty years, doesn't need to prove anything, whereas an edtech, govtech, or impact investor does. Be the perfect startup for them to prove that thesis.

Second, this is about people as much as organizations. Look for institutions, governments, or funders with strong leadership. This is ultimately personal, and a Jennifer Aument, Noah Raford, Miguel Gamiño, Joe Lonsdale, or Fadi Ghandour matters.

Third, look for structured programs relevant to your startup. Union powers programs for Transurban but also health systems, airports, pharma companies, airlines, and more. TechStars, Startupbootcamp, and Noah's Dubai Future Accelerators also have their own versions of these structured innovation programs.

The key is to find opportunities with a commitment to move toward a pilot or regulatory change or funding within a firm timeframe that aligns with yours. In the challenges that Union powers, there is always a ninety-day process for the institution and startup to work together to develop a pilot, at which point the institution has to make a decision. The worst thing for a startup is a never-ending "maybe."

SECTION 2

The Foundations of Regulatory Hacking

Chapter 6

NARRATIVE

If you ask enough startup founders to tell you their stories, you'll begin to pick up on some common themes. There are always some unique twists and turns and the characters will vary, but the standard narrative becomes familiar quickly. More often than not, it's a story about identifying a gap in the market, racing to build a viable product, rushing to raise capital, scaling as quickly as your team and your technology will allow, and ultimately disrupting the status quo.

Carolyn and her cofounders at HopSkipDrive tell a different story.

The HopSkipDrive story, to hear Carolyn tell it, is about frantically coordinating three different carpools with three different families for eight different children. It's a story about arguing with your spouse over whose job is more important that day. It's a story, she says simply, about an upset child who was late to soccer practice or was once again the last one waiting to be picked up from piano lessons.

The HopSkipDrive story is a story about working parents.

"We weren't looking for a problem to solve," says Carolyn, who with her cofounders Joanna and Janelle have eight children between them. "We were looking for a solution to a problem we all faced every day—a problem no one else seemed to be solving." Starting a startup was merely "our way to solve our own problem."

With that in mind, the cofounders set out to build a service they would be comfortable using for their own children, which meant going above and beyond when it came to safety and peace of mind. That's why the three designed and

implemented an extensive fifteen-point background check and driver certification process and integrated real-time vehicle safety monitoring into their app.[1]

As Carolyn puts it, "First and foremost, we're moms. We worry about our
kids, so we've built in safety measures before the ride, during the ride, and
behind the scenes that makes us feel comfortable sending our kids with Care-
Drivers, too."[2]

Joanna echoed the same sentiment a year later, telling mommy blogger
Emma Johnson, "It had to be something we would feel comfortable using with
our own kids," who she later noted were attending five different schools and
participating in a combined seventeen activities when HopSkipDrive was first
conceived. She was quick to add that "all of our children now use HopSkip-
Drive all the time."[3]

In addition, Carolyn points out, "We're three women, three mothers, all of
us first-time founders, and two of us were over forty when we started. We're
exactly the opposite of what you see in Silicon Valley."

That's the narrative they have carefully crafted: *for busy moms, by busy
moms.*

But there's more to their story.

The chapters Carolyn tends to gloss over with most audiences include her
fifteen years as an attorney after graduating from UCLA Law School, starting
and running her own practice, and launching and managing two nonprofits.
Joanna doesn't lead with her business degrees from both Stanford and Wharton, nor does she go out of her way to mention her senior executive roles at a
publishing firm, a bank, and a tech company. Depending on the audience in
the room, Janelle may never bring up her studies at Wharton, either, or how
the boutique marketing company she started has worked with the likes of
Nestlé and Visa.

Those were details that Donna and I heard when they pitched 1776 for a
seed investment.

The story they tell to most audiences is about three everyday moms
tackling the mundane challenges faced by every other working mom. It's
down-to-earth and relatable, bordering on homey, not entrepreneurial and
opportunistic. It's for moms, by moms. Not for moms, by savvy, successful, Ivy
League entrepreneurs.

After all, which would make you feel more at ease putting your child in a
car with a stranger?

Much of the credit for the story and the brand HopSkipDrive has crafted belongs to Janelle.

"Janelle is a branding and storytelling guru," Carolyn praises. "She knows how to convey the emotion about our brand in a way that's very compelling and approachable and in a way to create a sense of trust amongst families who five years ago would never have imagined using a service like this."

While the HopSkipDrive team had the luxury of understanding their target customers more intimately than most, the success of the brand comes down to one core value: empathy.

According to Janelle, "While Carolyn, Joanna, and I were all facing the same challenge of getting our kids where they needed to go, we each have very different parenting stories and sensibilities. The brand had to be relatable and understanding of every parent's unique struggle." The team dedicated time early on to working through exactly what the brand should stand for and why they believed so passionately in what they were doing as moms and as founders.

It starts with the way Janelle and the team frame their company to customers. In headlines, you'll find HopSkipDrive commonly referred to as "Uber for kids." But you won't find the cofounders promoting that analogy. Instead, they frequently describe the proposition to parents as "caregivers on wheels." It's a subtle distinction, but as Janelle points out, it's an important one for wary parents.

"We are very purposeful in the way we talk about what we do and how it supports parents and families. Our website breaks almost every digital marketing rule. We don't have lots of white space. The copy is long and explanatory. There aren't quippy analogies. We crafted our story to support obsessive parents, like us, who want to know every detail and need real assurances that choosing to trust their child's transportation to a CareDriver is safe." It helps that the voice they've created is easy to understand and authentic.

And it's not just potential customers for whom the story matters.

"We're dealing with the most vulnerable population in society, young children," Carolyn says. "When you're doing that, you have to live and breathe trust and safety, and not just in your actions, but in every interaction you're having with customers, with drivers, with employees, and with regulators."

Make no mistake, Uber's strategy and subsequent record of success early on wasn't lost on the HopSkipDrive cofounders. While they were building their own startup, they watched as the Silicon Valley poster child bulldozed its way into new city after new city with seemingly little regard for existing regulations, all in the name of innovation and a better consumer experience.[4]

"For us to adopt that same model and go into the California Public Utilities Commission like a bull in a china shop and say, 'We realize you don't have rules yet for transporting unaccompanied minors, so guess what, we're just gonna do whatever the hell we want' . . . that wouldn't have been the attitude that showed we were all about the same things they are—trust and safety," Carolyn says.

Instead, they leaned into sharing the same goals as their regulators, offering them the story about empathy and safety they told to every parent who would listen.

"We knew that the fundamental purpose of these regulatory agencies was safety," she says. "Once we could show them, because of who we were and where we were coming at this problem from, that safety was our top priority, too, the level of trust and the willingness to engage went up exponentially."

She adds, "We went in from day one knowing we didn't want to spend our time fighting with people all day long every day. We wanted to figure out a way to make it work for everyone. We wanted to find ways to negotiate that made everyone in the room, including the regulators, feel like they had won."

The Narrative Imperative

If you want to be successful as a founder, you'll have to become effective at pitching your startup, or have a cofounder who is. There's a reason why most accelerator programs spend at least as much time coaching you on your pitch as helping you fine-tune your business model. As nice as it is to believe that a superior idea or technology will win on its merits, the truth is that many ideas and technologies will never see the light of day if someone who believes in them cannot learn to tell a compelling story.

Narrative matters to all startups, but there are three ways in which it matters uniquely to regulated startups.

First, as a regulatory hacker striving to further the public interest, you're solving important problems that positively impact real people's lives. You can use that to your advantage. Everyone wants to believe that there are entrepreneurs in the world trying to cure diseases or save the planet or eliminate traffic.

Second, because you operate in a *complex* market, you need to find a straightforward way of communicating what you do. It takes skill and practice to explain your "artificial intelligence demand-response optimizer for electric utilities" in a way that people can intuitively understand and get excited about. Even more challenging, you have to explain your complex market in a way that overcomes people's often-mistaken assumptions. You don't want people to assume they know what your education startup does on the basis of *their* experiences at school, or the challenges of your healthcare startup based on *their* visit to the doctor.

Third, simpler startups are often preaching to the converted, sharing their narrative with investors, tech media, and perhaps end users. As a regulated startup, your narrative is so important because to unlock your market you often have to preach to the uninitiated as well, such as citizens, influencers, policymakers and advocacy groups, and other potential stakeholders, which is why crafting, refining, and effectively delivering your narrative is of paramount importance. If you want influential and powerful people to help you, and to engage other influential and powerful people on your behalf, then you need to arm them with a simple, compelling story that they can use and share.

Pitching Is a Process

Between 1776 and Union, I've coached hundreds of startups on their pitch. All that pitching has convinced me of one essential truth: As a founder, you are often the *worst* person on the planet to pitch your startup. Unfortunately, you're the only one with the credibility to do so.

I have some theories about why founders are uniquely bad at pitching their own startups. To some extent, as a founder, you're too close to your own startup. You've formed hypotheses, run experiments that invalidated those hypotheses, and gone back to the drawing board, over and over again. While your understanding of your business improves, your ability to communicate it in a clear way degrades.

Or perhaps it's because you have a background in your domain, say as a doctor or agronomist. Or, heaven forbid, you learned about your market as a consultant. Professions that require significant technical or business training often involve lots of jargon and buzzwords, which is the death of clear, compelling communication.

Because it doesn't come naturally, developing a great pitch takes *work*. Like a comic crafting their act, you have to get your material out in front of an audience, bomb, rework it, and bomb again, until regular people start to get the joke. It also helps to have someone you trust to tell you the truth, serving as a de facto editor, constantly forcing you to cut out your favorite bits that don't actually make much sense to your audience. At the end of the day, your narrative is a product in its own right and you should take the same build-measure-learn and iterate-like-crazy approach as you would in other part of your startup.

That said, there are points to bear in mind.

The process starts with owning your *core story*. Often referred to as your elevator pitch, this is the immediate answer you give if someone asks you what your startup does. It should be brief, simple, and able to get across the salient points about your company. Ideally, it should also inspire and intrigue. You should always be testing your core story and keeping it up to date as your understanding of your business evolves.

Once you have a core story that resonates with people, use it as the foundation upon which to build variations for different audiences, such as customers, investors, or regulators. The core story is always the same, but you should absolutely be telling it in different ways to different audiences, changing the framing and emphasizing the parts of the story most likely to resonate with that audience.

Once you have your core story, use it to build supporting materials, whether your investor pitch deck or your website. Use these assets to enhance your narrative, but never rely on them entirely. If you bump into a potential investor at a baseball game without your computer or iPad handy, you should be able to deliver the same compelling investor narrative you would if you had your deck at the ready. Similarly, if you give someone the thirty-second version of your story at a conference, and they go to your website later that evening, they should recognize the same narrative on your site.

As you go through the process of building your core story, refining it for different audiences, and building marketing assets around it, there are four key insights you should always remember.

The Four Keys to Telling Your Story
1. Start with *why*.
2. Tell a *story*, and keep it simple.
3. Know your *audience*.
4. Be authentic.

1. Start with *Why*

Airbnb's core story is *not* that it'll find you a low-cost lodging alternative to a hotel. According to cofounder Brian Chesky, Airbnb's mission can be distilled down to a single word: "At its core, Airbnb is about *belonging*. If we are to be understood as a brand, and more importantly as a community, we need to communicate this idea of 'belonging' around the world."[5]

Translation: Airbnb's story isn't about short-term rentals or hotel alternatives or even extra income for homeowners. It's a story about feeling at home in a foreign place.

The same goes for ID.me and their founder Blake Hall.* Blake could tell you that ID.me sells access to a digital identification verification network that allows individuals to easily prove their identity and whether they're, for instance, a military veteran or university student. Instead, Blake tells a markedly more concise story: "We sell trust."

Nothing about superior software or innovative processes. Nothing about unique features or competitive advantages. It's all about the *why*.

Simon Sinek, author of *Start with Why*, says in his 2009 TED Talk, "The goal is not to do business with everybody who needs what you have. The goal is to do business with people who believe what you believe."[6]

While this holds true for most startups, it's all the more important for regulated startups who need to show that their goals are aligned with the public interest. When you need to convince a city councilwoman to change a long-standing regulation that clearly favors entrenched, deep-pocketed interest groups, or when you need to convince a hospital or a court system to allow you to access sensitive data about their patients or their citizens, it won't matter nearly as much *what* you're doing as whether or not they trust that your motives and your beliefs align with theirs.

And yet, I find that most entrepreneurs spend their time telling anyone who will listen that *what* they have created is better than what others have or *how* their methods are superior to the competition.

Instead, start with the *why*—the mission—and work backward to the *what* and the *how*. If you're solving a problem in the public interest, then you are inherently a social-impact, mission-oriented startup, whether you find it useful

---

*You learned about Blake and ID.me in Chapter 3: Business Models.

to explicitly use those terms or not. Start your narrative with the citizens whom you benefit. Let your audience know that you have *empathy* for their challenge and *passion* for solving it.

Only once you have convinced someone that the challenge you are tackling matters will they grant you permission to essentially bore them with the details about how you are tackling that challenge. The *why* is what inspires and opens the doors.

If done well, focusing on the *why* can even break down deep-rooted emotional and cultural barriers. Just ask Guillermo Pepe.

In 2011, Pepe founded Mamotest, a telemedicine startup that provides free or low-cost mammograms to women in rural areas of Argentina by screening them where they live and then routing the images via internet back to a central location for analysis and diagnosis by a licensed radiologist. It's a promising potential solution to one of the country's most serious healthcare challenges. Every day, twenty Argentine women die from breast cancer, many of them losing a battle they might have won had the disease been detected earlier.

And yet it was a solution that could render him a villain in the eyes of the public, not a hero.

In Latin America, there's a bias against entrepreneurs in the healthcare sector. "When a private company looks to address healthcare problems in Argentina or in other parts of Latin America, they will say, 'Oh, you are trying to make profit from people's health problems,'" Pepe explains. While it's never ideal to have public sentiment working against you, it's particularly problematic for an upstart like Mamotest, which not only needs to work with government but would later lobby for policy changes that would support their mission and their business model.

Ever the entrepreneur, Pepe learned to frame his core story around the everyday women whose lives are saved by using Mamotest, rather than around his slick use of digital channels or creative partnerships with governments and nonprofits. He showed he is committed to helping those women rather than simply trying to make a profit.

So how do you best articulate the *why*? With a story.

2. Tell a *Story*, and Keep It Simple

I'll let you in on a dirty secret of the world of venture capital: I can't remember most pitches I hear, nor can most other investors. I don't mean weeks later. I mean that if I have four or five startups pitch me over the course of an hour at an event, I literally can't recall more than one or two when I'm heading home. When I'm judging a pitch competition and hear fifteen startups pitch one after the other, my fellow judges and I get back to the judging room and we literally cannot remember what more than four or five of the startups do. We're all flipping through our notes trying to remind each other.

If nobody can remember your pitch, then it wasn't worth the oxygen you used to deliver it. Being memorable isn't about being flashy or doing something special to stand out from the crowd, though. I once saw a startup founder deliver their entire pitch on stage as a nursery rhyme. When we got back to the judging room, we all remarked how clever the founder was. Then none of us could remember what her startup actually did.

The key to being memorable is really just about keeping it simple. A clear, concise story delivered in plain language is what sticks with people.

Across all cultures and throughout history, regardless of medium, every great story has shared several common elements. First, they have a compelling, relatable character. Someone with whom the audience can easily empathize. Second, that character inevitably faces a crisis or thorny problem that must be resolved. Often that crisis or problem is created by, or at least represented by, a villain. Third, the character discovers a heroic, cunning solution to said challenge. Finally, queue the "happily ever after" epilogue.

As a regulatory hacker, your core story should follow this recipe for success as closely as possible.

Simplistic and formulaic, sure. But straying from this storyline will generally lead entrepreneurs into a narrative that is too complex, abstract, or confusing—or all three. Charismatic hero confronted with important challenge caused by nefarious villain until saved by a clever solution—it's a tale as old as time, and it works.

The "just plain English" part of the formula is harder than it seems, though. The startup world is rich with jargon and buzzwords that don't make a lot of sense to actual humans. From "iterate" to "hack," you've read plenty in this book already (although I do try to define my terms). Each complex market in turn develops its own unique jargon, buzzwords, and—worst of all—acronyms. When you put those together, it's easy for your story to become incoherent.

Even if your audience is sophisticated in the lingo of your complex market, you should resist the urge to use anything but clear, simple words that anybody would understand. This is harder than it seems, but important. When I'm pitch coaching, I often take this to an extreme, forcing regulatory hackers to edit and edit their story until they have found the shortest, simplest words they could possibly use to take their audience through their story. It's basically impossible for your pitch to be *too* simple and clear.

A short, carefully crafted core story can get you that meeting you need with the mayor's office or the backing of an influential civic leader. In the case of Airbnb, it can convince you to stay in a stranger's home in a foreign country, or for HopSkipDrive, to send your child off to tennis lessons in a car with a stranger.

There are, of course, always tempting alternatives to telling a story, but you should resist them unless absolutely necessary. One weak alternative is narrative by analogy, otherwise known as "We're the Uber for energy" or "We're the Amazon for bananas." It's not wrong to use analogies to explain particular points, but they should never be your core story.

Another weak alternative is the "consultant" pitch. These usually start by throwing out a long list of facts and figures, designed to cow your audience into being impressed that your problem is important and that you did your homework, *without ever getting to the actual human story*. These kinds of pitches often start with statements like "75 percent of children in grades three through six perform 17 percent below grade standard" and proceed from there. Having data at your fingertips is great,* but the problem with the consultant pitch is that you lose the sense that you have empathy for the actual people who will use your product and whose lives will be better for it.

3. Know Your *Audience*

While your regulated startup's core story shouldn't change, as a savvy storyteller you must be able to tailor the narrative to the audience you're addressing, reframing and reprioritizing elements of your story to more effectively appeal to their differing motives of an investor, a customer, or a public official.

Pepe opted for an extreme version of this for Mamotest to overcome the biases in Latin America against profiting from new approaches to improving health. Around the same time he began working on Mamotest, his digital health startup, he also launched Fundación Telmed, a nonprofit focused on

---

*In fact, you're about to read an entire chapter on the importance of data in Chapter 7: Data.

expanding the use of telemedicine to reach underserved areas of Latin America. Fundación Telmed focused in particular on early diagnoses of diseases such as breast cancer, partnering with other like-minded nonprofits to encourage routine testing and expand awareness around available services, like Mamotest.

In this way, Pepe was able to clearly articulate that Fundación Telmed is pursuing a social mission while Mamotest builds technology. He can then emphasize one or the other depending on the audience.

Intentionally, Pepe introduces himself as the "founder of Fundación Telmed" much more often than he leads with "founder of Mamotest." On his business cards and atop his LinkedIn profile, you'll find the foundation, not the business. When he does bring up Mamotest, it's as the means to Fundación Telmed's end. Fundación Telmed is the *why* and Mamotest is *how.*

Routinely pitching the nonprofit as his primary focus—and framing the startup as an instrument to help that nonprofit pursue its mission—has cast a warmer light on Mamotest in the eyes of the public, the government, and the media.

"By doing that, we have the media interested in the foundation, and they have written positive articles in local newspapers and done interviews on television," he says. "That led to more civility around what we were trying to do, which made it easier to get meetings with mayors and governors of the provinces."

Of course, Pepe's default story—Telmed's mission first, Mamotest technology (and its profits) second—is not the story that every audience wants to hear. When meeting and pitching potential investors, for instance, Pepe switches hats, so to speak, emphasizing Mamotest and allowing Telmed to play a supporting role in the narrative, with the latter paving the way for Mamotest to more quickly garner visibility and scale their business model.

"When I'm meeting with investors, I have to almost forget about the foundation," he says. "Otherwise, what I will hear is that they think I'm a nice guy with a great mission but they can't be sure they will see a return on their investment. The only time I bring up the foundation is to show how it has helped us get public loans or make connections inside the government."

Pepe's approach isn't one that most regulatory hackers will find themselves in a position to use, but it highlights the creative tailoring of narrative to address market challenges.

Carolyn and her cofounders have been similarly thoughtful about adapting the HopSkipDrive story to different audiences. Remember that when meeting with California regulators and applying for permits, their narrative revolved almost entirely around the idea of safety.

While they've never abandoned that core tenet of their narrative, recent meetings with the Los Angeles mayor's office prompted them to shift other elements of their story into the spotlight.

With the permit in hand, what the HopSkipDrive trio really needed next was office space—but not just any space. Carolyn lives on the west side of the city, while Joanna and Janelle live on the east side, so they needed something downtown, a prime real estate market. Moreover, they needed a flexible lease to account for potential growth, and they needed one of the city's rarest perks—parking—so that prospective CareDrivers could come by for interviews and vehicle inspections. All at a price that a cash-strapped startup could afford.

In their conversations with the mayor's office, the cofounders leaned heavily on two elements of their story: One, that HopSkipDrive gives parents the flexibility to hold full-time jobs, and two, that the startup provides important income opportunities to caregivers.

"I would share the same story about my own experience, where I couldn't have a full-time job because I had to be there to pick up my children from school every day," Carolyn says. "We're enabling people, in particular women, to work and be productive, while at the same time we're creating this lucrative, flexible work opportunity for our CareDrivers."

It's a two-for-one economic empowerment message that hit home with the mayor's office, and within weeks the administration had helped HopSkipDrive secure a flexible lease at the city's new Maker City building right in the middle of downtown Los Angeles. When they had doubled in size four months later, the property manager asked them how soon they'd like to move into the other half of the space on their floor.

"I don't think we get that same treatment if we're not a mission-driven organization with a story to tell about enabling people to work," Carolyn says. "We made it easy for the government to get behind us."

4. Be *Authentic*

While your story can and should be a little fluid, your narrative is no place for fiction. For startups, a well-developed story is of little value unless it genuinely reflects the culture that defines the company. Here again, for entrepreneurs impacting the public interest, it's particularly important that your decisions from a business perspective are lock-step consistent with the story you preach.

Take Jonathon Ende, for example.

At SeamlessDocs, a NYC-based startup that helps government agencies turn traditional paper forms into easy-to-complete, easy-to-submit electronic documents, Jonathon's company motto tells the story: "Government is beautiful." More broadly, as the company puts it, "Our company was founded on the fundamental belief that interacting with government can and should be a beautiful experience."

It's a sentiment that runs counter to the common refrain that government is slow and inefficient and frustrating and corrupt, and as a result, it immediately signals to a mayor or county clerk that SeamlessDocs is different. It signals that Jonathon and his team believe that public servants have the best of intentions and that SeamlessDocs is there to help eliminate the barriers that stand between them and their desire to serve citizens.

That motto trickles down to affect everything from Jonathon's recruitment strategy—every prospective hire must demonstrate a genuine passion for government—to his marketing tactics. For example, SeamlessDocs recently launched a digital marketing campaign highlighting one of their users in government every month who has gone above and beyond in the name of public service. It's another way to show that SeamlessDocs genuinely values what their clients do every day and wants to help.

Even the company's sales strategy feeds the company's mission-driven narrative. SeamlessDocs structures their contracts around the volume of forms an agency needs to process, but for the most part it does not charge more for different features or add-ons. That's because, as Jonathon explains, "if we've added a new feature or done something to make the product better for the government and the citizens in Seattle, we want the government and the citizens in Eagle Mountain, Utah, to get those same added benefits."

If SeamlessDocs's mission was to sell e-document software to the government, that new-features-for-all strategy might not make sense. But because Jonathon's company is committed to "making government beautiful," the new-features-for-all approach aligns with the company's core story.

Ende adds: "Every day, we get a bunch of brilliant, passionate, talented people together and put them in a room to work on one thing—how do we make government better? It's that simple."

Pepe was similarly thoughtful from the outset about how his business decisions would influence Mamotest's story. When determining the company's first screening location, he could have easily set up shop in a relatively urban area, where there would be more women in need of testing and where internet connectivity would be better. It would have given his first trial a much better shot at success. But it wouldn't have served the narrative he knew needed to build.

"I knew that if we started in a city or a large town, the response would be, 'Well, maybe this can work there, but it will never work out in the difficult places, the rural areas that need it most,'" he said. Instead, Pepe set up his first imaging site in one of Argentina's most impoverished and ill-connected provinces, Chaco. Sure enough, there were some bumps early on, but eventually his team ironed out the kinks and only a few months later the model was working.

"We did it in the middle of nowhere," he says. "I can now show people this can work anywhere."

The Formula

In case I haven't driven home the point yet, your narrative should *not* sound like this:*

> SeamlessDocs is the Instagram of government forms. *Kill the analogy!*
>
> *Where's the hero in this story? What's their problem?*
>
> There are more than four billion PDFs on government websites. A recent KPMG study estimated that government workers spend more than four million hours per week processing these forms, costing taxpayers more than $480 million per week in waste from inefficiencies. *Consultant speak*
>
> *How do you make their life better?!*
>
> SeamlessDocs is an intuitive, collaborative process-improvement and paperwork reduction platform for the municipal e-government marketplace. The SeamlessDocs platform can convert a PDF into a responsive design eForm in less than 3.2 seconds. Overall, Gartner forecasts that the municipal e-government marketplace will be worth more than $20 billion by 2020. *Jargon and buzzwords!* *Irrelevant to your market!*

---

*This is a fictional example of a bad SeamlessDocs pitch rather than anything Jonathon would ever pitch.

Instead, by putting the insights of this chapter together, your narrative should sound something like this:

> *Sally is a single mother, working two jobs, who needs to apply for counseling for her daughter. Instead of spending her precious free time with her daughter, she goes to the Tennessee Department of Children's Services website and digs around for thirty minutes until she finds a PDF form to request subsidized counseling. She has to print out the PDF, fill out the form with a pen, write a paper check, find an envelope and stamp, and mail it in. Four weeks later, she gets a letter back in the mail with instructions on how to fill out more forms before she can someday start her daughter's counseling. Every one of us knows how frustrated Sally feels from our own interactions with government.*
>
> *Barry is a civil servant who manages the website for the Tennessee Department of Children's Services. He cares a lot about serving people like Sally. He also hates how all those PDFs make life inefficient for the other employees in the department. But he feels trapped by PDFs.*
>
> *At SeamlessDocs, we believe that government is beautiful. We wake up every day figuring out how to make Barry a hero and Sally's life just a bit easier.*
>
> *With SeamlessDocs, Barry just uploads his PDFs into our system and we automatically convert them into simple, elegant web and mobile forms, complete with online credit card processing. Barry can even automate what happens to the forms after Sally submits them, making him a hero to his team as well as Sally.*
>
> *We launched SeamlessDocs three years ago. In that time, we have grown to serve hundreds of government agencies. We make the PDF problem disappear for our clients while generating strong gross margins as a software-as-a-service business. There are more than twenty thousand municipal government agencies in the United States alone, making our immediate addressable market worth more than $1 billion per year as we continue to grow. Our growth strategy is simple: We've developed an efficient, highly repeatable inside-sales model that enables us to reach our target customer in a scalable way.*

The formula is as follows:

1. Introduce us to a sympathetic citizen (or citizens) to whom anyone can relate.
2. Show us that citizen's problem, using language that causes us to *feel* how painful or expensive this problem is for them.
3. Share your mission.
4. Show us how much better that citizen's life is with your product or service. (Do NOT rattle off a long list of features or technical specs. Nobody cares unless you've made it to due diligence.)

Once you've shared your story with us, you then get to share the "happily ever after epilogue" tailored to your audience. If it's an investor, then you might succinctly share the details I included above, such as market size, business model, growth model, and traction. If it's a customer, you encourage them to be a hero by sharing how easy it is for them to buy your product.

That's the formula. It sounds easy, but it takes an incredible amount of work to tell a simple story.

Chapter 7

DATA

Mark DeSantis doesn't have to pause to think. He has committed every number to memory, and they roll right off his tongue without a moment's hesitation, one statistic after the next, woven into the story he tells.

"Seventy-seven percent of the roads in our country are managed by local government."[1]

"Right now, 30 percent of our nation's roadways need to be completely rehabbed or replaced."

"To rebuild a road in a major city will cost between $500,000 and $1 million per mile."

"Bad roads are responsible for about $100 billion in unnecessary insurance claims every year."

"We spend more than $100 billion every year to maintain our country's 4.1 million asphalt lane miles. That's one-sixth of the defense budget being spent on roads every year."

For DeSantis, these are more than just facts and figures. They're his ticket into a conversation.

A serial entrepreneur who doubles as an academic and politico, DeSantis is the CEO of RoadBotics, a Pittsburgh-based startup that has developed a low-cost, smartphone-based monitoring solution that uses machine learning to evaluate road conditions for municipalities. The technology is both incredibly simple and wildly sophisticated.

It works like this: With the RoadBotics app running and your smart-phone mounted to the windshield of your car via suction cup, the startup's platform uses the phone's built-in GPS and camera technologies to capture images of every stretch of road you drive in your car. At the same time, the app taps your phone's motion-sensor technology to note where uneven condi-tions cause the phone to jolt or shake. The app feeds that information into a sophisticated algorithm (what DeSantis jokingly calls a "machine learning, artificial intelligence, neural network magic box"), which scans the images for cracks, crevices, potholes, and uneven surfaces, and compares those im-ages to others that have come in from other drivers on that same street. The "magic" algorithm then pits all those images against thousands of photos of similar road damage elsewhere to evaluate and provide a rating of the severity of the damage.

That information is then sold to municipal, county, and state govern-ments in the form of a map, helping them see where they should focus their maintenance and repair efforts. Different colors on the map show where a town's or city's roads are in good condition (green), where roads are starting to buckle (yellow), and where roads are beyond saving (red) and must be re-placed.

The core technology was originally developed at the Carnegie Mellon Uni-versity Robotics Institute, where DeSantis has been a professor for twenty years. Before that, DeSantis started and scaled several successful companies in other complex markets, from a web-based tutoring startup (Apangea Learn-ing) to several software ventures in the energy and power supply industries (MobileFusion, kWatera, and kWantix).

"I have spent my entire life in inhabiting every nook and cranny of this highly regulated startup world," he says.

In Chapter 4: Growth, we discussed inertia and the notion that the status quo, no matter how far from ideal for everyone involved, remains resistant to change. When you're working in a complex market and facing institutions with supreme aversion to risk and change, breaking that status quo can be im-mensely difficult. The mantra that "things are as they are and will remain as they are" tends to prevail.

DeSantis and the RoadBotics team know something about that.

When they tout the statistics about dangerous street conditions and soar-ing road maintenance costs in the United States, a common response from municipal leaders sounds something like, "Okay, but that's just the way it is";

or "Every city is in the same boat. We're all dealing with this same problem and no one has really figured out how to solve it."

And that's where data comes in handy again.

DeSantis traces his finger over what would look like a normal street map were it not for the seemingly haphazard shades of red, yellow, and green highlighting every road. On this one, the map is overwhelmingly red. He flips to another. It's almost all green with bits of yellow.

In just two images, DeSantis has illustrated the magnitude of the most costly challenge affecting every U.S. municipality—road maintenance—and put that challenge in a global context, showing what a typical color-coded roadmap looks like in the United States versus one in Australia.

"We know, and we can show them, that the U.S. is really bad at this," DeSantis says. "How do we know? Because we've run our own analysis with the RoadBotics platform in Germany, in Spain, in Australia, in Japan. We've compared the results. And it's not pretty."

The point he's trying to get across? One, that this is a big problem. And two, just as important, that it's a solvable problem. Some cities have figured it out using better data. Others can, too.

"This doesn't happen in Japan," DeSantis says. "In Tokyo, they inspect the roads every day. Every single day. In Berlin, they inspect their roads every week. They have a law that requires every city to have a person walk all of those roads every single week." Here in the United States, such frequent monitoring and maintenance has long been considered cost-prohibitive, especially for small cities and towns.

"With our technology, it doesn't have to be prohibitive anymore, though," he says.

Regulatory Hackers and Data

You don't have to go far to find tweets, blogs, or podcasts in the Valley extoling the importance of data. Data is *how* you should build your business, obsessing over the latest fashionable metrics that will lead you to product-market fit or optimize your growth strategy. Data is also the *basis* for many startups' products or business models. Facebook and Google are basically giant data-collection machines, designed to build incredibly refined graphs of our social connections, interests, behavior, and whereabouts. The same holds true in different ways for Amazon, LinkedIn, and numerous other iconic successes of the past decade. All of this is at least as true for regulated startups as it is for simpler ones.

In this chapter, you'll learn about four important ways that as a regulatory hacker you should be obsessing about data. The first is "outcomes data," or proving that your product or service has a positive impact on the public interest. The second is the use of data to create urgency around the need for your product. The third is using open data as part of your product or service. And the last is building regulated business models based on selling data to governments and institutions.

It's important to note that in all of the above, there are two distinct meanings and uses of "data." In the first meaning, "data" refers to *metrics*, or data *about* your business or solution. In the second, "data" refers to an *asset* that you are integrating into your business model. Both are important to regulatory hackers.

Before we get into the four ways that data is particularly important to *regulated* startups, let's take a look at how data matters to *any* startup today.

Building Startups Has Become a Math Problem

In decades past, startups needed to show investors exhaustive, forty-page business plans. These plans tended to revolve almost entirely around the company's product, operations, competition, and financial forecast models, often based as much on conjecture as anything else.

Today, as hacker culture has permeated the world of investing, sophisticated founders show prospective investors a twelve-slide pitch deck that lays out their narrative and an economic model showing how they intend to generate and spend cash, and—often most important—they supplement their pitch with data on their market and how their product is performing. I know of investors in the Valley who go so far as to not even ask to see a deck, just a cut of data from the startup's MixPanel dashboard. Building and investing in startups has become a data-driven game.

The startup world is brimming with blogs and podcasts touting key metrics that any founder needs to have at their fingertips. Some of the most obvious ones you hear in describing markets or products include:

Term	Definition
Total Addressable Market (TAM)	total potential market demand for your product or service, basically how massive your market could conceivably be
Serviceable Addressable Market (SAM)	the segment of the TAM that's most within your reach, basically what your market will likely be
Serviceable Obtainable Market (SOM)	the portion of your SAM that you expect to captvure over a period of time, basically the expectations you're setting for the market you can capture in a reasonable period of time
Monthly Active Users (MAU)	the number of users that use your product or service within a given month
Daily Active Users (DAU)	the number of users that use your product or service on a given day
Stickiness	your DAU divided by your MAU is a simple metric for describing how often users come back to your product or service, or how "sticky" you are
Churn Rate	the percentage of users that will become inactive within a given period
Average Revenue Per User (ARPU)	your total revenue divided by the number of active users on your product or service
Average Revenue Per Paying User (ARPPU)	your total revenue divided by the number of users that have subscribed to pay for your product or service
Annual Recurring Revenue (ARR)	the amount of recurring revenue (from subscriptions or regularly repeating transactions) you make in a period, then translated into an annual number
Monthly Recurring Revenue (MRR)	the amount of recurring revenue (from subscriptions or regularly repeating transactions) you make in a period, then translated into a monthly number
Net Promoter Score (NPS)	a survey metric that indicates how satisfied and enthusiastic your users or customers are
Lifetime Customer Value (LTV)	the ultimate metric you need to track on the value of a customer of your product or service, basically what a customer is worth to you
Cost of Acquiring a Customer (CAC)	the ultimate metric you need to track on the cost of acquiring a customer of your product or service, basically what a customer costs you
LTV:CAC Ratio	the gold standard for measuring how profitable a business model can ultimately be over time
Months to Recover CAC	how quickly the cash you receive from a customer covers the cost of acquiring that customer, basically how quickly a startup can become profitable

Source: Wikipedia

You'll also hear about funnel analyses, which show how your startup is performing step-by-step on converting potential customers into actual customers, and roll rates, or how often you're churning existing customers. Funnels and roll rates are often best measured through cohort analyses, which allow you to compare how key metrics have changed from the time you first engaged a potential customer, or sometimes based on another important segmentation variable.

All of this is just a sample of the world of startup metrics. There are many more esoteric measures that can quickly signal to a savvy investor whether you're showing promising signs of product-market fit and establishing a scalable business model into a large-enough market.

Let's apply these metrics to a classic example from the last decade in the Valley: the dating app. I was a small, early angel investor in Hinge, a popular dating app founded by one of my friends, Justin McLeod.

Justin has always been supremely diligent about sending investors a monthly performance report and updated pitch decks. He shows us how consumers are engaging with Hinge, using measures like daily and monthly active users, churn rates, net promoter scores, average time spent on the app each day, and similar metrics. He also shows us how people are getting results from the app by sharing the weekly number of conversations initiated per user.

Justin also shows us how his business model is performing, using his latest estimates of the lifetime value of a user based on data on their conversion rate into paid subscribers, their average revenue per paying user, and therefore their average revenue per user. He obsesses over how much it is costing Hinge to acquire new users, which involves viral coefficients and conversion rates from various paid user acquisition tools and strategies.

From all this data, Justin gives his investors remarkably insightful metrics each month into the health of Hinge's business model and whether various tweaks and interactions are moving Hinge in the right direction or not.

Knowing your data in the sense outlined above is at least as important for regulated startups in complex markets as it is for the founder of Hinge. The importance of your mission doesn't excuse you from applying meaningful rigor to measuring your business. If anything, the importance of your mission makes rigorous measurement even more important. This is even more true because as a regulated startup entering a complex market, you will probably face heightened skepticism from investors, particularly mainstream venture capitalists. Demonstrating that you understand and employ the same measurement and analysis strategies as other successful startups can go a long way toward easing those concerns.

To be clear, this is not only about winning over investors, though that's an enormously important part of the puzzle. That's merely a proxy for whether your business model and growth strategy have legs. Founders, including those in complex markets, should be constantly using these metrics to assess the path they're on and whether they need to pivot.

Complex Markets and Outcomes Data

Knowing your data is important in other ways that are uniquely relevant to startups in complex markets.

To illustrate the point, go back to the Hinge example, and let's run through all the things that Justin does *not* need to prove to investors, or users, or the media, or regulators. He doesn't need to prove to regulators, for instance, that the public interest is suffering due to a dearth of successful long-term relationships. He doesn't need to *prove* to users that more successful, long-term relationships result from using Hinge rather than Tinder or Bumble, or really that more relationships of any kind come from using Hinge. Heck, most investors do not even need to be convinced that more successful dates result from using the app. All they really want proof of is that a growing number of people are using the service and spending more time on it. While Justin certainly makes claims that Hinge is great at finding successful love connections, nobody really expects him to validate it through rigorous, peer-reviewed analyses. After all, the likeliest harm you'll suffer from an ineffective dating app is some wasted time and lowered self-esteem.

This isn't exclusive to consumer apps. Think about a typical SaaS marketing tool for small businesses. In addition to engagement and business model metrics, the founder of a new SaaS marketing platform may need to show her customers data that suggests her service helps companies improve marketing outcomes or reduce costs. But she does not need to rigorously prove to regulators that the success rate for small business owners is improved over a meaningful period by using her tool.

Now contrast this with RoadBotics. Like any other startup, DeSantis needs to show people data on engagement. He needs ready access to metrics like CAC, LTV, and the like so he can prove that he can profitably scale Road-Botics. Again, the social importance of reducing road maintenance costs doesn't excuse a lack of rigor in building his business.

But in addition to the data that any founder needs to show, as a regulatory hacker DeSantis also needs to show that RoadBotics actually helps municipalities, counties, and states reduce road maintenance costs. He might be able to close a few early adopters without this, but he will not unlock a mainstream market selling to municipal governments without meaningful data that shows genuine cost savings from the use of his tool. Governments tend to be understandably rigorous when spending public funds, particularly on new solutions. Given that traction with governments is crucial to RoadBotics's business model, it follows that savvy investors who understand these markets will want to see the same data before they make significant investments.

For an even more extreme example, consider a regulatory hacker scaling a new healthcare app. Again, she will need to show all the usual data around market size, engagement, and business model success. But she will also need to show that her product legitimately improves health outcomes for patients, or that it at least maintains outcomes while reducing costs. Depending on exactly what her company does, this may be relatively straightforward. At a minimum, hospitals and healthcare providers will need to see rigorous data on the health outcomes associated with a new technology in a way that a typical commercial enterprise may not. Or her burden of proof could be extremely robust, with, for example, a new medical device requiring FDA approval that might take years of trials and experiments.

Our healthcare founder not only needs this data for customers, but also for any investors, media, or influencers savvy in healthcare. And she will certainly need it for regulators like the FDA.

Why? Here again, it's because there is an obvious public interest involved in clinical healthcare solutions or autonomous trucks or nuclear reactors that simply doesn't exist when you're sharing photos or optimizing digital marketing or delivering takeout. And because there is public interest involved, there is regulation. If your startup is doing something that will impact the public interest, you are going to have a higher burden of proof than something that only affects private interests.

This holds true across complex markets. If you have an education startup and want to sell into school districts, it's not enough to show that teachers or students engage with your product. You have to show that it actually produces better educational outcomes. If you lack evidence of your outcomes, you're missing a necessary tool for unlocking markets. The same is true for startups in agriculture and food, financial services, space exploration, and numerous other complex markets.

And if you think FDA approval is hard, imagine the data that the recent handful of nuclear fusion startups will need in order to get approval from the U.S. Nuclear Regulatory Commission!

Obtaining Outcomes Data

All of this puts an even greater premium on early adopters, as we explored in Chapter 5: Arbitrage.

Geoffrey Moore's *Crossing the Chasm* is one of the greatest startup books ever written. Moore argues that disruptive technologies inevitably struggle to overcome the vastly different characteristics that distinguish early adopters from mainstream customers.[2]

Early adopters crave being the first to use new gadgets, tools, or services. Mainstream customers, conversely, want to see proof from early adopters that the gadget, tool, or service works. An astute founder understands this dynamic and proceeds carefully with early adopters, gathering evidence that their product is delivering value and found product-market fit before investing the big bucks to scale the company and take the product mainstream.

How does this apply to a regulated startup? In complex markets, because of the importance of proving outcomes, the chasm you must cross is often deeper and wider than in a simpler market. You're therefore going to need even better data to cross a regulated chasm.

You cannot get that hard data on outcomes without early adopters, and, depending on your market, a first-mover regulator willing to let you experiment. Perversely, while early adopters are all the more important, they may also be even more challenging to find for regulated startups, as early adopters must be willing to accept a higher level of risk than those in simpler markets. Think about the spectrum of risk. An early adopter of Hinge could be wasting some time without getting a date. An early adopter of RoadBotics could be wasting taxpayer funds without any benefit to show for it. An early adopter of a healthcare startup could potentially kill people. An early adopter of a nuclear fusion reactor could potentially wipe out entire populations.

In Chapter 5: Arbitrage, you learned some insights on why some governments and institutions may be willing to leap first with a new idea or technology, and how you can find them. Getting this right may represent a binary success or failure point for some regulatory hackers.

The importance of outcomes data also means you need to think about how you're going to capture this data as early as possible. Any smart founder should think about data capture as an integral part of their product. But this is doubly true if you're going to have to submit your data to Stanford or NASA or Kaiser Permanente or Duke Energy to pick apart and dispassionately analyze.

Depending on your burden of proof, you may need to invest funds—and no less important, time—to produce rigorous, peer-reviewed studies based on your data. That was certainly the case for Dr. Nancy Markley, founder, president, and CEO of MPowrx, a health and medical products startup based in Alberta, Canada, whose first product was a device to alleviate sleep apnea. When her company was preparing to launch in 2008, MPowrx invested the time and risked the scrutiny necessary to prove that the technology worked.

That meant conducting a first-of-its-kind randomized controlled crossover study with patients dealing with sleep apnea or severe snoring problems. The results provided empirical evidence that the use of MPowrx's device was effective in treating both problems, and the study was later published in the journal *Sleep and Breathing*.[3]

"We took the time to have our first product undergo clinical testing and peer review," Markley wrote in a column published by TechCrunch. "By the time we took the product to market, and as we raised capital later on, we had data to share that showed that our product was clinically proven and that the technology was scientifically sound."[4]

Four years later, results from a second peer-reviewed study were published in the *Journal of Clinical Sleep Medicine* by two of the industry's leading researchers showing further evidence to support the treatment of moderate to severe sleep apnea using the company's device.[5]

Markley, whose company now sells its products to customers in more than eighty-five countries, acknowledged that the proposition of holding your startup's product up to the highest levels of third-party scrutiny can be scary for a founder, but in a highly regulated field like medical devices, where the stakes are high, the practice is imperative.

"Founders must be open to the scrutiny of due diligence," wrote Markley, who emphasized the importance of having your data externally validated. "If your potential investors are bringing in scientists and experts to audit your company, you must trust them as they analyze your technology and data."

She later added: "Being able to share your data (under proper confidentiality agreements), having your technology validated in clinical trials and peer-reviewed in medical journals should be welcome. It is a good thing to be able to prove the effectiveness of your product. You want to be able to show investors that your product works and has valid applications."

This same principle holds true in other complex markets, including education startups like Baltimore-based Legends of Learning.

"The idea behind my company was that a unique approach to game-based learning—short, simple ed-games specially built and aligned to curriculum standards—would engage and teach students more effectively," Vadim Polikov, one of the founders, wrote in a piece promoted by EdSurge. "But the idea was a hypothesis, and hypotheses need to be proven."[6]

Polikov—who knows a thing or two about complex markets, as he has a PhD in biomedical engineering from Duke University and previously founded a solar energy startup—continued: "Typically, companies are started, a product is built, there are sales, and then, after a few years, a small study bolsters marketing claims. As a former research scientist, this strikes me as completely backwards; why start a company before you know something works? What makes sense is to start a company if and only if the product is effective."

Less than a year after the startup was founded, Legends of Learning partnered with researchers at Vanderbilt University to conduct an extensive academic study to test the effectiveness of the company's approach and, importantly, compare the outcomes with existing curricular tools.

Right from the outset, Polikov wrote, the study was "intended to be rigorous enough to be published in a peer-reviewed academic journal regardless of the outcome." The study included more than one thousand students in seven states, and researchers went above and beyond to ensure the sample included schools with differing student bodies, socioeconomic factors, and geographical locations. In other words, it was more than enough to "answer the hypothesis in a statistically significant manner."[7]

The results were what Polikov and his team had been hoping for. Researchers found that the students who played Legends of Learning's games, which are based on science curriculum for grades five through nine, performed better than their peers on standardized tests. Moreover, teachers reported increases in student engagement and performance when using the games.

"Even startups with limited resources can get the attention of academic centers if their product is compelling and their approach is rigorous," writes

Polikov, whose startup now offers around nine hundred games, works with more than four thousand teachers across the country, and in 2017 raised $9 million from the Baltimore Angels and other private investors.[8] "The key is working closely with academic institutions to design the studies and to be ready to publish the research regardless of outcomes."

Even better than using your own capital to fund peer-reviewed studies is getting others to invest those funds on your behalf. In some cases, an institution that serves as your early adopter may be motivated to fund a study on their own. If you're a healthcare startup, it's actually more credible for you if a major research hospital funds a study on the impact of your app on their patient population. You may also be able to get a credible influencer group to fund a study because it reinforces a point they want to be making anyway.*

Using Outcomes to Craft an Evidence-Based Narrative

As you generate outcomes data, and, even better, as you're able to turn that into evidence validated by third parties, you'll want to weave that into your narrative.

Tony Fratto is one of my favorite people in Washington. An economist by training, he's the former deputy press secretary for President George W. Bush, an on-air contributor to CNBC on economic policy, the managing partner of Hamilton Place Strategies, an angel investor with K Street Capital, and the owner of one of the best Twitter feeds in Washington. When he's not passionately discussing Pittsburgh sports teams, Tony spends his life explaining complex issues in simple ways, on behalf of major corporations and startups alike. He also sees startups do this poorly—and occasionally well—as an angel investor.

"Today, if you're a tech company serving citizens or public interests, we want to see all of your data and what the story behind it tells," he says. "Startup founders have to really understand their data and be able to use it as proof points for what they're trying to do—it's more important to be evidence-based today than ever before."

Tony joined Penny Lee and me as an early angel investor in ID.me through K Street Capital. You can see Tony's advice in play when Blake Hall says, "Of

---

*You'll learn more about influencer hacks in Chapter 8: Influence.

one hundred citizens that attempt online access, 85 percent are able to prove their legal identity through our digital equivalent of the DMV. The next closest comparable government program is in the thirties [of percentages], and they're still using knowledge-based verification, which is highly vulnerable to organized crime. We have stronger controls in place, so we've had zero reports of fraud."

As discussed in the last chapter, data shouldn't substitute for your core story—otherwise it's a consultant pitch—but weaving evidence into your narrative can turn a strong story into an exceptional one.

Evidence becomes even more important as you engage the media. In an era in which trust in media continues to erode, and journalists have become jaded about startup spin, it's more important than ever to be able to marshal credible evidence from trusted third parties to tell your story. There are even a growing number of media sites that tell stories entirely through data.

"There's a rise in analytical, data-driven journalism right now," Tony notes, pointing to examples like Vox Media and *The New York Times*'s Upshot blog. "If media attention is part of your strategy, you're increasingly going to need to be able to show data to help tell your story."

Using Data to Overcome Inertia or Break Iron Triangles

Outcomes data is the first—and most important—use of data for regulatory hackers. The next is using data to arm hero mayors or break iron triangles.

Mark DeSantis did this effectively with RoadBotics. It's easy for bureaucrats to acknowledge the inefficiency of the status quo while shrugging and saying, "But that's just the way things are." It's much harder to do when they're confronted with compelling data on an easy-to-read map that shows them how vast the gap is between what they're doing and what other governments or similar institutions are doing. The only thing better than data is a data visualization!

Evidence of the severity or urgency of the problem can be particularly powerful as ammunition for a hero mayor (or similar leader) looking to make a name for themselves. Political leaders in particular crave these kinds of simple, visual, data-driven narratives. As Tony points out, the same holds true for a growing group of evidence-based journalists. If you want to build momentum among political or institutional leaders, influencers, or the media, then hand them an easy-to-tell story with compelling data about how you could improve—or are improving—citizens' lives.

The same holds true if you're attempting to break an iron triangle. As discussed in Chapter 4: Growth, the key to breaking an iron triangle is to identify the weakest part of the triangle and focus your fire there. The weakest part is usually the one closest to whoever is losing from the iron triangle, most often citizens. Uber needed to break Big Taxi monopolies, so they targeted city councils and mayors rather than taxi commissions or operators. Uber used data to tell simple stories about the poor quality of taxi service in cities, for example, or about how poorly traditional taxies served minorities or low-income populations.

If you want to put maximal pressure on one part of an iron triangle, and rally citizens, media, or influencers to join your movement, you're going to need simple, evidence-based talking points.

Data-Centric Business Models

Beyond supporting your narrative, there is an entirely different sense in which regulated startups should be thinking about data.

As the *Economist* boldly proclaimed on its cover on May 6, 2017, "The world's most valuable resource is no longer oil, but data."[9] For many startups, data has become central to their products and business models, and this is no different for regulated startups. What make things interesting for regulated startups are the sources and customers of these data-enabled services. In some cases, like RoadBotics's, governments or regulated institutions may actually purchase your data or services powered by your data. The RoadBotics business model is predicated on the fact that municipal governments don't have quality data about the state of roads and are willing to pay handsomely for this data. In other cases, your product or service may actually be based on data that governments or institutions make freely available to the public, referred to as *open data*.

Sometimes you're doing both. One of my favorite regulated business models is one that has been around for decades. Esri, established in 1969, is a global provider of geospatial data and analysis software. Most of the raw geospatial data that Esri sells is available from governments for free. Esri takes this data, cleans it up, and licenses this easier-to-use data to their customers. The beautiful thing about Esri's model is that many of their customers are also governments and public institutions such as municipalities, hospitals, utilities, and schools. Esri gets data from governments and public institutions and then sells higher-value data back to governments and public institutions. Brilliant!

1. Harnessing Open Data

The open data movement had existed for a while among the civic hacktivist community, but it really took off in 2009 as President Obama came into office. Recovery.gov was one of the early wins for open data, and I had the privilege of helping to build it for the Obama administration as the CEO of Synteractive, working with officials like Aneesh Chopra, the first chief technology officer for the U.S. government. Aneesh promoted the idea that making government data openly available in machine-readable formats would both increase the accountability of government while unleashing a wave of startup activity. This idea spread from the federal government to public institutions such as utilities and hospitals, culminating in initiatives such as Blue Button—which started by enabling veterans to download their personal health records from Veterans Affairs, spread to other federal health providers, and eventually looped in other health systems—or Green Button, which did the same with utilities and your personal energy consumption data.

While there were early wins in making data available, it took a while for startups to leverage this data successfully. Many of the early initiatives focused on hackathons around open data, which attracted enthusiastic hobbyists. Serious entrepreneurs, though, struggled to see the business models around open data.

That has started to change recently as savvy entrepreneurs have started to find the lucrative business opportunities within the large swaths of data that government has been making publicly available. Alex Wirth, cofounder of D.C.-based Quorum, is one of those savvy entrepreneurs.

Started in 2015 while Alex and his cofounder Jonathan Marks were undergraduate roommates at Harvard University, Quorum uses big data analytics to pull in billions of data points annually about every member of Congress and every piece of legislation moving through the U.S. Capitol in Washington. Those data points include things like voting decisions, bill sponsorships, lawmaker press releases and floor statements, and social media posts from members of Congress.

The duo's platform crunches all that data and generates analysis and customizable insights dashboards that are sold to corporations, associations, nonprofits, think tanks, and anyone else who needs to know what's happening on Capitol Hill or in state legislatures.* In less than three years, Quorum's client base includes major brands like Proctor & Gamble, General Motors, Apple, UPS, Lyft, and Human Rights First.

"There's a lot of value in those documents and data points for those who need to be in the know, but there's just too much information coming out every day for even a large team of people to manually go through and make sense of it all," Alex says. "That's where we come in, and that's where technology and startups can come in."

The pace at which government is generating and spitting out machine-readable, publicly available data is only accelerating, Alex notes, which will provide new opportunities for his company and present untold new business opportunities for others who can find ways to collect it, distill it, and package it into useful, digestible information for others.

Not all regulatory hackers need to see a role for themselves in the open data movement per se, but you do need to think creatively about the data you need

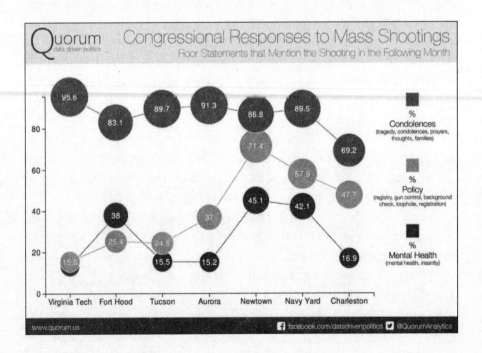

---

*Including startups, as you'll see in Chapter 15: Lobbying.

to make your product or service sing. In some cases, that might come from government, as in ID.me making use of government data to verify citizens' identities and attributes online. In other cases, it may come from institutions such as health systems or banks. In still other cases, associations and advocacy organizations may have data that's incredibly valuable to what you're trying to do.

As Blake discovered, though, the most valuable data is rarely truly *open*; rather, it's available if you know whom to ask in the right way. You'll have to think about how to partner with governments, institutions, or influencers to get what you need—and you'll probably need to show what's in it for them in the process.

2. Selling Data to Governments and Institutions

Governments and institutions may have stores of valuable data they should open up to the public, but the truth is that they *need* even more data than they have available. I've seen many more startups like RoadBotics gain traction through selling data to governments and institutions rather than exploiting open data. This makes sense when you think about it: Modern digital platforms have generated massive amounts of data that until recently were unavailable to individuals and institutions. Startups and savvy corporations are using this explosion of data to enable previously unimaginable services. Why would complex markets be immune to these same dynamics?

RoadBotics is one example of a business model based on selling data to government. Another example is Colombian startup 1DOC3, where citizens submit medical questions for free, which are answered by a combination of doctors and AI bots. With more than 1.5 million monthly active users from across Latin America, the platform collects, classifies, and processes significant amounts of health data, gaining valuable insights into health issues.

After testing various business models, Javier Andres Cardona Mora found his scalable business model in selling behavioral health data to insurance companies, public-private ventures that provide health coverage under Colombia's twenty-five-year-old universal healthcare system. As Cardona Mora dug into the data, he discovered that roughly half of doctor visits in Colombia are purely informational in nature, with no need for physical interaction or examination. That's hundreds of thousands of expensive in-person visits that could have been handled via digital communication. Today, 1DOC3 has delivered millions in savings to Colombian insurance companies by attacking that very inefficiency, using reams of data on what health problems are plaguing which patients in which areas during which times of the year. Cardona Mora learned that his most reliable and scalable business model wasn't selling his digital health solution directly to citizens, nor to governments on behalf of citizens, but using his platform plus the data it generated to help make public-private insurance companies more efficient.

Regulatory Hackers ♥ Data

As a regulatory hacker, data should drive almost everything you do. You will need data to communicate the urgency of your market opportunity, particularly if you need a hero mayor on board or you will have to bust through an iron triangle. You will need outcomes data to show the impact of your solution, and perhaps even peer-reviewed studies, which should drive much of your thinking around early adopters and influencers. Data as an asset may even become the foundation of your business model.

Although data has its own chapter, you should be thinking about data as a backdrop to almost every other chapter in this book—from crafting your narrative to thinking about launching a grassroots movement. Data is that important to a sophisticated regulatory hacker!

Chapter 8

INFLUENCE

Anne Wojcicki's company was ushering in a new chapter in medicine, the headlines breathlessly claimed.

Started in 2006, Wojcicki's direct-to-consumer genetic testing startup 23andMe offers customers a window into their genetic makeup, their ancestry, and their health risks for a hundred bucks and a few drops of spit. The company sells kits that let customers collect and mail in saliva samples, which are tested for some five hundred thousand genetic variants, with the results returned to the customer.

In no time, 23andMe was lauded as a game changer, promising untold benefits and unprecedented insights for consumers and marking a major step toward allowing individuals to take control over their healthcare. A *Fortune* magazine headline stated that the company could "change the face of healthcare,"[1] while *Fast Company* claimed that Wojcicki and her team had the potential to "herald an entirely new way of conducting medical research" with what the site later called "Wojcicki's $99 DNA Revolution."[2] Later, the *Wall Street Journal* hailed that she was on "a mission to genotype one million people worldwide."[3]

The buzz in and outside the Valley was electric.

Investors came running, too. Early investors in 23andMe included some of the Valley's most prominent venture capital groups, including New Enterprise Associates and MPM Capital, as well as the startup investment arms of companies like Google and Johnson & Johnson. In 2012, Russian billionaire Yuri

Milner, known for his early bets on the likes of Facebook and Zynga, led a $50 million funding round that brought the company's six-year funding total to $68 million.[4]

Then a letter arrived.

In November 2013, the FDA sent Anne Wojcicki a letter stating that the firm's service constituted medical advice, thus requiring FDA approval, and ordering 23andMe to immediately stop selling their kits. If 23andMe didn't halt sales, FDA officials threatened to take corrective actions that might include "but are not limited to, seizure, injunction, and civil money penalties."[5]

At the time, the letter was dubbed a potential death blow. Multiple media outlets railed against the company, with one particularly scathing story published by *Forbes* carrying the headline "23andStupid" and questioning whether Wojcicki's company was "guilty of the single dumbest regulatory strategy" the author had "seen in thirteen years of covering the Food and Drug Administration."[6]

What had gone so awry for such a promising startup?

When they started seven years earlier, Wojcicki and her two cofounders had cultivated an incredibly vast and strong network in the Valley—but they had not taken the time to build those same influential networks within the federal regulatory community. Consequently, when the FDA started digging into 23andMe and what Wojcicki and her team were doing, regulators had neither the context to understand the company nor the relationships through which to solicit information and develop a better understanding.

It wasn't too late, though. After receiving the letter, 23andMe launched a carefully orchestrated effort to start building trusted relationships with scientists who themselves had longstanding ties to the FDA. As 23andMe went through the consultative process with the FDA, those scientists were able to help the company bridge the gap between how 23andMe thought about their products' potential risks to citizens and how the FDA thought about that same risk.

Ultimately, the 23andMe team leveraged those relationships to cultivate a more trustworthy relationship within the regulatory community. Four years later, thanks in large part to 23andMe's efforts to build that sphere of influence, the U.S. Food and Drug Administration told the company it would be allowed to directly tell consumers whether their DNA puts them at higher risk for ten different diseases.[7] In March 2018, 23andMe received FDA approval to inform citizens of breast cancer risk from three gene mutations, making them "the first company allowed to test for cancer risk without a doctor's prescription in the United States."[8]

Influence: The Fourth Dimension

All startups are fueled by three precious resources: talent, capital, and brand. It doesn't matter what market you're in, which problem you're trying to solve, or where you're located: Wise founders are always stockpiling talent and capital while building their brand. Or, at the very least, they're always positioning their company to expand their *access* to talent and capital and build their startup's reputation in the marketplace so those resources are there when they need them.

For regulatory hackers, talent, capital, and brand are no less important.

But there's also a fourth resource that startups must continuously amass in the Regulatory Era: *influence.*

This chapter explains how to build and use this important resource, but let's start by defining influence, because the term can be tossed around pretty haphazardly, and the concept can seem abstract and ephemeral. Influence is your ability either to make specific things happen that further your interests or prevent specific things from happening that damage your interests.

Influence can be as simple as someone making a warm introduction on your behalf. Influence can be as robust as a trade association using their reach and resources to run a grassroots campaign that benefits your startup.

Influence can be as subtle as a call from a trusted friend to a policymaker reassuring them that your startup is addressing their concerns without the need for a public hearing. Influence can be as blunt a force as an association blasting an immediate call to action to their email list asking their citizen army to call their congresspeople with a demand that your startup not be shut down.

Without a doubt, 23andMe had mountains of capital and some of the most talented scientists and engineers in the Valley. They had built a brand with buzz through breathless stories in the media about the potential of home genetics testing to give citizens control over complex personal health decisions. But when the FDA started exploring the legality of their home testing, few of the major healthcare or scientific groups, or even individual scientists, stood up to vigorously defend 23andMe, either publicly or privately. Talent, capital, and brand are great, but if you're a regulatory hacker, you need *influence* as well. As you'll learn below, the inverse can also be true: Startups that build influence effectively can often use those relationships to grow with less capital and with a less-recognized brand.

Influence is like brand (and unlike capital) in that it is more art than science and hard to quantify. Oceans of digital ink have been spent defining brand and positing ways to measure brand. Despite that effort, you know a great brand when you see it, but it's hard to measure its absolute value or how to most effectively expand your brand's resonance. Influence works the same way.

Another way to think about influence is your regulated startup's network of relationships with individuals, groups, and institutions that are themselves connected to your complex market's decision makers, market leaders, media, and other influencers. We call these individuals, groups, and institutions *influencers*, as they have the reach and sway to help shape your market in favorable or unfavorable ways. You can best measure your regulated startup's influence as a matrix of connections to influencers, weighted both in terms of quantity and quality.

Influencers and Types of Influence

Who exactly are influencers?

Some are more formal than others. Influencers may be institutions like trade associations, advocacy groups, think tanks, universities, lobbying firms, or major media outlets.* In a way, many of these organizations exist to be influential; influence is their game, their purpose, their forte. Others may be less formal, like a blogger or the friends, colleagues, and advisers of key decision makers.

Some influencers may hold influence over massive swaths of the population, like celebrities, major media outlets, or high-profile government officials. Others may have a more niche reach, like prominent experts or insiders in a given industry, but that niche reach may include precisely the group of decision makers your startup needs to befriend or convince.

What makes influencers so important to complex markets? How might they prove valuable?

For starters, healthy relationships with influencers are the fuel that will power many of the regulatory hacks you'll learn about throughout this book. An influencer can help you better understand your power map, identifying key players you may have overlooked or helping you understand the interaction between players on your map. They may help you shape and share your story

---

*You went through a comprehensive analysis of the types influencers in Chapter 2: Power.

with the right audiences or create or gain access to the data you need to help tell that story. Influencers can also prove invaluable as members of grassroot or grasstops coalitions.

Deploying influencers can also be a strategy in and of itself. There are five key ways in which influencers can directly help you build your regulated startup:

- Access
- Credibility
- Reach
- Resources
- Domain Expertise

Access

The most basic currency that influencers provide is *access*.

One inherent truth about complex markets is that their power maps are thick with gatekeepers. Influencer relationships can be the keys that unlock those gates. Whether it's a direct link to a pivotal decision maker or a more roundabout route that slowly puts your startup in front of the right group of people, you should be constantly building relationships with influencers who can help you access the people who can knock down the hurdles you face today and the ones you expect to face in the future.

Note that this holds true even if you've already established your own personal network within your market. It's often better for an introduction or a meeting request to come from someone else with credibility, as it shows that someone else of stature is willing to advocate for you.

Almost every type of influencer—from massive organizations to private individuals—can provide your startup with access, whether introductions to customers or calls placed on your behalf to a policymaker or reporter. But certain influencers are better at certain things. If you are looking for validation of your outcome data, then a respected organization without any vested interest in your success can prove invaluable. If you are looking for market access, then an association with significant reach into your market and an openness to a formal partnership can present a breakthrough for you.

Influence can prove just as valuable for playing defense as playing offense. Even in a market as laissez-faire as Kenya. Just ask Grant Brooke.

Grant may be my favorite founder in the 1776 portfolio. We first met at the Challenge Cup Nairobi in 2014. Grant comes across as part mad scientist and part Oxford tutor, teaching anyone who will listen about the fascinating world of informal markets in Africa. When we met, Grant had taken his obsession to a new level by cofounding Twiga Foods with Peter Njonjo, at the time the country manager for Coca-Cola.

At the time, Twiga was delivering bananas to mama mbogas, or informal stalls on street corners across Africa that sell everything from fresh produce to Snickers bars to batteries. Before Twiga, a Nairobian would pay as much for a banana from a mama mboga as I would from my Whole Foods in a trendy neighborhood in D.C. By using smartphones and data analysis to power sophisticated supply chains, though, Twiga was able to provide a better price to both farmers and mama mboga proprietors, while generating a healthy profit. Grant and Peter had their eyes on much more than bananas, though. Bananas were to Twiga what books were to Amazon.com, and the ultimate prize was that $900 billion in high-velocity commerce that flowed through informal markets in sub-Saharan Africa.

In 2015, we invested in Twiga after Grant won the global finals of that year's Challenge Cup, then doubled down in 2016 when Twiga raised the largest seed round of capital in East African history. In 2017, we made our largest investment to date from our fund when Twiga followed up with the largest Series A round in East African history. My role as a board member with Twiga gave me an eye-opening view on the application of regulatory hacking to a market like Kenya and in particular on the critical role of influence.

Grant had spent several years working and studying in East Africa before launching Twiga, and over that time, he built important relationships with influential individuals in the public and private sector. Through his role at Coca-Cola, his cofounder Peter was also deeply embedded in commercial and government circles and understood how the two interacted. He would later become Coca-Cola's general manager for all of East Africa and then president for West Africa.

Other influencers that Grant developed close ties to in Kenya before and while launching Twiga Foods came through connections from Peter's wife, Justine, who leads the legal division for Safaricom, the dominant mobile carrier in the country, as well as other national and city-level government leaders who wielded power and, no less important, were respected throughout the region. By the time I joined the Twiga board, Grant's Rolodex was teeming with names of those who had the access and networks to help open doors and clear hurdles for Twiga.

And that has proved critical.

"Kenyan politics and the regulatory system is a mess," Grant says. "In many ways, the legal and regulatory frameworks in the country have intentional gray area built in to encourage the practice of bribes and corrupt agreements. That was particularly challenging for Twiga because there really aren't rules to govern our type of business, so everything Twiga does is in a non-regulated gray area."

As a result, local government officials in the region had taken to harassing Twiga's staff and Twiga's farmer clients, demanding bribes to allow both to continue operating and demanding to see licenses and permits that otherwise wouldn't be necessary. For a while, the ill-intent visits became so frequent that they posed a real risk to Twiga's operations and started to threaten the company's ability to attract new farmers and vendors to its system.

Fortunately, Grant has his Rolodex.

"When one of these low-life officials shows up making demands and trying to shake us down, we need to have somebody to call. Luckily, we've developed relationships at this point that can help us turn them back without much trouble," Grant says. "Having influencers like that who not only know you but are willing to take action to defend you in times of need is important, especially when you are small and just starting out."

While startups in complex markets anywhere in the world will benefit from constantly cultivating powerful allies, if you operate in areas or in industries that are rife with corruption, then you will find that your ability to stockpile influence early on may make the difference between fizzling out quickly or finding long-term success. Powerful friends are important everywhere, but they're particularly important when the rule of law is a fuzzier concept.

Credibility

The importance of *credibility* to a regulated startup should be obvious.

Any statement or claim made by a founder that serves the interests of the startup understandably should be taken with a grain of salt. There's no way around it. Even with the most compelling narrative or the most reliable data, the statement simply won't carry as much weight coming from the founder.

If Anne Wojcicki, for instance, tells a reporter or a policymaker that home genomics testing is perfectly safe, she will be viewed as inherently biased, and her claims will consequently be met with some degree of skepticism. Conversely, if a prominent scientist not employed by 23andMe makes that same statement in the same forum, it will carry considerably more credibility.

If Carolyn from HopSkipDrive testifies before a city council meeting to proclaim that there are urgent public safety concerns with minors using Uber, Lyft, and traditional taxis, she's likely to be dismissed as promoting her company's service. On the other hand, if the National Child Safety Council or the Association for Missing and Exploited Children were to testify before Congress making the same argument, it may well spark a national discussion about how parents should keep their children safe while taking advantage of modern transportation networks.

The same applies to Mark DeSantis at RoadBotics. His startup's red-lined street maps are much more powerful visuals when they're presented by the American Society of Highway Engineers or by a well-respected university researcher unaffiliated with RoadBotics.

In the same way, your investors may have influence with other investors, but their financial interest with you makes them biased supporters in the public sphere.

None of this is to say you shouldn't be your startup's most vocal advocate, nor should this be taken as a disincentive to be out there sharing your narrative. The point is that your narrative becomes more credible if someone outside your company is helping tell that story and advancing your mission with you.

While many types of influencers can provide credibility, whether the Association for Missing and Exploited Children or a retired FDA scientist whose opinions still carry weight with his former colleagues, influencers who have cachet in your market—and ideally a reputation for objective analysis—can be particularly effective. Universities, think tanks, and major media outlets are great examples of this credibility amplification. A Harvard Medical School study detailing the effectiveness of your digital health solution may prove to be immeasurably valuable to your health startup.

Another variation on this theme is formal standard setting. The American Petroleum Institute sets the standards and certifications globally for an incredible array of valves, pipes, lubricants, and whatnot in the oil and gas industry. An organization like API can provide you with credibility, but in certain scenarios they can do even more through formal endorsement, certification, or setting a standard around your product.

Reach

Reach is another important way in which influencers can be directly valuable to your startup. Reach can be fuel for grassroots and grasstops campaigns, but it can also simply provide direct market access if an organization so desires.*

While various influencers can provide access and credibility, reach is more typically associated with major organizations like trade associations, advocacy groups, or major media outlets. The U.S. Chamber of Commerce can activate many thousands of businesses in the United States with the push of a button, requesting action from, and likely getting a response from, their CEOs. AARP can engage more than thirty-seven million Americans over the age of fifty-five. The Sierra Club can reach two million members globally via their email list and countless more via their 318,000 Twitter followers. *The Washington Post* reaches more than seventy million readers around the world in a typical month.

Of course, reach isn't always about getting your message out to the biggest audience. Reach can operate on a smaller scale but with greater effectiveness: For example, the American Hospital Association can connect you to executives at 4,500 member hospitals, if they want. The Virginia PTA can engage 1,200 local PTAs and 30,000 parents across Virginia.

Of course, there are also individuals who bring reach as well. If a social media influencer like Neil deGrasse Tyson endorses your new approach to energy storage on a podcast and tweets it out to his 10.9 million followers, he can reach a lot of people. But individuals with the kind of reach that the U.S. Chamber of Commerce, AARP, or the Sierra Club can bring are the exception, not the rule.

Resources

Influencer organizations can bring not only access, credibility, and reach, but also *resources* like money and data. If you can align with an influencer with a shared agenda and the financial wherewithal, then you can get them to contribute or cover the cost of an advocacy campaign.** Or perhaps you can get

---

*You'll learn more about grassroots and grasstops campaigns in Section 4: The Regulatory Hacker's Toolkit.

**Kidde, which you learned about in Chapter 2: Power, is a great example of this approach working with their child health coalition in support of mandates for carbon monoxide alarms.

them to fund a peer-reviewed study on how your new technology is impacting their members.

As we explored in the last chapter, data can also be a valuable resource that influencer organizations have available. ID.me was able to expand their identity authentication solution beyond military veterans and into areas like first responders by partnering with major associations that had underused data just waiting for a regulatory hacker like Blake Hall to make use of.

Domain Expertise

The final way that influencers can be directly valuable to you, without powering any of the tools in Section 4: The Regulatory Hacker's Toolkit, is through what they know. Influencers of all types—from major organizations to individuals in niche fields—tend to know a lot about their domain. That might be formal knowledge about the rules you'll encounter on your power map or tacit knowledge about which players work well with one another—and which always seem to clash.

Given the foundational importance of understanding your power map, this domain knowledge is critical and might be prohibitively expensive for you to hire into your startup. But it also comes in handy as you think about your business model or growth. Influencers tend to carry institutional knowledge on behalf of entire complex markets—and in that sense they know where the bodies are buried, the hacks that have worked in the past, and what might seem appealing but always seems to fail.

Domain expertise can also be actual content that can power your product. David Fairbrothers, the founder of Dorsata, learned this after a lot of trial and error.

David, a former University of Virginia offensive lineman turned serial entrepreneur, was building another healthcare technology company when he began to realize how inconvenient it was for physicians to access industry-established best practices research on various treatment options when trying to decide between available courses of action. Often, that information, including relative costs and outcome expectancies for different treatment options under various conditions, would be buried on a healthcare system's intranet or printed and shoved in a filing cabinet somewhere.

"This is some of the best information doctors have available to help them make the best treatment decisions," David says. "But it's not readily used."

David and his cofounder, Greg Herrington, a fellow University of Virginia graduate with a background in computer science, embarked on an entrepreneurial mission to change that. Together, they began developing an easy-to-use software platform that would let clinicians view and create new clinical processes and suggested treatment pathways based on that best practices research. In the process, the Dorsata platform would help doctors engage with electronic medical records in a way that would help them more easily and effectively compare all the available pathways to treatment for a given patient and choose the one that would provide the best outcome and, often, also reduce the cost of care for the patient and the provider.

In response to early customer interest, David and Greg would later narrow Dorsata's scope (at least initially) to focus on one area of medicine in particular—women's health; namely, obstetrics and gynecology. That meant they would need to find a source for established best practices and cultivate a baseline bank of physician-generated treatment pathway content from physicians in those fields.

That meant talking to ACOG.

The American College of Obstetricians and Gynecologists is a nonprofit trade association composed of and representing fifty-eight thousand obstetricians and gynecologists across the country. Over half a century old, the group advocates for high standards of practice and pushes public awareness of women's healthcare issues. In a nutshell, ACOG and its leadership represent the influencer of influencers within that particular field of medicine.

"It didn't take long for us to realize we needed to get on their radar and start building relationships there," David says.

Armed with grand visions and a basic prototype of their platform, David and his team registered for a booth at ACOG's major annual conference in Washington, D.C., in May 2016. As he describes it, "We had the smallest booth set up over behind the bathrooms, because that's all that was left." But that's all they needed.

"A gentleman walked by at one point and expressed interest in what we were doing," David recalls. "It turns out we were talking to Dr. Steve Hasley, ACOG's chief medical information officer. When we explained what it was we were trying to accomplish, that we were trying to reimagine the way doctors interact with their health records and make decisions, he was bought in."

Not long after the conference, the CMIO set up a meeting with Dr. Barbara Levy, ACOG's vice president of policy, who had run her own practice for twenty-five years and was among the most well-connected individuals in the industry. Hasley and Levy would quickly become advocates and champions for Dorsata—and not merely for selfless reasons.

"We were helping them solve two of their most significant challenges," David said. "We were giving doctors a better experience and allowing them to spend less time doing routine tasks on electronic record, and two, through data, we were creating a new way for ACOG to study the impact of its best practices content and expertise. In a way, we were helping them thrive in the digital age, when their members were expecting more for their annual dues."

Highly motivated and ideally positioned, Levy organized a small group of stakeholders at ACOG that accelerated a formal partnership between ACOG and Dorsata, which would provide David's company with a tremendous accelerant: content, reach, and credibility. ACOG's massive library of established best practices and expansive network of physicians helped Dorsata source a baseline of initial content and recommended treatment pathway information for its platform.

"Dorsata brought us a fresh outlook on how to leverage the power of computers to remove administrative tasks from doctors while presenting clinical information in an accessible, efficient, and actionable way," Levy says. "One of our senior physicians watched the Dorsata demo yesterday and told me that it made him want to start practicing again."

Today, in part through its partnership with ACOG, Dorsata has more than a thousand OB-GYNs on its platform, meaning that tens of thousands of babies will be born in 2018 to women whose care was managed on their platform using ACOG content.

Building Influence

As you use the tools in this book to execute and refine your strategy, you will want as much access, credibility, reach, resources, and domain knowledge as possible. Therefore, just as you're constantly accumulating talent and capital and building your brand, you should be constantly cultivating influence by growing and nurturing your network of influencer relationships.

Even if you don't need to call on that network right this moment, and even if you don't know exactly how you'll use that influence in the future, more influence provides you with more options and more paths to success.

As much as the notion of influence can feel a bit nebulous, the process by which you build influence can feel even more so, especially to a regulatory hacker who may be new to the field or who hasn't yet established a known presence within the complex market. Starting from square one and penetrating the inner circle of power players in your field may seem like a game of chance encounters and lucky relationship bounces.

But that isn't so. The same way you can construct formal processes and pipelines to methodically build your customer base, you can implement concrete strategies to systematically build influencer relationships as well as informal and formal partnerships with those who can help you break down barriers, advance your objectives, and provide protection when you're threatened.

The first step is determining which influencers you ought to target, which brings you back to your power map.

As you build your power map, you should be asking the following questions: Who has interests that align with your interests? These players represent your potential natural friends. On the flip side, who has interests that conflict with your interests? These are likely to become your natural adversaries. Third, who are the adversaries of your adversaries? These are what you might call your potential friends of convenience. They may not feel passionately about helping you, per se, but their influence may prove to be useful under the right circumstances.

If an individual or organization with significant access, credibility, reach, resources, and expertise seems to be your natural friend, then they should be in your relationship-building pipeline—and at the top of your priority queue at that. In the same way, if someone or some group with influence appears to be a potential friend of convenience, in that you share a common adversary or would benefit from some decision or outcome, you should be actively pursuing ways to engage with them.

When I say you should have formal processes and tools to manage your influencer relationships, I mean this literally. Personally, I use a combination of LinkedIn and HubSpot to build a list of relationships that I want to cultivate and to formally keep track of those relationships. In some cases, for an important influencer on my power map, I will set reminders in HubSpot to reach out to someone every few months for coffee. In other cases, I'll build small-scale email campaigns to regularly share personal notes about success or progress in my activities. If something is important to you, then build a system, track it, and measure it. And influencer relationships are important.

If you identify an influencer on your power map whose interests are opposed to yours, first, as discussed in Chapter 2: Power, make sure to verify that through actual engagement with that influencer. There are times when flying under the radar can make sense, but in general the insights you'll gain override most other concerns.

If you have validated that you have an enemy, then resist the temptation to immediately start pursuing ways to combat them or circumnavigate them. Instead, start by asking the question: Can you convert them?

It's a strategy that Christine Boyle from Valor Water has tirelessly pursued with some success.

After graduating from Columbia University in 1998, Boyle found her way to an e-commerce startup, riding the wave from boom to bust over three years. "During that time, I learned a lot about logistics, distribution, and managing complex systems, and how data fits into that picture," she says. "I decided I wanted to pursue something like that, but I wanted to do it in a way that had bigger social impact."

That's when Boyle started to become obsessed with water. "I gravitated toward water and water utilities because it seemed like a way to use some of the skills I had acquired, to do good work, and to impact human rights and effect human change," she says.

Boyle returned to school, and while earning her PhD in Environmental Policy and Planning at the University of North Carolina at Chapel Hill, she began working as a research assistant at the school's Environmental Finance Center, where she would help organize and analyze water utility data, like how much utilities were charging or how much water consumers used in different areas. Along the way, she started applying new and revolutionary analytics methods and platforms to the data sets and began writing software code that could spit out insights about how much utilities should charge to maximize profits and which customers were likely to stop paying their water bills.

Boyle describes those initial coding applications as "pretty simple statistical models." But for the water industry, into which advanced technology and data analytics had yet to seep, those resulting insights were nothing short of astounding.

Boyle, who had become something of a water data savant along the way, quickly recognized that there was commercial value in what she and her peers had uncovered. Lured by the droughts, she eventually relocated to California, where today her startup, Valor Water, provides water utilities with a SaaS tool that uses sophisticated data analysis to identify faulty meters and eliminate waste. The company's signature product offering, what Boyle calls a "hidden revenue locator," has eclipsed annual sales of a million dollars and keeps tabs on more than five hundred thousand water meters, helping utilities ensure that they're collecting payment for all the water they distribute to citizens.

While at first Valor Water seems like something everyone would want to get behind, it turns out not everyone agrees with Boyle's approach.

"In our industry, there's this particular group of high-level influencers," Boyle says, noting that the group comprises primarily retired utility or engineering officials who now serve as consultants. "It's a group of about fifteen people, and they are tough old birds who know everything there is to know about water utility hardware. They hold a lot of influence and power."

What's important is that the group is, in Boyle's words, "old school." They subscribe to a longstanding but outdated "sampling" method of doing the same work Water Valor seeks to perform with modern technology. "They'll go in and look at ten meters, they'll do all this testing on those ten meters, and then they'll say, 'Okay, if these ten meters are this way, then I can assume the following about your other hundred thousand meters.'"

"It's the way things have been done for a long time," she adds.

Rather than positioning herself as an adversary to this elite group, she has worked hard to convert them.

"Over the past couple years, I've been trying to win these guys over one by one," she says. "Most of them have dug in, and at this point, they haven't been really helpful to me. They don't want to see some up-and-comer swooping in and disrupting things."

However, she says she has managed to turn two converts.

"One of them is from North Carolina, and eventually, I was just like, 'Alright, you're from Winston-Salem, and I started this company in Chapel Hill,' and I started talking with him about funny things about being from North Carolina," Boyle says. "Eventually, I said, 'Let's sit down, have a beer, and get through this.' I basically made him talk to me, and now we're friends. He has become a supporter of what we're trying to do, and having him on board is important."

She adds: "It takes a long time, because they're all very skeptical. But we're getting somewhere."

Boyle's experience highlights one other important insight about working with influencers: Even when you've identified a group you need to engage, it's really all about people, and therefore, relationships.

"When you're working with a big organization, you need to remember to make it about the people, not the institution," David from Dorsata says. "You need to identify those two or three people—the ambitious, entrepreneurial, startup people within the organization who are aligned with the problem you're trying to solve and are willing to fight to see a solution."

He adds: "The moment I stopped thinking I had all the answers, the moment I started engaging and listening to experienced people within these institutions who wanted to solve the problem I did, that was the moment where things started taking off."

Play to Your Strengths

Once you've established your target influencers and built the systems and tools to track your progress, the next step is to begin understanding what would motivate an influential person or institution to want to help you. In short, what's your pitch to them?

Luckily, there are actually plenty of reasons that powerful organizations and individuals would want to work with you.

This is where your narrative becomes important. If you've crafted a compelling story, you should be emphasizing that story at every turn, particularly when you're trying to win over influencers. You provide solutions to problems that may otherwise seem intractable, and being able to clearly articulate that will help you expand your network with important players.

First, startups, being small, scrappy outfits taking on big challenges, are endearing. This is especially true for regulated startups, which are working for the public interest. The more admirable your mission, the more you'll find that well-connected and credible individuals and institutions want to be linked to you. As a regulatory hacker, this is a perception you should be aware of and lean into at every opportunity.

Second, you may present an appealing way to introduce or talk about a complex issue. For a think tank that wants to seed a conversation about genomics testing or a policymaker who wants to show the urgent need for infrastructure funding, using startups like 23andMe and RoadBotics as a vehicle to discuss those issues can make them more accessible and compelling than waving a forty-page report. Likewise, presenting the faces and voices of entrepreneurs like Wojcicki and DeSantis, or even better, everyday citizens who have benefited from these solutions, can make the issue more human and relatable.

And third, while many influencer relationships are informal partnerships in which you're exchanging favors or "chits," in some cases you may establish a formal economic relationship with an influencer. Maybe you pay to retain a lobbying shop or join a trade association. Or perhaps you can establish some form of revenue-sharing model through which an influencer gains financially from your wins.

David Fairbrothers discovered this as he deepened his partnership with ACOG. ACOG provided invaluable best practices content on women's health, but Dorsata needed more. David needed to start getting on the radar of more women's health groups and gynecology practices to begin to build a potential trial customer base. At first this was informal, as Dr. Levy and others at ACOG introduced David to many of the OB-GYN practices and other healthcare groups that would become Dorsata's early adopters and customers.

Over time, however, this grew into a formal partnership, which brought immense credibility to Dorsata's work with OB-GYN practices. As he explains: "Our partnership with ACOG gave us a brand name that we could use to gain credibility when reaching out to potential new customers. No one knew who the hell Dorsata was, but every OB-GYN office in the country knows who you are talking about when you say you're working with the American College of Obstetricians and Gynecologists. There's no doubt that helped us with our sales efforts, particularly early on."

Coalitions

Another way to build partnerships with influencers to expand your access, credibility, and resources is through coalitions.

A *coalition* is a temporary alliance between individuals or organizations to achieve a common purpose. Most commonly, as with Kidde in Chapter 2: Power, that purpose involves a policy change or other government action. In most cases, coalitions are formed between groups of similar values, interests, goals, or common enemies, allowing the individual members to pool their resources and their influence to become more powerful than they could be if they were operating independently.

More specifically, coalitions allow their members to attach their objectives on more than one front and from multiple angles, increasing the chances of success, and they tend to allow each organization to tap into more expertise, resources, and personnel than they would otherwise be able to access on their own. In addition, being part of a coalition also increases your available resources—not just financial resources, but also additional contacts and connections.

Coalitions can also make it much easier to garner favorable media attention, as the banding together of a group of companies or an entire industry makes for a much bigger and better story than a single company or organization launching a policy battle.

Most important, being involved in a coalition means you have more people who understand what you want to accomplish and more people advocating for your side.

Mamotest's Guillermo Pepe can attest. Since launching the company in 2011, Pepe has forged numerous strategic partnerships with institutions that share Mamotest's interests and the interests of his complementary nonprofit organization, Fundación Telmed. Through the foundation, he organized and now leads a coalition of groups focused on all women's cancers, including ovarian, cervical, and breast cancer.

"We knew that we would be able to access more resources and get more visibility if we worked together," Pepe says. The coalition continues to get support from medical groups, insurance companies, pharmaceutical companies, churches, and law firms, which are working together on a comprehensive list of policy recommendations to present to the country's minister of health.

"We want this to be radical," Pepe says about Mamotest's and Telmed's shared mission to expand telemedicine throughout Latin America. "We can't do that on our own."

As perhaps the best evidence of the potency of coalitions, even the most powerful and heavily funded lobbying groups and trade associations in Washington, D.C., regularly form coalitions to advance their most important policy issues. Even though they sometimes compete for funding from the same clients, when it comes to high-stakes debates about issues like healthcare or education policy, you'll inevitably see massive coalitions take shape on either side.

Coalitions aren't a silver bullet, but as with anything, teamwork can go a long way. When you need to spur a change in government that could help your startup, or when you need to thwart a change that could hurt your startup, the collective financial resources, political influence, and access to power that come with coalitions can mean the difference between success and failure.

One important consideration when thinking about building or joining a coalition is, in fact, ideology. Coalitions are the exception to the rule that ideology and political parties matter much less for regulatory hacking than you might think. While the *disruptive technologies* involved in regulatory hacking rarely fall into predefined ideologies, the *individuals* or *institutions* you want to work with may have meaningful ideological or partisan constraints or motivations.

"It's important to understand the political leanings of individuals and groups," Penny Lee from 1776 says. "While your product or service might be politically agnostic, your champion or coalition partner may have a political agenda or at least a perceived one. It's important to understand how an affiliation with someone like Bernie Sanders can either help or hurt you. Choose wisely."

The Sierra Club and the American Petroleum Institute may both have powerful reasons to support a new technology, but it may or may not be to their advantage to be publicly seen working together. You need to understand these dynamics carefully as you think about coalitions.

Influencers as Investors—and Investors as Influencers

There's another way to bring influencers onto your team and give them a vested interest in using their credibility, access, reach, resources, and expertise to benefit your company. It's something that Blake Hall at ID.me has excelled at.

"When I moved the company from Boston to D.C., I made a conscious effort to create a synthetic portfolio of investors that would bring the right mix of advice and influence," Blake says, meaning he targeted potential investors not just for their financial investment, but for how they could help him build the business in other ways. "For us, that meant accruing product and engineering advice, sure, but it also meant gaining access to government know-how and influence, as well."

Blake took the time to identify and meticulously build relationships with a small group of D.C.-area angel investors with public sector backgrounds, including K Street Capital, the angel group that Penny and I helped launch. Today, his cap table includes multiple former congressional chiefs of staff, as well as Penny herself, who was Senate Majority Leader Harry Reid's senior adviser and deputy chief of staff.

"That was all very much on purpose," Blake says.

Blake's approach underscores the importance of thinking about influence the same way you think about other fundamentally critical ingredients for startup success, including capital. For startups in complex markets, the normal considerations when identifying and courting investors or when weighing funding offers must be married with due consideration to what relationships and how much access a given investor or investors bring to the table, too.

The strategy paid dividends for Blake at a key moment in 2015. Congress was considering a bill that would have created an expensive government program to create digital IDs and charge veterans for their use, which would have been a serious threat to ID.me. Blake found out about the proposed program twenty-four hours before the various committees were preparing to vote. Blake emailed Penny and within a few hours had meetings with the key staffers to share with them that ID.me was already doing what the program aimed to do. And ID.me was free for veterans, unlike the proposed program.

As a result of those conversations, Blake was able to educate the relevant committees about the greater work that ID.me was doing and redirect the emphasis of the bill.

"Our investors have been able to make sure that we have access and that our position on these issues is heard by the right people at the highest levels of government, and they give our voice some added juice and credibility," he says. "That doesn't happen unless they're truly invested in our success."

In the opposite direction from Blake's strategy, influencers can also become investors, as David Fairbrothers discovered with Dorsata and ACOG. After partnering around content and lending their credibility to Dorsata's go-to-market strategy, ACOG would eventually throw in another C—capital. When David was raising Dorsata's latest investment round in early 2018, ACOG accepted his invitation to be part of the round and take a financial stake in the company—a first for the group.

Influence Is a Tool

Influence is one of the most important assets you can cultivate, and relationships with influencers can provide direct benefits. But ultimately influence is useful because of what you can do with it as you develop your strategy.

"In a complex industry like ours, I see having those connections to influencers more like paying the blind in poker," David said. "That's just what opens the door to be able to compete—you still have to go out and win the hand."

SECTION 3

Business Models

Chapter 9

SELLING TO GOVERNMENT

It was quarter to nine on a cold night in March 2014, and Jonathon Ende was the last one in his company's small office when the phone rang. He thought he knew who to expect on the other end of the line. He was wrong.

It would prove to be a call that completely altered the trajectory of his business.

Jonathon, a straight-talking New Jersey native and serial entrepreneur, had three years earlier founded SeamlessDocs with a very specific goal in mind: to create a more useful PDF. The idea took hold while Jonathon was running a New York City–based paper-processing center for paralegal clients. All day, his firm processed reams of hard-copy government forms, and over time, he came to loathe the inefficiencies of traditional paper forms. As he recounts, "A typical form took four people, seventy-four sheets of paper, one industrial-strength printer, two eFax numbers, six phone calls, five revisions, and six weeks, at best, just to get submitted."

Looking to bring form filing into the twenty-first century (and save more than a few trees in the process), Jonathon partnered with Chachi Camejo, a software wizard who had helped Jonathon's company automate some of its routine operations, to launch SeamlessDocs in 2012.

With SeamlessDocs, any static PDF form can be converted into an interactive e-document that allows users to fill it out using any web-enabled device, eSign it, and submit it, after which the completed form is automatically and securely routed to the appropriate individual or department. The form can alert users if, say, required fields are missing, saving additional time and hassle on the back end. And perhaps most important to the recipients, the contents of the completed document are more easily organized and searched than a scanned paper form completed with human handwriting.

Early on, Jonathon set his sights on professional services companies, not unlike his paralegal services firm, and traditional small businesses, for instance, law firms, insurance agencies, and real estate companies—anyone who needed to routinely complete simple administrative tasks, such as waivers or tax forms.

The company quickly raised about $1 million and was building an eclectic client list, but Jonathon struggled to get to product-market fit. By casting a wide net in terms of customer segmentation, he and Chachi struggled to make decisions about marketing strategy and product roadmap. It became difficult to articulate exactly what SeamlessDocs was, what problem the company was solving, and for whom. Interest from both customers and investors tapered, and Jonathon's frustration mounted.

Which brings us back to that phone call late one evening in March 2014. As Jonathon reached for the phone, he expected the voice on the other end to be one of SeamlessDocs's customers, calling with a mundane question about their account.

Instead, it was Barry Jones* from the Tennessee Department of Children's Services.

Barry had heard about SeamlessDocs and wanted to learn more. Sending, receiving, scanning, storing, and searching government forms were all part of the daily routine at his agency, Barry explained, and he was eager to take a look at any technology that might reduce the corresponding headaches.

Not an hour later, Jonathon had set up a screen-share demo and was walking through the SeamlessDocs portal with Barry, who got more excited with every passing minute. Barry then sent over a sample foster care release form, and Jonathon converted it in minutes. The next day, Barry set up a follow-up web demo with all eight people on his team.

"It was an 'aha' moment for both of us," Jonathon recalls.

---

*Name changed.

His continued conversations with Barry over the coming days revealed that, unlike his private-sector clients who tended to need minor customizations for nearly every form, the public sector mostly needed what he had already built—it was plug and play. In addition, Jonathon gravitated toward the mission of making government work better for citizens.

There was another advantage, too. Whereas it could take weeks or even months to get a small business owner on the phone or arrange a meeting with the right decision maker at a real estate firm, government offices, Jonathon notes, "have to pick up the phone." He and his team started cold-calling local government departments with a surprisingly high rate of success. One of their first calls was to the municipal clerk's office at a small, four-thousand-person Victorian town called Atlantic Highlands, New Jersey, about an hour south of Manhattan. Within hours, they had the clerk on the phone. Within a day, they had showed him a demo. Within a week, they had signed a $1,000 contract.

For Jonathon, it was a game-changing realization. He had found, as he calls it, his "perfect customer."

"As soon as we chose government," Jonathon says, "everything got easier." Improving the product, explaining the business to investors, streamlining the website . . . every decision became simpler. "In particular, with investors, the game became far easier," he says, noting that the pool of investors for govtech companies was much smaller but that his conversion rate increased markedly (see Chapter 5: Arbitrage). "In a pitch, you need to convey two things: what you do and, I think even more importantly, who your customer is. We couldn't convey the second part before; now we can. Now, we're the company that helps government go paperless."

We at the 1776 seed fund were in that smaller pool of investors enthusiastic about govtech startups. Jonathon delivered a short, confident pitch to us over the phone at the end of June 2014 as he was wrapping up a seed round after his pivot to government. We said yes within a week. After watching Jonathon execute with maniacal focus for a year, we wrote another check into SeamlessDocs's $5 million Series A and then another check in 2016 into their $6.5 million Series B.

From the moment when Barry from Tennessee first called, Jonathon became, in his words, "completely obsessed with understanding government and being the best at selling to government."

Today, SeamlessDocs works with hundreds of governments in forty-eight states, has raised almost $20 million total, continues to grow exponentially every year, and perhaps most important has a 115 percent revenue renewal rate. SeamlessDocs has found product-market fit in selling to government.

When the Government Is Your Buyer

If your business model involves selling directly to government—either a B2G2C startup like SeamlessDocs or a B2G startup like SpaceX—then the crux of your business model will be navigating the perils of government procurement. Selling to any institution involves some degree of procurement hassle, but the hassles of selling to government are of a different type and degree.

Let's start with the basics. What kinds of things do governments buy? Depending on how you look at it, just about everything, from warships and sprawling office complexes to janitorial services and sticky notes. The U.S. federal government alone buys about $1.8 *trillion* worth of goods and services every year. And that doesn't include the $3.2 *trillion* of goods and services that the country's thousands of state and municipal governments are purchasing. And taken in the aggregate, the European Union buys even more goods and services than the United States!

If you're selling to a government, you need to ask:

a) Do I have a superior product or service to what the government is currently using or providing to citizens?
b) Do I have a comparable product or service that will cost the government less than what they're currently buying?
c) Or do I have something the government isn't currently buying but could be of value in helping their mission?

The answers to these questions will guide you down different approaches to procurement.

Governments Like to Save Money

Let's start with the first two options. Given government's aversion to risk and ever-present budget constraints, there tends to be a premium on goods and services that reduce costs. That is, all else being equal, a procurement officer may get far more jazzed about a new platform that will deliver the same outcomes at a 2 percent cost reduction than a platform that might cost 2 percent more but deliver 25 percent better service. Be prepared for that if you want to sell a "better" but more expensive solution directly to government.

What about a startup that could cut costs by a significantly greater margin in exchange for only a slight reduction in the quality of outcomes? It depends: When you're talking about internet speed or office supplies, a 20 percent cost reduction for products that are 2 percent lower in quality might be awfully appealing to the government. But when you're talking about dropout rates in school districts or mortality rates in a hospital, a government can rarely stomach even a minuscule dip in expected outcomes, no matter how great the cost savings, and understandably so.

In either case, whether you have a superior product or a cheaper alternative, you'll need to prove that you're better or as good as your competition. Here, too, the burden of proof may be trickier for superior product startups, in that they must prove both that the product is better (which means you have to know your data) and that it's better *by enough to justify the higher costs.* For cost-cutting solutions, you still must convince your customers that your product is at least level with what they're accustomed to, and that may not be an easy feat. As always, evidence matters.

Selling Something Entirely New to a Government

The trickiest path may be when you have something a government isn't currently buying at all but could be of value to citizens. In this case, you're going to need strong data to build a case that there's an urgent and painful problem that the government needs to address as well as to prove the outcomes you can achieve for them. You may also need to find a hero mayor to overcome the inertia inherent in government. On the plus side, though, you're unlikely to have to beat out an incumbent who has had time to build its own little iron triangle!

How Governments Buy Things

The one thing to know about government procurement is that the process isn't designed to be efficient or innovative, but rather to ensure a fair use of public funds. As a result, government procurement isn't efficient or innovative, and, ironically, can at time feel unfair to startups, particularly ones who are new to the game.

Government Procurement Process

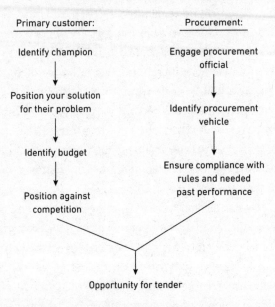

Primary customer:

Identify champion

↓

Position your solution
for their problem

↓

Identify budget

↓

Position against
competition

Procurement:

Engage procurement
official

↓

Identify procurement
vehicle

↓

Ensure compliance with
rules and needed
past performance

Opportunity for tender

When selling to a government, you have to manage two parallel paths. On one path, you have to find a primary customer for your solution. On the other path, you have to work through procurement officials to find a procurement vehicle so the agency can purchase from you. These two paths are represented by two different parts of a government's bureaucracy, often formally separated by rules and processes designed to ensure fairness. The procurement official isn't necessarily looking out for the primary customer's best interest, or yours, but rather for the best interest of the taxpayer. While not every government has quite such distinct divisions, most governments, even fairly small municipalities, will have at least a single procurement officer tasked with overseeing their purchasing.

"You have to be even smarter than your government buyer about procurement, because sometimes you will need to be able to show them how to buy your product," Zac Bookman from OpenGov* says. "It's a two-part process. You have to convince someone in government that, yes, your product will help them solve their problems, and then you have to close the deal with the procurement process."

---

*You met OpenGov back in Chapter 5: Arbitrage.

Tenders

Procurement vehicles come in many forms, but the most obvious is a request for proposal, often called a *tender* outside the United States. A tender outlines something the government would like to buy, details the constraints the government is working under, and asks companies to explain how they would provide a solution under those constraints. Companies can then submit proposals, bidding on the work and explaining how they would do the work or what they would deliver. The procurement official then considers all proposals and awards the contract to the most attractive one. This is common practice in the United States at the federal, state, and municipal levels, and the basic principles apply around the world.

However, the particulars of how governments implement tenders can vary widely outside the United States. CitizenLab cofounder Wietse Van Ransbeeck, whose citizen engagement startup has contracts with governments in countries throughout Europe, notes that in the Netherlands, for instance, his team may send over a quote for a €25,000 project on Monday and receive the signed contract and a check by the end of the week. Conversely, in France, even a relatively small €4,000 project will almost always need to go through an open tender.

In addition, tenders often require the government to accept the proposal with the "lowest price that is technically acceptable."

Other Procurement Vehicles: Schedules

Tenders aren't the only procurement vehicles you should understand, however, or even the most common.

Let's suppose your startup has a new solution to a thorny government challenge. In your case, there's nobody currently addressing this problem, or at least there's nobody solving it the way you are. How do you sell something to a government if it's not something they know they need yet?

If you can find a customer within the federal government, as an example, who wants to experiment with your new idea, it may be easier to use an alternative procurement vehicle rather than an open tender. The tender process is as cumbersome for government officials as it is for you, so procurement officials will sometimes attempt to simplify things by going to the market and saying, in effect, "Hey, we're looking to buy a lot of this category of thing, you should compete for the right to be able to sell those things to us over an extended period of time!"

These prenegotiated procurement vehicles, or schedules, essentially give a small group of vendors an oligopoly over selling that category of goods or services to a federal agency, in return for agreeing to terms that the agency deems favorable.[1] You can think of them as almost "closed" tenders. In many cases, state and local governments can also purchase through these federal schedules. But here's the hack: The vendors on that schedule can often let other companies use their schedule in return for a pass-through fee. These schedules may be odious, but they can provide a much faster and easier path for government to buy your solution than open tenders.

Blake Hall from ID.me discovered this as he started expanding the market for his digital identification solution from the private sector to government agencies.

"The next thing I needed to understand was procurement vehicles. All it really is, is a way for the government to limit the number of companies that can submit proposals. They don't want to review proposals that come out from the woodwork, they just want prevetted companies to be bidding, because it makes their life easier and ostensibly raises quality. There's no rhyme or reason to it. Once I understood that, hey, you just need to partner with a company that's on that schedule. Once you got that, then if you have a buyer that's interested, and they go, 'Hey, how can we procure you?' You can go, 'Hey, we're on this schedule, we're partnered with so and so, and our price is out there and if you want to procure us, that's the way to do it.'"

As Blake discovered, government procurement can feel unfair when you realize that the fastest way for a government to buy your solution is to use a preexisting procurement vehicle, but whichever companies have access to that schedule get to take a cut of your revenue for the privilege. Many government officials I know would agree, and find procurement frustrating, but in most countries government procurement is a form of an iron triangle in its own right.

Over the past decade, many government leaders have attempted to pioneer more innovative procurement approaches, such as "challenges," but have encountered significant resistance from their bureaucracies and the industry that serves them. In cases where the law does allow more innovative approaches to procurements, bureaucratic norms often prevent their actual use.

Past Performance

When navigating government procurement, you need to keep in mind the paramount importance of your *past performance*. Past performance doesn't simply mean that you have existing customers. For state and local procurement, it often means that you have sold your solution to a similar government before. For federal agencies, however, past performance can mean that you have previously provided your solution to the government agency that you're selling to. But wait: Why are you navigating their procurement process *if they're already your customer?* Welcome to the painful paradoxes of government procurement.

Why is past performance so important? Procurement rules generally give huge advantages to providers who have previously delivered successfully for that agency. If you're trying to get into an agency for the first time, your next best alternative is to get some "points" for past performance with an agency similar to theirs, which can often be sufficient at the state and local level.

All of this means that landing your first sale with an agency, or any government at all, is monumental. The quintessential hack is to find a way to do a small pilot. Perhaps, like ID.me, you'll use someone else's schedule to gain past performance. Or perhaps, as you'll learn soon, you can sell a pilot at a low enough price point to bypass certain procurement rules.

Past performance is another way in which early adopters can be critical for regulatory hackers.* Government procurement rewards insiders and sets up high barriers to outsiders. It's hard to get inside, but once you are, government procurement can quickly snowball on itself.

Rewards Come to the Patient

David Yarkin, former chief procurement officer for the state of Pennsylvania and now president of Government Sourcing Solutions, a consulting firm, is probably the smartest person on procurement in Washington, D.C. "Government procurement generally takes longer and will be more expensive to pursue than private-sector procurement, plain and simple," he says. "You need to be

---

*For more on early adopters, refer back to Chapter 5: Arbitrage.

prepared for that." A good rule of thumb is that closing a deal with government may take two or three times as long as a similar transaction with a private institution, at least your first few times through the process.

"Procurement is a black hole," Zac Bookman puts it more colorfully. "Often, you'll work for months on a deal, it'll go into procurement, and they'll tell you everybody has to go dark, and then it never comes out, and you might never hear from them again. That's enough to destroy a company."

However, the benefits can be immense for those with enough patience and runway to sell to the public sector, as OpenGov has shown with more than 1,800 municipalities now using their platform. For one, Yarkin says, with very few exceptions, governments aren't going to suddenly go bankrupt next month. They also tend to be reliable payers, and they are, as Yarkin puts it, "pretty sticky." That is, if you're doing a halfway decent job, you can usually count on a contract renewal.

At SeamlessDocs, Jonathon had to adapt to the pace of government procurement and balance that against the expectations of his investors, who would encourage him to close deals quickly and move on to the next sale. However, his team soon learned that investing twice as much time with a government official up front could result in contracts that were three, four, or five

Profits/Time

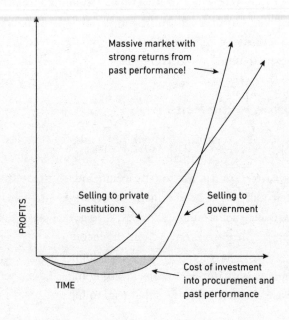

times larger than what was initially on the table. What's more, Jonathon discovered that the larger the initial contract, the greater the chances a government client would renew or even expand the deal later on.

In each municipality, the SeamlessDocs sales team would takes notes about nuances like decision-making authority and procurement thresholds (the deal size at which the purchasing process becomes more complicated). Salespeople would also track how many hours were spent inking a $5,000 deal versus a $25,000 deal so that the team could ensure they were allocating appropriate time and resources toward capturing each new deal.

His team learned to identify the opportunities in which a little more time could pay a lot more dividends—and that sometimes meant going against their investors' advice. Going after smaller, quicker municipal deals using a telephone sales model was working for them. Over time, though, they learned that investing a lot of time and resources going after larger state contracts would give Jonathon and his colleagues a license to hunt additional contracts with other agencies throughout the state because they had relevant past performance. A contract with the New York DMV, for example, opened up many new doors and eventually paved the way for contracts with the New York Energy Research and Development Authority and the New York Gaming Commision, too.

Like everything else involved in building a regulated startup, Jonathon and his team had to build-measure-learn over and over again to find the optimal customer acquisition and procurement strategy for *their* product with *their* customers.

While patience is required for B2G and B2G2C business models—and you should manage investor expectations accordingly—there are four procurement hacks that can make the process less painful.

Procurement Hack #1: Find Your Hero

I've shared this before but it is worth repeating: Find your hero mayor, or hero governor, or hero superintendent, or hero whatever.

The idea of finding a champion isn't unique to government sales of course. In *The Challenger Customer*, Brent Adamson[2] encourages anyone selling into a large organization to start by finding and developing an internal champion. But the insight is doubly important when selling into government. Most bureaucrats face asymmetric incentives that lead to inertia, so you need to find the handful of government leaders willing to take a risk in order to make a name for themselves.

"If you have a new or unique solution, you need to look for that government official who's out there stating publicly that tackling that challenge is a top priority for their administration," says David Yarkin. "If you hear that and think 'I have that solution,' go full gusto after that one city, get that win under your belt, so that way, when you meet with anyone else and they ask, 'Have you actually done this yet?' your answer is 'yes.'"

Your hero doesn't always have to be at the top of the organization, either. Often, it's about finding the official who feels the most pain. At SeamlessDocs, Jonathon deployed tried-and-true data-driven sales and marketing techniques that SaaS startups use to sell to small businesses but applied them to selling to municipal governments. In the process, his team started tracking how much time they were spending on the phone with communications directors versus secretaries versus information technology specialists versus city clerks. It turned out that they were spending much more time talking with the former two, whereas it tended to be the clerks and IT directors who greenlit a contract. His team adjusted their sales strategy accordingly.

"We started to learn that, even if you're talking to this person and they seem super interested, you're still going to need them to get buy-in from this other person," Jonathon explained. "But then we started to learn that each town has a different process, and over here, you may need to take a different route than you did in that other town."

In addition, he started to realize that the sales process with governments wasn't just about convincing the person on the other end of the line that his product had value. It was about empowering that person to go into another room with someone else and convincing that decision maker that the product has value. "While that's often the case in B2B sales, it's even more critical in government," Jonathon said. "You have to know what has to happen after you hang up the phone, and you have to understand exactly what Janie or Jimmy needs in order to go sell your product to their bosses." Even with a hero leading the way for you, you have to close the sale, and that's tricky when you're a startup without much past performance to show. As much as you're convincing your hero that you can make their citizens' lives a little better, you're also enticing them to want to be connected to *your* story because of what that means for *their* story. They should be as fired up about it as you are.

Why? Because you don't just need them to be that early customer. You also need them deeply invested in your success so that when you run into turbulence, they double down and help ensure the project succeeds. You're going to need them to become not just your customer but your champion in the market more broadly. You want them to tell every other mayor or health executive or superintendent they meet that your startup is a winner. In order for that to happen, they need to be passionate about your mission and what you've done for them. They need to believe in the *why* behind your startup.

"Don't just get that first win," says Yarkin. "Execute the hell out of it so it's a story that first client is telling to others."

Procurement Hack #2: Know the Procurement Officer

Another procurement hack to remember derives from the dual-track nature of government procurement. You may be pursuing one contract with one government, but you really have two customers: the agency that will use your solution and that government's procurement official. Overlook the procurement official at your peril.

"Ultimately, you have to get in to see your primary customer and sell them on the benefits of your product," Yarkin says. "Where startups make a mistake is that they end there. They forget about the ultimate executor of that contract, which will be the procurement director."

Yarkin recommends arranging a meeting with the procurement official immediately after you meet with your prospective customer, say, the department of health services or energy. While you won't need to make the same compelling case you made to the user, you should take the time to help them understand the problem you are solving and how. This way, the procurement officer isn't blindsided when a request comes in from the customer, and you're a real human being to them, not just some unknown company name scribbled on a form.

This can pay dividends in two ways. First, it helps you find your way into the good graces of the procurement official, so when there are hiccups or you have questions, they're going to be more inclined to help.

Second, it can open up doors that you didn't know were there. As Yarkin explains, "Procurement touches everything, every department, and they know everybody and they know what problems those people are trying to solve." They may tell you that the artificial intelligence engine you're currently selling to prisons sounds like something the healthcare system could use, too, or that the drone system you've built with the public works department in mind could also be valuable to the parks department. This might help you land customer number two, number three, and so on, maximizing the value of the past performance you earned with customer number one.

"If you can find the right person in procurement, they can be a great resource for you," he says.

Procurement Hack #3: Pricing

Of course, the way you price and package your product or service is important with almost any type of business model. But pricing is uniquely important with government procurement, because of procurement thresholds.

The most common and effective pricing hack when it comes to landing early adopters in government is to price your solution below the threshold at which the law requires government to use a formal tender. The rules may dictate that projects under, say, $10,000 can be awarded without a formal procurement process. In some cases, bureaucrats have the authority to pull out a government credit card on the spot and make the purchase. Projects between, say, $10,000 and $25,000 might have go through a limited process and get at least three quotes from three different bidders, but those exceeding $25,000 must go through the entire procurement process. For a larger city, or a state or federal agency, each threshold might be ten times higher.

If you can price yourself just under the right threshold, you'll make it easier for early adopters, because the process is shorter and simpler. "That can be a great strategy to get you started, when you're trying to land those first few clients," Yarkin says.

At CitizenLab, Wietse Van Ransbeeck and his team did precisely this.

"Here in Belgium, the upper limit for not going through public procurement was €8,500," he says. "For a startup that's trying to move quickly, it's crucial to have very short sales cycles, and for us that meant avoiding that public procurement process. So, what we did for the first customers in Belgium was we always sold to them at €8,499. It worked well."

You can run into problems with this approach, though. At least in the United States, Yarkin says, setting your prices just below contracting thresholds will eventually raise eyebrows, and in certain cases, you can face legal liability for deliberately skirting the formal procurement process. With this in mind, Yarkin adds that just-below-threshold pricing "isn't really a sustainable strategy" for most startups, even if it helps you win early adopters and prove past performance.

Jonathon Ende at SeamlessDocs and Zac Bookman at OpenGov have also experimented with different pricing models and have similarly come to the conclusion that lower prices don't always translate into success with government procurement.

Jonathon notes that the prevailing wisdom in selling to government when he started the company was to always bid the lowest price for your services. Early on, Jonathon embraced this "race to the minimum dollar figure" mentality when pricing SeamlessDocs for public-sector customers.

But he realized the approach had two major drawbacks, in addition to yielding less revenue on each sale. For one, customers associated low-priced services with low value. When SeamlessDocs only cost a department, say, $1,000 to implement, few felt compelled to learn all that the platform could do and take full advantage of the product.

Conversely, when a department paid $15,000 for a pilot, there was urgency to squeeze as much value out of the product as possible, and customers took more time to learn about it. Customer satisfaction and renewal rates for the latter group were far higher.

And two, Jonathon realized that he was, as he calls it now, "pricing for the sale, not for success." In agreeing to nearly break-even contract prices, he explained, he wasn't building in the financial flexibility necessary to hold an in-person tutorial for a customer at a moment's notice in order to ensure their satisfaction.

Soon, he began pricing for success instead, with much better results. His team recently sold a ten-form pilot program for north of $30,000.

Procurement Hack #4: Councils of Governments

A procurement hack that can help you *scale* your B2G or B2G2C model uses councils of governments, or CoGs. Mark DeSantis, the CEO of RoadBotics, has worked with countless CoGs during his career. He explains it best:

"Take a small town with five hundred people, for example. They don't really need to own their own fire trucks, nor does the town next to them or the town next to that. So they're starting to look at their local governments and think, 'Okay, we want to retain our own autonomy as a government, but we also have to lower our costs, so let's go to the three towns that are contiguous and similarly sized and let's share fire trucks. While we're at it, why don't we just do all our buying together. As a matter of fact, why don't we even share some of our employees by collectively contracting people to do the same job for three different governments."

Thus, CoGs were born as buying consortia for multiple municipalities. Some may include only two or three small towns, whereas others may include a large group of major governments spanning a metropolitan region, like the Metropolitan Washington CoG or the South Bay Cities CoG in the Los Angeles area.

CoGs aren't new. They've been around for as long as DeSantis and Yarkin can remember, but both agree that their role and their membership have expanded exponentially in recent years.

"The concept really took off in the wake of the recession, because procurement budgets got slashed," Yarkin says, noting that "cooperative purchasing has been the trend over the last decade in our industry" thanks to the savings governments can find by going through one procurement process and by purchasing goods and services in larger quantities. Understandably, these can be coveted and fiercely competitive contracts.

Yarkin adds: "CoGs really got their start with simple things like buying office supplies or maintenance supplies, but now you see them purchasing more complex goods and services. I think you'll see that trend continue moving forward."

So when can CoGs help your startup?

"When you're scaling, not when you're starting," Yarkin says.

"On the one hand, CoGs are great for sharing information," he explains. "If you land a project with the city of Arlington and you do it well, there's a chance the Arlington representative on the Metropolitan Washington CoG will take you to the next meeting, vouch for the work that you've done, and encourage the other governments' representatives to listen to your pitch. It could be a great way to expand once you get that first customer."

As for looking at CoGs for early adopters, Yarkin advises against it.

"Not only is that less likely, because you essentially need to convince a larger group of governments to take a shot on you before you've proven your concept, but getting ten or twenty different governments to agree on what that first contract should look like and how everything should work could be very difficult," he says. "Plus, even if you could do that, then you may find yourself, on your first go, trying to make twenty different people from different local governments happy, and in that scenario, your chances of success diminish considerably."

The Potential of the Government Market

It's not just CoGs that can help you scale once you've had success with those all-important first government customers.

Earlier, I quoted Yarkin's adage that governments neither want to be the first nor the last. Once you've been successful with those early adopter government customers, the second part of the adage—that "nobody wants to be last"—immediately plays to your advantage.

This is especially true because, as Yarkin has learned, "government circles are pretty close-knit." If you manage to solve an important problem for one municipality or state, "there's a good chance their counterparts in other towns and states are going to hear about it, and you can scale that way."

CitizenLab's Van Ransbeeck echoed a similar sentiment.

"The government market is very complex, for sure," he says. "You need to develop a lot of expertise about how things work and how public procurement works in each government you want to sell to, and what you'll learn is that there are a lot of rules about the decision making processes that are totally different from any other market."

However, he says, "Once you gain this expertise, and once you have that first reference and case study to show, then it's also a huge market that becomes available to you."

Chapter 10

SELLING TO CITIZENS
AND PRIVATE INSTITUTIONS

For Matt Caywood, it was the same guessing game every morning.

From his house in San Francisco's Haight-Ashbury district to the University of California, San Francisco's Parnassus campus where he was pursuing a PhD in neuroscience, Matt had three public transportation options. He could take the 43 bus, he could walk a couple blocks south and catch the 6, or he could hop on a nearby streetcar. A wrong decision could put him at school twenty minutes later than a shorter option. And yet, the actual time on the bus or train varied by less than a minute. The question was which one would be leaving next.

For Matt, it was a question without a readily available answer. This was 2007, and there were no open data APIs feeding transit data to app developers. In fact, the iPhone App Store didn't yet exist. There was no way to quickly compare route options to find the fastest path to school and back.

So he built one. He hacked together three separate web pages with real-time rail and bus information, combining them to form a single online interface (what he now fondly calls a "Franken-TransitScreen"). He would pull it up for review before leaving for his commute to help him select the speediest route to campus or back home.

In San Francisco, the project remained just that: a personal hack for personal benefit. It wasn't until he moved across the country to Washington, D.C., in 2010 to work at a national lab that it started to become more.

Matt's daily commute took him through Arlington County, and he started volunteering with Arlington's Department of Commuter Services, which was created to find ways to increase demand for public transit in the region.[1]

While Arlington and their private sector partners were focused on traditional consumer marketing tactics, such as putting transit maps and bus schedules in apartment lobbies, Matt and two others volunteered to lead a small, four-month taskforce seeking new technology-driven solutions to meet that same objective.

One of the projects Matt and the team started piecing together was a larger scale and slightly more sophisticated version of what he had mashed together back in California: a real-time transit options dashboard.

In January 2012, the group mounted their first screen in a local coffee shop called Java Shack right in the heart of Arlington's main transit corridor. Displayed on a small flatscreen in the corner of the shop were up-to-the-minute departure times for the next Metro bus, Arlington county bus, and Orange line Metro train from their respective stops a few blocks away.

"Early reviews were overwhelmingly positive," Matt recalls.

"The owner loved it, the employees loved it, and customers loved it," he said. "We heard that people were regularly checking the screen before leaving, so the vibes we got back were good."

In March, the initial funding for the project ran out and Arlington opted not to extend the project any further. Discouraged, the team members went their separate ways. Matt put the project and the prototype out of mind for a few months to focus on his day job, working on artificial intelligence and neuroscience projects for government clients.

Until he returned to Java Shack.

Matt popped in for coffee in early June, and to his surprise, months after anyone had last tinkered with the program, there was the little screen still working perfectly, still pulling in and displaying real-time transit data. "Hmm," Matt thought. "Maybe we built a promising MVP after all."

Matt started kicking around the idea of starting a business built around what he had started calling the "TransitScreen" platform. He sat on the idea for six more months, unsure what the business model would look like but convinced there was something there. But how to unlock it? Who would pay for it? Was there any way to make money off this technology?

That's when Matt met Ryan Croft at a startup networking event in D.C. Ryan was an adventure-seeking entrepreneur with his own travel company, and he had spent years leading excursions around the world. In the more than one hundred cities he had visited, he had observed a common problem: congestion. Ryan was looking for ideas for how to help cities solve this problem.

When Matt mentioned what he had built in Arlington and why he believed it held promise as a startup, Ryan jumped on board, and the two incorporated TransitScreen later that year.

Right away, Matt and Ryan envisioned two potential customers who might recognize enough value in TransitScreen to actually pay for the product: governments, particularly transit agencies, and real estate companies, particularly apartment and office buildings. Without knowing it, Matt and Ryan were instinctively taking their first steps in building TransitScreen's power map.

Real estate seemed particularly promising as a potential customer because of two important trends: One, Americans were migrating to cities at an ever-accelerating clip; and two, builders were increasingly focused on transit-oriented and commuter-friendly real estate projects.

"We knew enough to know that governments generally wouldn't be the greatest client to work with in terms of speed and adopting new technology, but at the same time, we knew governments had the biggest interest in solving transit and congestion issues," Matt says. "So we focused on both, though most of our attention went to getting meetings with real estate companies."

Although Matt and Ryan met with several interested real estate developers, reaching a viable deal with them was a challenge. Developers were intrigued by the idea but not motivated to invest in the screens, with some expressing uncertainty about what the return on that investment would look like. Matt and Ryan started looking for ways to provide incentives for real estate companies. Could they rethink their pricing structure in a way that would make it more appealing? Could they tack on additional features or otherwise derive some added value from the screens?

Then they found their regulatory hack.

When Matt and Ryan began researching which cities around the country were most aggressively trying to address their traffic congestion issues, they learned that many city governments already offered incentives, like tax breaks, to real estate developers who took measures to promote mass transit and other sustainable transportation practices. These measures could be as simple as placing bus maps and schedules in an apartment building lobby to more involved programs like educating employees on public transportation options when a company relocated to a new office.

"We've been able to use these existing incentives to our advantage when marketing TransitScreen to developers," Ryan explains.

And that's what's so uniquely effective about the company's growth strategy. With TransitScreen, the city arguably has the most to gain in the form of reduced congestion and pollution—much more than any one apartment building manager or any one commuter. And yet, the city, Matt and Ryan realized, wouldn't be writing them any checks. Real estate developers would buy TransitScreen in order to unlock the incentive offered by the city.

"What you have to ask is, 'Who really owns a city?'" Matt says. "If you think about it, 80 or 90 percent of any given city is buildings. Thus, 80 or 90 percent of the city is actually owned by and controlled by the real estate industry. That was a critical realization for us in identifying our market. Sure, we're essentially a public good, but that didn't mean government had to be the customer."

The Pervasive Role of Government

In the last chapter, you learned about business models based on selling to government, such as SeamlessDocs. You can build a great regulated startup selling to government, but many more regulatory hackers will find their interactions with government less direct, but no less important.

If you're building a B2C, B2B, B2B2C, or a marketplace business model in a complex market with lots of regulation, then governments aren't your customer. Governments may not even be your direct regulators, but they will nonetheless determine your ability to access your market in overt or subtle ways. In healthcare, education, agrifood, energy, transportation, security, and numerous other highly regulated industries, government is pervasive, setting the rules of the game, creating markets, nudging behavior in certain directions, outright banning other activities, or all of the above at the same time.

If you ever want to understand the extent to which governments shape the behavior of private players, take some time to browse through the tax code for your country, state, or municipality. Studying most tax codes is almost like doing an archeological dig on our modern societies, where you can see the layers of behaviors that policymakers either wanted to help or hinder at any given moment in time. Often, you'll see a tax appear for a particular activity, only to later find a waiver for that tax for people who engage in some other desired activity. For an even fuller picture, start digging through the layers in a government's building codes, health codes, and fire codes!

As a regulatory hacker, mastering this arcana may be the difference between banging your head against a complex market that won't open for you and finding a spare key sitting under the doormat. If you want to win, you shouldn't assume your goal is simply to get government to leave you alone. As TransitScreen learned, many of the best regulatory hacks in selling to private citizens or institutions actually involve getting government to do some of your work for you.

Governments Can Help, Hinder, or Do Both Simultaneously

The formal rules and regulations that shape a complex market are usually fairly obvious. Less obvious but no less important are all the subtle ways that government can provide incentives or disincentives for your customers to purchase and use your solution.

Incentives/Disincentives

Excise taxes	Subsidies

←——— Hindering   Helping ———→

Bans	Licensing & registration	Waivers	Mandates

It's easiest to think about the ways that government can help or hinder your ability to sell to citizens or private institutions as a spectrum. At one end of the spectrum you will find governments issuing explicit mandates with teeth behind them, such as a requirement for new homes to have carbon monoxide detectors. In those cases, governments can create an entire market from nothing, almost overnight. At the other end of the spectrum you'll find governments banning activities, such as the trading of bitcoin in China, or human cloning in many countries. In those cases, governments can obliterate your market just as fast.

However, chances are the opportunities for the most creative and impactful regulatory hacks will reside somewhere in the middle of the spectrum. For example, governments may provide complete or partial subsidies for certain products or services while raising the cost of others through excise or sales taxes. Governments can impose licensing or registration requirements on certain kinds of services, or other regulations that dictate or constrain how you operate, while simultaneously relaxing these requirements if you engage in other activities that the government wants to encourage.

Let's start going through the spectrum from one end to the other and explore ways regulatory hackers have found to win despite—or because of—regulation when selling to citizens or institutions.

When Governments Help

The ultimate regulatory hack is to get governments to create a market for you where none existed before. Hackers do pull this off, as in the case of Kidde getting states to mandate that new homes have carbon monoxide alarms, or Opower getting certain states to mandate that utilities provide comparative usage data to citizens in their energy bills. Governments will almost never mandate that citizens or institutions have to use a particular provider's products. But Kidde owned the best intellectual property for carbon monoxide monitoring, so a mandate for alarms in general was almost certain to significantly benefit them. In the same way, Opower quickly emerged as the dominant provider of comparative usage data for utilities, so a mandate to provide a service like theirs was going to benefit them.

Getting government to create a mandate around your solution will almost certainly involve a mix of favorable circumstances and excellent hacking. You need a significant problem with an obvious and comparatively inexpensive solution. You need a strong coalition of influencers. And you need to be a regulatory hacker who understands how to leverage those influencers to work across the grassroots, the grasstops, and the media. Kidde was able to find their way to all of these. Opower was able to in certain states.

For most regulatory hackers selling to citizens or private institutions, however, you'll be looking for hacks that take advantage of *existing* incentives or finding opportunities to encourage governments to create more or different incentives.

One of the easiest and most common ways for governments to nudge citizens or private institutions to do something is by providing subsidies, often through tax incentives. In this case, while government isn't writing your regulated startup a check directly, they are indirectly providing a financial boost if your customer purchases your product or service.

Tesla is a great example of this. Governments around the world want to cut carbon emissions, and one of the ways they seek to do that is by providing subsidies to consumers who purchase eco-friendly vehicles like electric cars. The U.S. government alone has pledged to put a million electric cars on American roads, setting aside billions of dollars in available government subsidies and other incentives to help reach that goal.[2] Of course, these are taxpayer dollars that are being spent to encourage a desired behavior by citizens, with the rationale being that the public would collectively benefit from major pollution reductions if electric vehicles become a mass-market product.

It's important to note that the U.S. government didn't put in place subsidies for electric vehicles *for* Tesla, although they certainly did so with the *encouragement* of Tesla. Rather, the government put the subsidies in place in 2008, in a law signed by President Bush, to help stimulate the emergence of a mass market for electric vehicles. Tesla was just the startup that was first able to take advantage of the program, actively helping customers secure the subsidies in the form of tax credits that can exceed $10,000 when various state subsidies are included. Analysts generally agree that the program has been critical in helping Tesla build a market for their electric vehicles.

Tesla has also received billions of dollars in research and development subsidies from governments in the U.S. and abroad.[3] This includes subsidies to promote battery research and manufacturing by the governments of Japan and China. In recent years, for example, Japan's New Energy and Industrial Technology Development Organization, a public-private partnership, has invested $400 million in the form of various subsidies into developing more advanced battery technologies, which have benefited Tesla. The company has also received research and development subsidies to expand its battery manufacturing facilities in Kasai and Osaka.[4]

And of course Tesla received a guarantee from the U.S. Department of Energy for $456 million in low-interest loans in 2010, at a critical juncture for the cash-strapped company as it pushed to complete its shift from selling its proof-of-concept Roadster to its showpiece Model S. Tesla famously repaid the loan many years before it was due, a public-relations coup for Elon Musk.

When subsidies aren't viable, government can provide incentives in other ways. For example, governments might grant tax waivers in return for taking certain actions. An obvious example relevant to the startup world is that many governments provide reduced capital gains tax rates for investors in startups.

Other waivers can be even more subtle but no less powerful. Matt and Ryan at TransitScreen discovered, for example, that some governments reward apartment-building developers who implement congestion reduction technology, like TransitScreen's, by reducing the amount of parking they are required to build. Building parking is many times more expensive for developers than buying a TransitScreen display. These hacks are powerful because everyone wins. It costs a government nothing to achieve a desired outcome: more use of public transport and less use of cars. Property owners show their commitment to the government's goals in a way that also makes their projects more profitable. TransitScreen finds a market of real estate developers eager to buy their service. Citizens who travel in and out of those buildings get better real-time data to guide them through the city's multimodal transportation system. Even citizens across the city—who don't necessarily use the TransitScreen service—benefit indirectly from less congestion and pollution.

When Governments Hinder

Turning back to Tesla for a moment, it's easy to see ways in which governments have helped Tesla create a mass market for electric vehicles. But governments also hinder Tesla with numerous regulations. From safety belts to battery technology, automobiles are one of the most regulated products we use in our daily lives. Many of those regulations have clear benefits to the public interest, but there is at least one notable exception: car dealerships.

Many U.S. states forbid a car manufacturer from selling directly to citizens and instead require the presence of local middlemen, otherwise known as car dealerships. It's easy to see the benefits to car dealerships in this system, but it's harder to see the benefits to the public interest. Tesla is selling a fairly radical new approach to car ownership and wants to control the end-to-end experience for their early adopters and emerging mass market. But state rules make that unnecessarily hard.

As I've said before, it's in this sense that many in the Valley reflexively think about startups' involvement with governments. There are numerous ways in which governments can hinder your access to markets, or your ability to create a new market, as in the case of Tesla. And some of them will in fact be blatant rent seeking or market protection supported by iron triangles.

It's important to remember, though, that not every regulation that is a hindrance has as questionable a basis as the car dealerships. I've already discussed my belief that many of the regulations Uber railed against actually make sense. In the case of 23andMe, you can understand why there's a legitimate public interest in the FDA regulating home genomics testing that could inform health decisions by citizens.

Overall, the most common way in which governments will hinder your regulated startup are through well-intended rules interpreted or implemented poorly, most likely because regulators never imagined the impact on your new technology or business approach. As you saw with HopSkipDrive, the best regulatory hacks for these circumstances often come through engagement with regulators, rather than Uber-style confrontation.

Governments can also put in place regulations that are direct barriers to the growth of new technologies or ways of doing things. Drones are one such example. The FAA wasn't out to crush innovation when they imposed rules that most commercial drones be registered and that they must operate in line of sight to licensed pilots.[5] But the FAA's main priority, understandably, is safety. They just aren't nearly as concerned about innovation.

Governments can also hinder your regulated startup through taxes targeted at the purchase of a particular class of products or services. Many cities are starting to look at taxing Uber and other ride-sharing providers as a form of tolling to pay for the upkeep of their roads and transit systems. This actually makes a lot of sense for the public interest, but it will surely hinder Uber's growth and add more complexity to their compliance.

And of course, as with 23andMe, government can simply ban your product or service, at least until you address their concerns.

Paradoxically, governments can also hinder new technologies or approaches by *not* having any regulations. This is happening increasingly often as new technologies smash into legal codes that could not possibly have contemplated their existence when they were drafted. Why *would* states have regulations governing self-driving cars until recently? Why *would* national governments have mechanisms in place to govern cryptocurrencies?

Without appropriate regulation, nobody is exactly sure of the rules of the game. In areas like e-commerce or media, with minimal consequences from failure, it's easy to forge ahead and beg forgiveness later. In complex markets, where consequences can be life and death from self-driving cars, or systemic impact on economies from cryptocurrencies, a lack of clarity on who bears liability can hamstring startups. It's hard to put self-driving cars onto roads when nobody is sure who gets sued when people inevitably die.

In much the same way, mainstream institutional investors have hesitated to get too involved with Bitcoin until governments start to provide clear regulatory guidance, such as allowing the trading of Bitcoin futures contracts at the end of 2017. (At the time of publication, Bitcoin has continued to explode in value. The total value of Bitcoin in existence is now measured in hundreds of billions of dollars. But it's worth remembering how niche that still is in a world that trades around $5 *trillion* in traditional currencies *every day*.)

This is why Ola Doudin's approach with BitOasis is so interesting.* By knowing the laws and regulations and building her cryptocurrency exchange and wallet startup as if she were as rigorously regulated by the UAE national bank as any other financial services firm, she's not waiting to ask permission, but she's likely avoiding having to beg forgiveness down the road.

Finding the Hacks to Win

As you build your power map and explore all the ways that regulation can help or hinder your regulated startup in selling to citizens or private institutions, your head can start to spin in confusion and frustration. But you should look at this as a genuine opportunity instead.

Uber became a massively valuable company because mobile phones suddenly opened up entirely new ways to manage transportation networks, but *also* because iron triangles around the world had left massive value available for a startup who could break them apart. Uber won with technology but also with regulatory hacks.

Most founders have no idea how complex markets or regulations work, which means that taking the initiative to understand them and find creative regulatory hacks can give you a massive advantage.

As you iterate through build-measure-learn cycles to find the hacks that will unlock a market thick with regulation, you should keep the following nine tips in mind.

The Nine Tips for Selling to Citizens and Private Institutions
1. Do your homework.
2. Don't be a cynic.
3. Decide whether to beg forgiveness or ask permission.
4. It's often simpler to comply.

---

*You learned about Ola and BitOasis in Chapter 4: Growth.

5. It's easier to tweak than start from scratch.

6. Use the local, esoteric, and indirect to your advantage.

7. Think twice before poking big, scary bears.

8. Rules are meant to be broken (or at least changed).

9. Never forget that hacking is creative.

1. Do Your Homework

My father spent nearly twenty years lobbying the Virginia General Assembly on behalf of the Metro system without losing a major fight. I grew up hearing these stories. When I was young, they involved my father outworking or being more creative than his opponents. Over time, though, his job became a lot simpler: He had helped to write so many of the laws and regulations that he gradually gained an advantage over new entrants who didn't understand the rules of the Virginia transportation game as well as he did.

Before you even start to play this game, you have to do your homework to understand the rules that govern your power map. Many people in your complex market may have read an article in *The Washington Post* that summarizes a few laws or regulations in your market, and may sound clever for citing them. But they don't actually know what the rules say. Don't be that person. Do your homework and make sure you really know what these laws and regulations say, how they apply across geographies and levels of government, and even more important, *why*.

Dr. Nora Khaldi took an extreme approach to doing her homework with Nuritas: She taught her AI to do it for her!

"We knew we needed to find a way to get Chinese approval on our peptides," Nora says. "Everyone told us early on that that would be impossible, though, and that it was very rare for peptides to be approved for use in the Chinese market." The resulting risk, Nora explained, was that Nuritas would invest months or even years targeting, unlocking, and testing a peptide for use in new personal care products only to have Chinese regulators in the middle or at the very end of the process block products using that peptide from hitting the shelves.

Nora's solution: Code, quite literally, China's regulatory approval process into the earliest stages of her company's product development processes.

"We basically took those regulations and taught them to the artificial intelligence software we use to generate potentially valuable peptides," she explains, essentially adding a regulatory filter to the genomics data that Nuritas researchers use to generate potential product leads. "This way, we don't move forward with a product or an ingredient and invest all the necessary time and resources on something we know wouldn't be approved later."

Through a deft regulatory approach and software that seems to come from an episode of "Star Trek," Nuritas has turned what many biotechnology companies perceive as a business risk—regulatory approvals—and turned it into a massively valuable competitive advantage.

"In these areas, you can only fight regulations so much," Nora said. "There's a reason for these regulations, they serve an important purpose, so you can't just go and try to break them. Instead, you have to find an interesting or advantageous way to deal with them, and for us, that meant computationally building them into our initial discovery process."

Do your homework. Or train your AI to do it for you. Either can work.

2. Don't Be a Cynic

It's easy to assume that rules exist to protect incumbents, or that subsidies are only giveaways to well-connected insiders, but as Nora points out above it's more productive to start with a presumption of good intent. Why was this rule originally created? How might it support the public interest, even if it's inconvenient to your business? What was the historical context?

In the case of Uber, most of the rules governing taxi services were established many decades ago, after public scandals rocked the nascent taxi industry. The rules were established to protect citizens. Even if those rules are now antiquated, such as requiring paper receipts, or have mutated in ways unfavorable to citizens, they weren't necessarily created to support a Big Taxi monopoly at the expense of those sitting in the backseat.

You'll usually have easier conversations with policymakers if you start with empathy for the intent and goals of the current rules—even if you're proposing new and better ways to achieve those same ends. Moreover, you'll also have far better luck by framing your regulated startup's mission in a way that flows from that public interest.

3. Decide Whether to Beg Forgiveness or Ask Permission

Once you start testing possible regulatory hacks through cycles of build-measure-learn, you should have a view on the fundamental question we introduced in Chapter 4: Growth: Are you begging forgiveness or asking permission? Are you, like Uber, facing an iron triangle that you'll need to break to win? Or are you simply trying to overcome inertia, in which case you might want government's help in creating a market, like TransitScreen?

Part of what you're learning as you experiment with hacks is what's viable. If you're dealing with more of an iron-triangle scenario, *can* you simply launch your product, build momentum, and respond when governments eventually catch up? At that future point, will you simply deal with the additional costs of compliance? Will you attempt to have rules or laws changed? If you can't beg forgiveness because the costs of noncompliance are too significant or the ethics too uncomfortable, then what hacks are you planning to deploy to break one part of your iron triangle? In either scenario, what's your hacking strategy and what resources will you need to have ready to make those hacks work?

If you're asking permission—perhaps even asking for government's help in creating or unlocking your market—then what regulatory hacks will make that happen? Again, what resources do you need to make those hacks work? What expectations should you set with your investors about how long those hacks will take and what milestones to expect along the way?

4. It's Often Simpler to Comply

It's a fact of life that regulations are rarely convenient for the regulated. Just because a rule exists doesn't necessarily mean you should find a way around that, particularly if an honest reading shows how that serves the public interest and doesn't prevent you from operating. In most cases, your best hack is to suck it up and get good at compliance.

5. It's Easier to Tweak than Start from Scratch

When regulation, or the lack of regulation, does stand in the way of your startup furthering the public interest, your easiest path will usually be to find an existing law, regulation, incentive, or tax that you can reinterpret or repurpose, rather than creating something from scratch. This should be obvious, but to see the opportunities for these kinds of subtle hacks you really need to have done your homework.

Reinterpretation is often the easiest approach. Laws and regulations are never perfectly precise and always require some amount of interpretation. It's why many countries have robust judicial traditions. Judges aren't the only ones tasked with interpreting these rules, however. It's the responsibility of regulators and bureaucrats as well. If these officials can change their understanding of what a regulation means with regard to your startup, you may be able to accomplish what you need without having to officially change anything.

6. Use the Local, Esoteric, and Indirect to Your Advantage

Similarly, it's often easier to get things done when you're dealing with something local, esoteric, or indirect. Uber benefited from the fact that it's easier to change laws and regulations at the municipal level than it is at regional or national levels. Kidde benefited from changing esoteric public-health regulations, rather than something more prominent with more stakeholders. TransitScreen benefits from hacks that take indirect advantage of regulations providing waivers to real estate developers. The more local, esoteric, or indirect your hack, the less likely you are to run into opposition and the faster you can get it done.

7. Think Twice Before Poking Big, Scary Bears

The corollary to the last point is that if your hack is to change prominent national regulations, you will face stiff resistance. If you want the U.S. federal government to reduce tax benefits for the oil and gas industry, no realistic amount of capital or creative hacking will lead to success. Big Oil is extremely well organized through the American Petroleum Institute, a single organization with deep pockets and clear priorities, which start with protecting Big Oil's generous tax benefits. You may win the fight. Many things are *possible*. But the odds would be overwhelmingly stacked against you.

8. Rules Are Meant to Be Broken (or at Least Changed)

My father taught me to do my homework if I want to win a game. But he also taught me that rules are meant to be broken, or at least changed. Every year he went to the Virginia General Assembly with a clear focus on a rule he needed changed, eliminated, or added to benefit Metro. He almost always came home having achieved it.

It is possible to bend regulation to your benefit. As you'll read in Chapter 15:

Lobbying, Opower successfully passed a law in Texas mandating their service simply *as a test* as to whether their business model could work. It's actually more common than you might think.

But you cannot assume that policymakers will look at your startup, immediately understand its potential, and go out of their way to figure out the rule changes that need to be made to unleash it. The better you understand why the current rules are the way they are, the better positioned you'll be to propose reasonable and measured changes that help your startup *and* governments further the public interest together.

Remember that new subsidies or tax rebates or waiver programs do not get created on a whim, and your startup may not have the clout to push through a totally new incentive mechanism. On the other hand, getting public officials to simply tweak, repurpose, or reinterpret an existing program can be a much more expeditious route.

Similarly, if you're thinking about proposing a new government rule that could provide incentives to citizens or private institutions to use your product or service, persuading policymakers to create a waiver to a tax or fee is often easier than getting them to provide a subsidy. Money that never arrives hurts less than spending on something new!

If your hack involves changing a rule, then do your homework, sharpen up your narrative, know your data, build your influence, and carefully study the tools in Section 4: The Regulatory Hacker's Toolkit, because you'll want all your firepower ready to go.

9. Never Forget that Hacking Is Creative

Finally, don't limit your creativity when it comes to ways that governments can help you build a market for your product. The public sector interacts with the private sector and citizens in many subtle ways, and you may be able to tap into those interactions for your gain. TransitScreen certainly has.

Having never abandoned the idea of selling to government, Matt and Ryan eventually landed contracts to place their screens in the lobbies of the D.C. Department of Transportation (DDOT) and the D.C. Department of Consumer and Regulatory Affairs (DCRA). The deals themselves weren't big revenue drivers, but then, that wasn't the point.

"If you're going to a meeting at the DDOT or DCRA offices, you're probably a real estate developer coming to talk about the transportation implications of your new project," Ryan explains.

This was better than free advertising. These were two perfectly placed billboards reaching the right audience, and they were billboards that Transit-Screen was being paid to operate. To date, Matt and Ryan say the two screens remain among their most effective promotional strategies.

"We started to see government contracts as a marketing opportunity to our bigger market," Ryan says.

Chapter 11

SELLING WITH SOCIAL IMPACT

Tom Davidson likes sports analogies, and one of his favorites is that "no game has ever been won in the locker room." In other words, he wants his employees out in the field, meeting with clients and partners and other stakeholders, learning everything they can about the environment in which their company operates, not sitting around for hours in meetings or mocking up ideas on whiteboards. "Get out on the field and go learn," he says.

The irony is that, from a business model perspective, Tom has drawn up—and successfully executed—one of the more complex, crisscrossing game plans ever conceived. He explained his unusual business plan and personal journey to a 2015 Georgetown University masterclass coproduced by 1776 on building a company around social impact.[1]

An Oklahoma native who still wears cowboy boots under his jeans, Tom's fascinating career began in politics when he managed to win an open seat in the Maine House of Representatives during his senior year at Bowdoin College. He decided not to seek reelection after three terms, but one of the issues he had worked on during those six years in office would stick with him. Public schools, especially those in poor and underfunded districts, struggled with digital literacy and other areas of education that had been shown to greatly affect student performance.

Tom continued to examine the underlying reasons for the challenges and—even more important—the disparity in the magnitude of the challenges from one school to another. He even traveled across the country in an RV, talking to teachers and parents and superintendents to develop a richer understanding of why schools in low-income areas have a harder time preparing their students for success later in life.

Not surprisingly, a lot came down to money and government funding mechanisms.

More alarming was the realization that, in Tom's view, it simply couldn't be fixed.

"The school funding formulas that run every school that your kids go to, if they go to public schools, are really, really screwed, they make no sense, and they are wildly unfair to kids who grow up in low-income communities," Tom said during an interview in 2015. "The reason why is that so much of it is funded by the local tax base."

He later added, quite emphatically: "This funding inequity is never going to get solved—ever—and there's nothing you can do about it."

Still, this was a massive and important challenge affecting millions of children and their communities, and Tom was hell-bent on finding some way to crack it. He knew parents wanted to solve it, and he knew school districts and their communities wanted to solve it, but none of those stakeholders had the money to pay for it. Somehow, he thought, he had to find a way to motivate institutions that did have the money—namely, well-heeled private-sector institutions—to foot the bill.

And that's precisely what he did.

In 2008, working alongside his cofounders, Tom launched EverFi, a Washington, D.C.–based startup that provides life-skills education curriculum and content to schools without charging students or many of those schools one cent. Instead, the company finds corporations, universities, foundations, and other institutions that benefit from those lessons being taught or that benefit from being seen as helping provide those lessons.

Which lessons? In Tom's words, EverFi's programs "teach kids the things that we all should have learned but nobody actually learns about," subjects like financial literacy, digital literacy and emerging technologies, violence and rape in schools, nutrition and health, and other topics that have been shown to make a major difference in whether students succeed not merely in school, but in life beyond the classroom.

To pay for these courses to be taught in schools that otherwise could never afford them, EverFi has worked with institutions such as American Express,

JP Morgan, Honda, Intel, Comcast, the U.S. Chamber of Commerce Foundation, the John Calipari Foundation, and every NHL and NBA team.

Why do these institutions pick up the tab for the courses?

In many cases, Tom explains, "these are companies that care a lot about the communities where they're based or where they have large employee bases, and we tap into that." He would later add that "these are organizations that have been tied to these schools for a long time. They just haven't been sponsoring curriculum and life skills, they have been doing scoreboards and bake sales and library book giveaways."

A logo on a high school scoreboard, though, doesn't provide the same return as life lessons.

"If you are Principal Financial Group in Iowa, you have a huge interest in kids in west Des Moines becoming technically proficient, understanding big data, coming out with the skills that are going to make them really successful as potential employees," Tom explained. For other companies, like financial-services firms, making sure millennials and the generations behind them are financially literate is an industry-wide imperative. For still others, the simple optics of backing education around a given issue is a major brand win.

Now, that doesn't mean the three-legged business model Tom has cobbled together is easy—quite the opposite, according to Tom, who has called it a "wild west" approach.

"I take issues that are devastatingly difficult issues for families and kids— like bankruptcies and mortgages and payday loans and campus violence and rape—and I put them in front of schools and then I ask corporations to wrap their brands all over it," Tom said with a chuckle in that same 2015 interview. "It's not the most intuitive business model."

What it requires, he added, is "going really high up in the organization, as high as you can possibly go, usually to the CEO, and get them really excited about this." One of the things that gets them most excited, he added, is that EverFi's technology allows them to scale the type of impact they want to have. "Often they already have relationships that they love with other nonprofits or school systems, but what they don't love is that even in their best year they may reach and help sixty-seven students or a hundred and ten students. With our technology, we can bring much greater scale to their efforts."

Tom's "wild west" business model is working. Today, EverFi is working with twenty thousand primary and secondary schools, and more than sixteen million students have completed an EverFi course, thanks to support from more than four thousand partner institutions. As discussed in Chapter 5: Arbitrage, the firm's longtime investors include Jeff Bezos, Eric Schmidt, Ev Williams, Allen & Company, and New Enterprise Associates. In April 2017, EverFi, which has reportedly been profitable for years, raised a $190 million Series D round to fuel and accelerate growth from investors including the TPG Rise Fund, whose cofounders include Bono and Jeff Skoll, eBay's first president.

Business Models Based on Social Impact

In Chapter 3: Business Models, you learned about business models that depend upon social impact, mostly multisided B2C or B2B2C models. Like EverFi's, these business models tend to be complex, but for certain regulated startups they may be the only way to profitably scale your business.

EverFi's business model is B2B2C with a strong social impact component to it. Let's run through everything this involves. EverFi has to identify gaps in life skills for their target students, such as financial literacy, that their online learning tools can address. They need to find schools willing to provide the program to their students. They need to find an institution willing to fund a supplemental learning program for those students. And in order for that corporation to fund the program on a recurring basis, EverFi needs to demonstrate real outcomes, and in certain cases also ensure that the institution looks good in front of citizens or policymakers.

Those are a lot of moving pieces that need to fit together, which makes

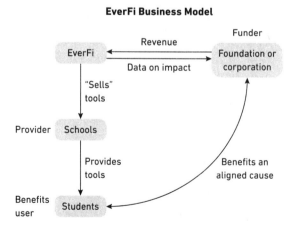

EverFi Business Model

these kinds of business models scary for the faint of heart. But if your goal is to use digital tools to improve life skills for underserved students, then you're going to need to understand the often underappreciated and misunderstood world of social impact and get creative about hacking it.

While regulated business models based on social impact are complex, they share important attributes with more familiar indirect or multisided business models, such as ad-supported models. In ad-supported models, such as Facebook, Google, or *The Washington Post*, a company provides a service to users in return for capturing detailed data about that user. The company then uses that data to precisely target ads for brands willing to pay to reach those audiences.

Why couldn't EverFi provide their programs to schools for their students in exchange for data on the students they could sell to advertisers? Why aren't ad-supported models more common in regulated startups?

Some regulated startups do use ad-supported business models, for example, lightweight health apps selling information about users to brands, most notably pharma companies. But capturing data and selling it to brands can be difficult in complex markets for a variety of reasons, notably privacy concerns. If you're collecting data from an educational tool for kids, like EverFi, or perhaps a mental health app, then it can be difficult to sell that data to third parties in the United States, due to laws like the Family Educational Rights and Privacy Act (FERPA) and the Health Insurance Portability and Accountability Act (HIPAA) that give parents or patients strong protections about what data stewards are allowed to do with their data. In other cases, the barrier may be less regulatory and more about societal norms, where citizens simply aren't comfortable sharing data about sensitive topics.

In these circumstances, you might be able to change your product in ways that allow you to skirt these rules or norms, but doing so might reduce your value proposition significantly. While some health advice apps do generate revenue from pharma companies, these tools have to be careful that they don't capture certain data about you lest they become subject to HIPAA. Unfortunately, much of the data they can't collect is exactly the data that would make them most valuable to a citizen seeking online health advice.

As an alternative to undermining the value of your solution, you can find other ways to get institutions who care about these problems—*or want to be seen to be caring*—to subsidize your users. This is where social impact becomes powerful.

Understanding Social Impact

Social impact is a broad term that can cover different behavior from different types of institutions. I find it helpful, though, to classify the types of institutions supporting programs for social impact into three categories: foundations and nonprofits, governments and NGOs, and corporations.

Foundations and Nonprofits

One form of social impact that's straightforward and intuitive is when foundations or nonprofits choose to support an initiative for philanthropic reasons, meaning because it supports the public interest. Many foundations and nonprofits have been looking to the world of startups and digital technologies to help them crack previously intractable challenges. Foundations with a mission to reduce educational gaps for underserved students may see a startup like EverFi as a more cost-effective way to accomplish their mission than, say, funding in-person after-school programs. For example, Pharrell Williams's foundation, From One Hand To AnOTHER, supports a full range of EverFi courses in his hometown of Virginia Beach. In the same way, the Allan Houston Foundation uses EverFi to provide African American history courses to communities in need, and The Calipari Foundation (founded by John Calipari) uses EverFi to provide financial literacy education to all high schools in Kentucky.

Governments and NGOs

Internationally, donor-funded NGOs and government-backed international development and foreign aid programs can complement foundations. These can be a boon for startups that are trying to solve problems in the public interest that align with those organizations' respective missions. Like foundations, many NGOs and government programs have been experimenting with working with startups to provide new capabilities to help them address their missions.

Grant Brooke, the cofounder of Twiga, has made great use of this kind of social impact funding. Twiga is building agricultural supply chain infrastructure in Kenya that drives cost efficiencies for farmers and vendors alike. Grant recognized that the problem Twiga is solving was one that fell squarely within the mission of certain governmental aid programs. That is, foreign government entities and NGOs had already committed funds to tackle the same challenges Twiga was already addressing.

Two entities that Grant identified were USAID, an arm of the U.S. federal government committed to combatting poverty and furthering socioeconomic development in foreign countries, and Mercy Corps, a global NGO based in Portland, Oregon, whose stated mission is to alleviate suffering, poverty, and oppression by helping people build secure, productive, and just communities. Both entities, Grant learned, were investing millions into major economic development, financial inclusion, and sustainable agriculture projects in East Africa.

Still, historically, they had limited reach into informal farming markets.

With Twiga's work in Kenya, "they knew that 98 percent of the agricultural output is sold within that country, but they had been stuck working with companies that were exporting that other 2 percent, because they needed a formal entity to work with, to funnel donations through, to report back with data on impact, and that just hadn't been possible in this fragmented, informal farming market," Grant explained. "Immediately, it was clear that by bringing farmers and vendors onto our digital platform we could help them do work in those markets they could not reach previously, and that was of value to them."

As a result, for instance, Mercy Corps supported Twiga by providing credit-scoring specialists and liaisons with credit partners in Kenya. This support expanded into a Mercy Corps–backed project with IBM Research to develop algorithms for delivering daily microloans to Twiga's vendor base. IBM was able to use the algorithm to persuade financial institutions to provide microloans to Twiga vendors, which helped Twiga deepen their engagement with clients. Twiga's average drop-size increased 30 percent and cash deliveries waned in favor of mobile money. Mercy Corps, IBM, and Twiga are now working together to scale financing to all of Twiga's vendors and suppliers. This could be a game-changer in African markets where, though 70 percent of the population works in agriculture, only 2 percent of credit goes into the sector.

For Twiga, the nondilutive investment is one that benefits the startup in many ways, most notably by helping its vendors buy more product. For Mercy Corps officials, they get to go back to their donors and provide data-driven evidence to show that they're making real headway toward their stated mission and partnering with a local, innovative company as an added bonus.

"What they want in return is impact data, in the form of vendors reached, and other evidence that they're making an economic impact through the grant," Grant says. "It's really a win for everyone involved: Mercy Corps, IBM, Twiga, our vendors, and consumers."

Corporations

Corporate social responsibility, or CSR, refers to the basket of business practices that many corporations engage in to be a good corporate citizen—and often, as important, to be perceived as one. CEOs and boards are increasingly recognizing that generating value for the entire ecosystem of stakeholders that support the business is vital for the sustainability of the business. These can include not only customers and shareholders, but employees, suppliers and their employees, the communities in which a business operates, and the environment that sustains a business. In turn, citizens are becoming increasingly conscious about the responsible business practices behind a corporation. For many corporations, responsible business practices have become essential to their brand. For others, responsible business practices are a way to mitigate the risk of damage to their brand.

Steve Rochlin, a friend and fellow angel investor with K Street Capital, is one of the more thoughtful people in D.C. about this as the CEO and founder of the consulting film IO Sustainability and the author of CSR management books.

"Customer attitudes in America are finally catching up to those in other countries," Steve explains. "Research shows that up to 20 percent of a company's customers are ready to be activated to make their purchasing decisions based primarily on socially responsible considerations. An additional 40 percent are open to being heavily influenced by CSR in their purchasing decisions. This translates into an opportunity for large established brands to increase revenues from sales by up to 20 percent from their socially responsible activities. For regulatory hackers, these trends represent something else—it's a pathway for them to compete with the large incumbents, outflank them, and seize market share. You can see this starting to happen in the processed food sector."

Depending on whom you ask, CSR can be defined narrowly and focus on the responsibility business practices of a corporation. Or it can be defined more broadly, to include traditional corporate philanthropy, volunteering, and cause marketing, such as the shoe company Tom's giving a bit of their profits on each pair of shoes to a charity. For your purposes, you should be thinking about the opportunities that CSR can represent to your business model as broadly as possible.

There are a variety of reasons why corporations engage in CSR activities—from genuinely altruistic to fairly cynical. In some cases, a company's leadership team or owners have a sincere, personal, and intrinsic motivation to pursue certain causes. Other corporations may see CSR as an extension of their PR efforts, in order to improve the perception of their company to the media, their customers, or policymakers. They may see CSR initiatives as a way to look good to their employees and make them proud to work where they do. Most commonly, such efforts are in line with maintaining a general positive image of the company, but often a company will use it to "whitewash" a negative reputation in one area of their business by doing something positive in another area.

A powerful example of this "whitewashing" (or perhaps "greenwashing" in this case) is Shell. Shell ran an advertising campaign in the UK promoting a factory with flowers coming out of their smokestacks and claiming: "We use our waste CO_2 to grow flowers." There was a grain of truth to this claim. In the Netherlands, Shell did in fact capture CO_2 and use it in floral greenhouses. However, Shell only used 0.325 percent of their CO_2 output in this way. The UK Advertising Standard Authority eventually banned the ad as grossly misleading.[2]

Understanding the underlying motivation can be important for startups seeking to engage with a corporation's CSR efforts. You need to understand what the company wants to get out of it, and how permanent their focus on a given cause or challenge may be. Is this a project near and dear to the current chairman, meaning it may be axed when he steps down next year, or is it aligned with the causes that matter to the firm's customer base, which aren't likely to change anytime soon? Similarly, is this just a short-lived project to distract from a crisis the corporation is dealing with this month? My point being, if you plan to engage in this area, seek to understand the *why* behind the initiatives.

The Scale of the Social Impact Opportunity

It can be easy for startups to think of the world of social impact as a niche opportunity, but that would be short-sighted.

A quick reference to understanding the breadth of challenges that are facing our world is the list of the United Nations Sustainable Development Goals, which include poverty, hunger, health and well-being, education, gender equality, clean water and sanitation, affordable and clean energy, decent work and economic growth, infrastructure, inequality, sustainable cities and communities, responsible consumption and production, climate change, healthy oceans, endangered species, and justice and the rule of law.

Governments, foundations, and corporations around the world are growing in their appreciation of the urgency of these issues, and in particular their interlocking nature. Almost nobody is immune from the risks that inaction on these issues represent in a deeply interconnected world.

The Sustainable Development Goals represent a staggering $12 trillion market opportunity.[3] The Global e-Sustainability Initiative finds that solving these problems represents a $2.1 trillion[4] opportunity for technology startups alone.

These challenges and the opportunities they represent are central to the rise of the Regulatory Era. They represent unprecedented opportunities for innovative, market-driven solutions to address societal challenges that were previously the providence of governments and nonprofit sectors. Tesla is just one prominent example of this. Elon Musk unfailingly argues that Tesla exists to increase the usable life of our planet, profitability merely being a way to make Tesla sustainable, and yet their growth and success in a short time is staggering.

"As we enter the regulatory hacking era," says Steve Rochlin, "the business opportunity is enormous. The range of issues covered by the seventeen UN Sustainable Development Goals would've been viewed in the past as demanding an unfeasible amount of public spending, and by association onerous taxation. Instead, the SDGs are helping us do a one-eighty to look at the tremendous potential of launching innovative and disruptive business models that can be used to address urgent societal challenges."

One exciting idea within the world of social impact is the circular economy, in contrast to the linear economy of make, use, and dispose. The circular economy focuses on business models that keep resources in use for as long as possible, extract the maximum value from them while in use, then recover and regenerate products and materials at the end of each service life. Accenture projects a $4.5 trillion[5] global market opportunity for businesses in these areas.

Another idea gaining traction that presents incredible opportunities for regulatory hackers is the voluntary standards industry. Voluntary standards organizations exist outside government but nonetheless work with businesses to create voluntary standards, regulations enforced by the collective action of citizens. The Forest Stewardship Council is one of the most famous examples. These voluntary standards systems are finding that they need to create for-profit business models to sustain and scale, such as for-profit certification companies. More and more of them are looking to digital technologies for their business models.

Startups and Social Impact

Of course, many of these challenges have existed for a long time. Societies looking to business to solve these challenges isn't new either—it's known as privatization. What's new is that tech startups are able to use software and mobile devices to create radically new solutions to previously intractable challenges, such as Twiga's approach to food inflation in Africa. As emerging technologies like artificial intelligence, autonomous vehicles, robots, synthetic biology, distributed ledgers, and cryptocurrencies bring science fiction to reality, this is only accelerating.

Think about some of the social impact models that digital technologies can enable:

- Reduce the cost per person of critical public services through radically improved efficiency.
- Use data analytics to optimize the right solution delivered at the right time, rather than analyzing social outcomes after the fact through a protracted evaluation process conducted by third parties often under a cloud of resistance and concern over who will be blamed.
- Engage and involve the beneficiaries of social services efficiently, by using digital technologies to empower them to express their needs and feedback, rather than patronizing them with ideas imposed from someone else.
- Enable creativity regarding payment of services, such as creative ways to price and charge for services, ways to generate pay-for-performance schemes, and innovative financing like social bonds.
- Find creative, ethical, and participatory ways to enforce socially responsible regulations, such as a startup that might change the way brands monitor garment factories overseas by giving factory workers private

smartphones and surveying them to ensure they are safe, healthy, and that their rights are protected.

The World of Corporate Social Responsibility

Regulatory hacking holds immense potential across the world of social impact, but arguably holds the most potential in the context of CSR.

"In the CSR arena, regulatory hacking opens up an exciting array of business model opportunities," Steve says. "We're seeing startups that are succeeding by enabling large organizations to outsource societal problem solving to creative entrepreneurs. We're seeing others that are directly competing with anyone and everyone from governments, to nonprofits, to big corporate brands. The opportunities are limited only by the imagination of the entrepreneurs."

To identify CSR-related hacks, you have to understand the forms CSR takes and why corporations invest so much into these initiatives. As discussed, one end of the CSR spectrum involves corporate philanthropy, cause marketing, and volunteering. For your purposes, you can think of those as behaving much the same as other foundations or nonprofit institutions pursuing philanthropic aims. Some of the biggest opportunities for regulatory hacks, however, involve the other end of the spectrum with cause promotions, which refer to company-funded advocacy campaigns that support a certain social policy change, corporate social marketing practices (through which the company finances behavior-change campaigns), and responsible business practices.

Responsible Business Practices

Any large corporation that sells a product or service to consumers will inevitably have an extensive supply chain, which means that they buy many intermediate goods and services in the process of producing their final goods and services. The decisions they make about whom to work with along that supply chain have the potential to significantly impact the public interest—either positively or negatively. You should be thinking about this as a regulatory hacker if only because of the scale: Responsible business practice initiatives now cover a significant proportion of global value-chain activity and therefore cover a huge amount of economic activity.

Corporations that don't take responsibility for their supply chains expose themselves to the risk of severely damaging their reputations, which can cost an enormous amount of time and money to amend, both in legal courts and in the court of public opinion. Examples include the tragic collapse of the substandard Savar building in Bangladesh in 2013, which killed more than a thousand garment factory workers and pushed companies in the apparel industry to reconsider the impact of their operations on society and the environment. That same year, a horsemeat scandal broke out in the United Kingdom, affecting scores of retailers, including Tesco, the nation's largest retailer, and leading to the supplier's dismissal.

These events and others like them have pushed corporations across numerous industries to pursue standards for suppliers in relation to human rights, labor practices, and sustainable environmental impact. Companies are no longer sitting around waiting for the next unwanted surprise to spring up in their supply chains.

How is this relevant to you as a regulatory hacker? Let's say you have an app that helps small farmers in underdeveloped countries monitor food quality and safety. Chances are, those farmers are already operating on razor-thin margins, and they aren't going to have cash lying around to invest in your app. However, Amazon's Whole Foods, or Walmart, or even Dole or Nestlé might be willing to pay for it on behalf of those farmers to 1) ensure strong food-safety compliance, and 2) show the public that they are invested in food safety.

The play here is to find a cash-rich corporation that cares about or benefits from solving the same problem you're trying to solve for your cash-strapped customer. If you can do that, you can easily find yourself with a profitable and scalable regulated business model that leverages social responsibility.

Cause Marketing

Cause marketing, or initiatives that serve the dual purpose of increasing profitability while simultaneously bettering society, hold some of the biggest opportunities for regulatory hackers to leverage CSR in their business model. EverFi has been masterful in building this into their regulated business model.

It works like this: EverFi identifies the sweet spots between what students need and what causes corporations want to support. For example, they've gotten more than 750 banks and financial institutions to fund financial literacy programs in primary and secondary schools across the United States. These programs help these institutions create more responsible, financially informed citizens. They also help students and their parents associate the institutional sponsor with these products. More important, though, they demonstrate to a much broader range of citizens and policymakers that the institution is committed to supporting their communities.

In a similar way, Mondelez International, one of the world's largest makers of snacks and candy bars, uses EverFi to provide their "After School All-Stars" initiative, providing nutrition and fitness education to middle schools students across America. The GE Foundation uses EverFi to provide their Brilliant Career Lab initiative, exposing Boston students to innovative, digital, industrial jobs of the future using online and hands-on STEM education. (GE recently moved their headquarters to Boston.)

The Sustainability of Social Impact Hacks

As you can see, the world of social impact, whether philanthropic or CSR, presents interesting opportunities and tools for regulatory hackers. Before you move too far down this path, though, you should explore some key questions.

Six Questions to Ask Before Selling with Social Impact
1. Should you use social impact as a supplement to your business model or as its foundation?
2. Is the social impact initiative sustainable?
3. Are there enough social impact partners to build a market?
4. Is providing value to your social impact partner compatible with your users and providers?
5. Is providing value compatible with regulation?
6. Can you be transparent and produce a win-win-win?

First, are you using social impact initiatives as a supplement to your business model—for example, helping you to enhance your product or unlock a market? Twiga has made excellent use of social impact initiatives in this way, but their business model does not depend upon them. Rather, they're using CSR as a form of nondilutive investment capital, reducing the need for equity investment. Or alternatively, are you making social impact initiatives a structural element to some or all of your business model, like EverFi, where foundations and CSR budgets provide a primary source of revenue for many of their products?

Second, if social impact initiatives are going to be a structural element of your business model, is this sustainable? Or, put another way, is the initiative a pet project or is it something structurally important to a company's business as well, such as a maker of snacks and candy needing to promote health and fitness? If it's a CSR cause marketing play, are you able to help drive profitability for the corporation as well as its benefits to the public interest?

Third, still assuming social impact initiatives are going to be fundamental to your business model, are there enough potential partners out there to build a market? EverFi has done this exceptionally well, finding numerous foundations and CSR programs willing to fund a relatively uniform set of educational programs.

Questions two and three point to the imperative for sustainability in your social impact partner base. As you explore your regulated business models, you don't want to confuse a few corporations pursuing short-term pet projects with a billion-dollar market into which you can scale your startup.

Fourth, can you provide the value that your social impact partner seeks in a way that's compatible with providing a service in the interest of your beneficial users (students, in EverFi's case) or providers (schools, in EverFi's case)? Are the compromises that you might need to make to satisfy the people giving you revenue going to turn off the people you're ultimately trying to benefit? For example, at 1776, Philip Morris, the maker of Marlboro cigarettes, approached us about funding a program for health startups. We were clear that while *some* health startups might participate in such a program, most would not want to be associated with Philip Morris on any terms.

Fifth, continuing on that theme, can you provide value to your social impact partner in a way that's compliant with regulations, such as HIPAA or FERPA? If not, can you get those regulations waived or modified, given your impact on the public interest?

Finally, the ultimate gut check, can you make your business model work based on social impact in a way that's transparent and enhances everyone's brand? This is crucial to sustainability. Everyone involved in these complex business models should understand everyone else's involvement and what they hope to gain from it. Nobody should be surprised if a journalist someday writes an article implying that evil Big Business is secretly trying to convince our impressionable middle schoolers to eat more candy bars under the guise of a nutrition program. Rather, everyone should be able to proudly respond with excitement about the team of partners that have come together to enhance the public interest!

Competing for Social Impact Funds

There's another wrinkle to consider when wading into the social impact arena, and that's whom you may be competing against. While every startup is competing with other for-profit ventures to gain customers, a company like EverFi is vying for business that might otherwise go to endearing nonprofits—something that Tom is keenly aware of when making his pitch to potential customers.

"We compete against longstanding, amazing nonprofits," Tom said, noting that when pursuing CSR customers for its financial literacy programs, EverFi could be vying for the same dollars as a nonprofit like Junior Achievement, and in its emerging nutrition and childhood obesity curriculums, EverFi may be trying to secure money that could have gone to a foundation like Michelle Obama's Let's Move program. He continued, jokingly, "So here's me, saying 'Don't go with Junior Achievement, those awful people helping great kids learn great things,' or 'Don't go with Michelle Obama, who's trying to help kids lead healthier lives, forget that.'"

More seriously, he noted, when you're competing for social impact revenue that might otherwise go to a nonprofit, you can find yourself at a financial disadvantage given the tax breaks afforded to your competitors. Speaking about the tax disparity, Tom noted, "In many ways, we often feel like we're fighting with one hand tied behind our back."

Pursuing Social Impact Hacks

If you think that the world of social impact, either traditional philanthropy or CSR initiatives, could help you find a business model that scales, then you should reread Section 2: The Foundations of Regulatory Hacking and make sure you're incredibly strong on narrative, data, and influence.

Many of your social impact partners will want to be associated with your brand and therefore you'll need to clearly communicate your *why* and how you're helping improve the lives of citizens. In this sense, your brand really does become part of your product, almost like a media company selling ad space to brands. You have to make sure that the brands want to be associated with you in a way that helps them show they're benefiting society.

Data is also incredibly important. Many foundations, nonprofits, government aid programs, and CSR initiatives struggle to find evidence that validates the impact of their programs. One of your biggest advantages as a sophisticated regulatory hacker should be that your startup has built data into the core of what you do. Whom have you served? What outcomes have you achieved? How do you compare with alternative approaches to solving this problem?

Finally, foundations, government aid organizations, and CSR initiatives can be a world unto themselves. Many of them are increasingly interested in what startups are doing and how they can work with them, but you'll find that having a strong network of influencers will help you gain access to people who can help, so you can quickly execute build-measure-learn cycles to see how social impact can help you find a business model that scales or can complement your existing business model in powerful ways.

SECTION 4

The Regulatory Hacker's Toolkit

Chapter 12

THE MEDIA

Nora Khaldi's first hire for Nuritas was a computer scientist, which was an obvious move when you're building AI software that must sift through billions and billions of data points about plant and animal genomes in a quest for new treatments and medicines.

Her second hire, however, was Meaghan Lee-Erlandsen.

An American from Atlanta, Lee-Erlandsen graduated with degrees in sociology and film from Georgia State University before working as a legal assistant for law firms in Georgia. She moved across the pond in 2013 to pursue a master's degree in popular literature from Trinity College in Dublin. She was, in other words, a surprise third employee for a startup ripped from the pages of science fiction.

"I can still remember the response from the VCs I was meeting with at the time," Nora recalls with a smile. "One of them asked me, 'Why would you hire a writer and a regulatory person rather than investing in another computer scientist or a commercial person?'"

Khaldi knew what she needed.

"At that point, I needed someone who could do two things: someone who could read and make sense of these heavy regulatory and legal documents, and someone who knew how to write and work with the media," she says. "I wanted to get the word about us out there." It actually helped, she adds, that Lee-Erlandsen didn't have a scientific background at all, because it forced Nora to learn to translate what Nuritas was doing into plain language.

"Meaghan helped us put things in simple language and reach a broader audience," Nora says.

The strategy paid dividends, as Nuritas quickly began generating earned media in major pharmaceutical journals and other industry-specific publications. One story in particular, which was published in a prominent journal in 2015, caught the attention of a major investor more than ten thousand miles away in Singapore. He would go on to lead Nuritas's seed round a few months later. "That story in the journal was where the conversation started," Khaldi says.

"For us," she adds, "the media and conferences were the best way for us to reach the audiences we needed to reach, including industry leaders and investors. They were both very valuable as I started trying to build a business network, because my entire network when we got started was in academia. There was no better way to let the world know what we were doing."

Nora and Lee-Erlandsen's skill at using the media to explain the intricacies of peptides and food science to a mainstream audience continues to pay dividends, with Nuritas recently raising a $20 million Series A led by Chicago-based Cultivian Sandbox Ventures. This brings the total invested to date to approximately $30 million, including early funding from Singapore-based VisVires New Protein, Marc Benioff, Ali Partovi, and U2 rockers Bono and The Edge.

The Media

This chapter has a catchy but misleading title. Commentators love to speak knowingly of "the media" as if there were a single, monolithic medium of communication with the public. In fact, this chapter might more aptly be titled "the many mediums." Think about a journalist with *The Washington Post*. Talking with that reporter is one avenue of communication that an organization might use to reach the public. Then again, that organization could also choose to write a post on Medium and reach that same public in a different way. The organization could share that post on Facebook and run ads to promote it to a targeted audience. Same message, same organization, same public, but different media and somewhat different audiences. In fact, I would argue there are more media available today to reach the public than at any time in human history.

Although there are many media through which startups can reach the public, this chapter is primarily, though not exclusively, concerned with reaching the public through the persuasion of credible third-party storytellers. The art and science of developing a favorable public image for your startup through third-party storytellers is called public relations. Public relations is about getting those with access and credibility among a public audience to like you and say things that make others like you, too. Or when the crap hits the fan, to at least mitigate the damage.

Media in general, and public relations specifically, are useful to virtually any startup. A *Fast Company* cover story about a hot, new dating app could result in hundreds or even thousands of new signups, whereas a piece in the *Wall Street Journal* about an up-and-coming social media site raising a new round of funding can help that startup continue to expand awareness and visibility. Likewise, a local television hit or a cable news segment that features a startup's new e-commerce or delivery technology can provide new inbound marketing leads or land on the radars of additional investors.

As you'll learn throughout this chapter, though, public relations is particularly important to you as a regulatory hacker, and is a tool that you should have natural advantages in wielding, if you know what you're doing.

Media: Earned, Owned, and Paid

Before we get into the specific of public relations for regulated startups, though, it's important to run through a primer on the kinds of media you have at your disposal as a regulatory hacker.

Every medium to reach the public will cost you, but not all will cost you in the same ways. Public relations, or working through credible third-party storytellers, doesn't involve the exchange of money, but it does require a lot of work. For this reason, it's often referred to as *earned media*. Earned media includes traditional news publishers such as *The Washington Post* or the *Financial Times*, television news such as CNN or your local news station, and digital-only sites such as Axios or BuzzFeed. Depending on the level of credibility and independence, it can even include bloggers and podcasters.

Almost all media that isn't earned is either "owned media" or "paid media." Owned media means using the channels that you build and control to reach the audiences who have chosen to follow and listen to you directly. This might include social media channels, a blog, a video channel, or other content repositories over which you have total control. Meanwhile, "paid media" means forking over cash to place your message or your brand in front of the audience you want to reach. This might include digital advertising, like sponsored content or promoted social media posts, or traditional advertising, like magazine ads or billboards.

There are advantages and disadvantages to each method. With owned media, you retain total control over the message you're distributing and the story you're telling, but your reach will be limited to your existing network or those who have chosen to listen to you, and it can take a while to build that audience. With paid media, you retain nearly total control over the message and the story, depending on the platform or channel you're using, and you gain the benefit of reach. And, especially with modern digital marketing tools, you can with sometimes frightening accuracy segment and target the audiences you most want to reach. Just like owned media, the main drawback with paid media, in addition to costing a pretty penny, which can be prohibitive for cash-strapped startups, is again related to credibility. An audience knows that you paid to put that message in front of them. They know it's a message and a story that has been shaped by you and you alone, and they know you're biased. Consequently, both owned and paid media strategies suffer from significant trust deficiencies.

For regulated startups that will impact the public interest, credibility, as you've learned throughout this book, is essential. And that's exactly why earned media is most likely to be your most effective means of sharing your narrative and seeding goodwill toward your startup.

Of the three options outlined above, only with earned media does your story or the message you're trying to share get communicated via an unbiased, credible source. Only with productive earned media, then—which, again, is generated by successful public relations activities—can you mitigate skepticism from citizens about new products or services that could impact their health or how their kids are educated.

Of course, the downside of earned media is that you retain far less control over the message, as you ultimately turn over the story to someone outside your organization. At best, this may lead to stories about your company that aren't told precisely the way you would have framed them. At worst, you may run into reporters or bloggers who downright misquote you or misrepresent your company, or even cast your company in an unfavorable light, for one reason or another. But this is the price you pay to achieve a higher level of credibility than you would otherwise through owned or paid media strategies.

Three Types of Media		
Earned	*Owned*	*Paid*
Message interpretation	Message control	Message control
Reach	Limited reach	Reach
Credibility	Limited credibility	Limited credibility
Hard work	Hard work	Expensive

Stephanie Cutter, best known as the deputy campaign manager for President Barack Obama's 2012 reelection campaign and now a founding partner with Precision Strategy, knows how to drive a message with the media with force and clarity.

"Traditionally, earned media is worth much more than paid media because it's a more credible source than tooting your own horn," Stephanie says. "It can help you shape your own storyline, market your product, and appeal to people who may not be open to you through direct marketing. It's also free, which for a startup, means *everything*. For some companies, investing in a public relations person or agency is one of the best investments they'll make."

With that in mind, think of public relations in much the same way you think about influencers. They are both third-party validators with enough access to help you build awareness about the problem your startup is trying to solve and enough credibility to limit any inherent skepticism about your company and your solution. And they both require effort and investment to get right.

The difference is that influencers tend to help you reach and sway a small but pivotal audience of decision makers and power players, whereas earned media can generally help you reach and sway a larger but less-well-connected audience.

For most regulatory hackers, both are enormously important. Luckily, success in one area can breed success in the other. A feature story on your startup in a prominent publication could help get the attention of influencers you have been courting, or ones you didn't even know were out there. On the flip side, many influencers are naturally well connected with journalists, especially ones who cover their fields of expertise, and the influencers you recruit into your fan club may be able to make connections with journalists, or their editors, and otherwise elevate your public relations efforts.

In short, public relations can help your regulated startup *credibly* share your story, improve your public image, and garner goodwill among your current and potential customers, investors, regulators, and other stakeholders by transmitting your story and your message via a trusted third-party validator.

Wietse Van Ransbeeck can attest to the power of public relations.

Van Ransbeeck is the CEO and cofounder of CitizenLab, a Belgian civic engagement startup that seeks to bring town hall meetings online and allow citizens to more easily contribute ideas and provide feedback to public sector officials. Launched in 2015 with a working prototype, Van Ransbeeck says his team struggled to establish credibility before they had acquired any clients, and even getting meetings with the right city officials to pitch their product was laborious.

"We struggled quite a bit to land out first customer," he says. "We just didn't have any references. So instead, we relied on public relations to gain access and credibility."

Van Ransbeeck pitched the CitizenLab platform to an online community called Springwise, which relies on a network of more than twenty thousand individuals who essentially crowdsource ideas and content about the most disruptive new trends and technologies from across the globe.[1] That pitch resulted in a glowing article about CitizenLab that was published on the Springwise blog in September 2015. In the days after the story came out, the phone began ringing nonstop for Van Ransbeeck and his team, and not just from Belgian cities. Government leaders across the world, from Rio de Janeiro to Riyadh, saw the story and reached out to learn more, too.

"That shows you the kind of credibility you can gain from investing in public relations," Van Ransbeeck says.

Of course, to some extent, the credibility of earned media is valuable for any startup, but it's *particularly* important for regulatory hackers.

The dating app founder need only convince bliss-searching singles that her service will create collisions with promising prospects. The social media founder need only convince users that they can connect more easily or in new ways with their social or professional networks. And the e-commerce founder need only convince buyers and sellers that her company's service makes it easier to process transactions or cheaper to move goods from one place to another.

Compare that to the credibility bar that a healthcare startup's founders must clear. They will need to convince hospitals or health systems that they will save money or be more efficient by deploying the startup's technology. They may need to assure patients and patient rights groups that the deployment of the technology leads to better or at least neutral health outcomes for those who are being treated. They may need to convince doctors and nurses that their solution will make those individuals' jobs easier. And they may very well need to convince regulators at multiple levels that their product or service is safe or secure.

That's a much harder sell. But it's easier if you have credible voices helping you make that sell, and that's where earned media can become so powerful for regulated startups in complex markets. Ola Doudin has seen firsthand how powerful the credibility of earned media can be for BitOasis, her Dubai-based cryptocurrency wallet and exchange, especially with specific and important audiences.*

"Some of the press we've received has helped me start conversations with regulators," she says. "In the media, we're talking about BitOasis and our approach to regulations and compliance, but we're also talking about the benefits of Bitcoin and why we should be embracing that technology, and that has been well received by regulators, too."

And You Should Crush Public Relations

Beyond credibility, there's another reason why, as a regulatory hacker, you should focus on earned media: You *should* have significant natural advantages. Think about it: Every reporter wants to write a story about an endearing founder with a new idea who has overcome daunting odds to solve a previously intractable problem to the benefit of everyday citizens.

Put differently, if you've nailed the basics of regulatory hacking you learned about in Section 2: The Foundations of Regulatory Hacking, then you should already have the tools at your fingertips to give reporters exactly what they already want.

Your narrative is the foundation of any public relations strategy. If you've followed the framework you learned in Chapter 6: Narrative, then you're already adept at telling a great story about your regulated startup. Even more important, your story is all about the *why* of your business, laying out your

---

*You first met Ola and BitOasis back in Chapter 4: Growth.

mission in a way that ties directly back to what it means for citizens. The hardest part for most startups is simply answering the "so what" objection to reporters, or why their audience should care about yet another SaaS marketing tool. Your regulated startup is inspiring, though, precisely because it's not yet another SaaS marketing tool, but rather something that impacts our real, gritty lives as citizens. You are doing what everyone secretly hopes that *someone* in the world is working on. So be that person and give that story to reporters.

There is a catch to your narrative, though. You have to be *really* good at telling your story in a simple way. Even great reporters struggle with complexity. By definition, you operate in a complex market. What that means is that it's your job to distill all that complexity down into a simple, clear, compelling story, like Lee-Erlandsen helped Nora do for Nuritas. If you rely on a reporter to do it, then they will probably get it wrong.

In addition to your narrative, if you've followed the framework in Chapter 7: Data, then you should have compelling data, which is pure gold to a journalist. In an era of diminishing trust in any source of authority, data-driven evidence becomes only more valuable. This is certainly true for the growing number of sites focused on storytelling through data analysis, such as Nate Silver's FiveThirtyEight.com and the *New York Times*'s Upshot blog. But evidence-based storytelling is valuable for almost any journalist.

Again, though, just because journalists love data, it doesn't mean they're adept at understanding or working with it. It's up to you to take the data about the urgency or size of the problem you're solving, or the outcomes that your solution is having for citizens, and turn that into clear evidence that journalists can use. The simpler and more compelling the evidence you compile, the easier it will be for a journalist to write the story and the greater the odds will be that they get it right.

Of course, data isn't the only form of evidence you can provide a journalist. You can also give them the stories of the real-life citizens who have benefited from your solution. The trifecta for a reporter is a simple story about an endearing founder, clear data to validate impact, and an actual citizen whose life is better because of that impact.

"Regulatory hackers have something that a lot of other companies don't have: a good storyline," Stephanie emphasizes. "Hackers are fixing glitches in the system, making our world work better, saving money, and producing better outcomes. So, by the nature of what you're doing, you're an interesting story to the media, you just need to figure out how to tell it. Hard numbers give you credibility, while colorful anecdotes of people you've helped or money you've saved write the story."

Finally, as discussed above, influence matters. If you've executed on the advice in Chapter 8: Influence, then you should have a strong network of influencers with their own access and credibility with journalists relevant to your complex market. Use them. If you've built the trifecta, then your influencers are actually earning currency with the journalists they know by giving them your compelling story.

The Two Ways to Earn Media

Okay, so public relations is important to any startup, but particularly important to your regulated startup. And you've built the foundation of narrative, data, and influence to execute a great public relations strategy. But how do you "do" public relations? How do you land, or land in, that favorable story? How do you do it over and over again for your startup to create that ephemeral asset called buzz?

Let's start by talking about the two ways your startup can earn media:

Option one: Create a story.

Option two: Ride a wave.

Create a Story

Creating a story is the more common but slightly more challenging tactic. Here, you're trying to persuade a journalist to write or produce a story that's about you, your regulated startup, or something your regulated startup has done lately. Commonly, this is done when your company has news to share, as most, but not all, journalists will want to have what's known as a news "hook" or "peg." The hook is basically the "so what," or the reason they are publishing the piece now and why their readers, listeners, or viewers should be interested in reading, listening to, or watching that story right now.

For any startup, including regulated startups, common news hooks include product or market launches, closing a funding round, a merger or acquisition, a new senior hire, an award, or something of that nature. For regulated startups in particular, regulatory actions or unique partnerships between your regulated startup and a government or institution can also be compelling hooks. The Uber playbook spun earned media gold from every attempt by a

taxicab commission to shut them down in a city. Although certain media outlets, such as magazines, may be inclined to publish "feature" or "interest" stories that don't depend on a news hook, you will generally find better success
creating a story if you have news to share.

"Journalists like to identify a problem, and then provide a solution to that
problem," Stephanie stresses. "Regulatory hackers can offer both, and often can
play into a narrative that's long been out there—that regulations can sometimes
impede creative and cost-effective solutions."

Once you have your news hook, the standard procedure is to create and
distribute a press release. A well-crafted press release will clearly and succinctly articulate the news you want to share, provide the voice of the founder
by way of a quote or statement, provide a validating quote by a credible partner
or official, and provide adequate background on your regulated startup for
those reporters or producers who may be unfamiliar.

If you have a great hook, then you may actually have competition amongst
journalists to be the first to make your story public, or "break" it. In this case,
before you issue a press release, you'll be pitching your story to reporters and
determining to whom to give an *exclusive*. With story pitches, you provide
enough information about the story to entice journalists, but you do it *off the
record*. As you pitch journalists and determine who is interested, you negotiate
the parameters of an article before granting an exclusive. In general, when
granting an exclusive, it's fair game to negotiate the placement or location of
an article or segment, when it would be released, who will be interviewed and
quoted, and perhaps even what topics will or won't be on the table. Implicitly,
you're also trying to glean the angle that the journalist would likely take in
writing the story. It goes without saying that you want to find one who will
present your story in a favorable light, or at least fairly.

Of course, the inverse is also true. While you might think everything your
regulated startup does it interesting, journalists may not find your hook particularly compelling, in which case placing a print story or generating a television segment all about your company and its recent developments can be
awfully challenging. Remember that although closing a Series A round or hiring a new senior engineer may be big moments for your regulated startup,
there are probably dozens of other startups who have done the same that week,
and many of them may have pitched the reporter a very similar story.

It's helpful to understand and consider the questions a journalist is going
to ask when reviewing your pitch or your press release. Some of these include:

Do I really care about this? Will my editor care about this? Will my readers care about this? Will they care about it enough that they will not only click to read this story but also share it and talk about it online? Would publishing this story give me any type of advantage or a win over my competitors? How does this story fit in with what I have published recently or the assignments I'm working on currently?

If you're going to need to work to get your story out there, then it's very important that you be able to answer these questions for a reporter. That means doing your homework, starting with the audience you want to reach, understanding where they go for information, researching which journalists produce well-regarded pieces in those places, and then figuring out what other articles those journalists have written. That process should give you great context in being able to answer those questions and craft your story in a way designed to appeal to the most important journalists for your audience.

And again, if your goal is to place an authentic story in which your regulated startup is the focal point, focus on the ways your startup's new technologies, products, or services are improving the lives of citizens, and by extension, the lives of that media outlet's audience. You need to do the work to give the journalists the trifecta.

Guillermo Pepe, the founder of Mamotest, has also carefully leveraged public relations to gain access and credibility.*

"The media have written many positive articles about us in local newspapers and done interviews on television," Pepe says. "That led to more civility around what we were trying to do, which made it easier to get meetings with mayors and governors of the provinces."

Another proven method to generate earned media? Offer data.

The media is increasingly looking to tell data-driven stories, and new research can provide an excellent hook for a journalist. This might be the results of a study you're conducting for other reasons, but it could also be a study conducted specifically to spark media coverage. HopSkipDrive, for instance, conducts a survey of working parents every year to produce a State of Back to School Transportation in America report,[2] which has fueled stories mentioning HopSkipDrive on the likes of Parents.com[3] and WorkingMother.com.[4]

Sometimes, you may not need to generate external data; rather, you can

---

*You met Pepe and Mamotest in Chapter 6: Narrative.

simply package insights you're already gleaning into bait for a reporter. Airbnb does this beautifully by sending out press releases about travel destination trends and the most sought-after types of vacation homes, all by simply compiling and distributing data-driven lists or reports that make for simple but compelling stories for the media.[5]

Ride a Wave

As an alternative to creating a story, you can look to ride a wave. This move is all about being opportunistic and actively looking for stories where you may be able to insert yourself or your company into the broader zeitgeist. Maybe the stock market plunged, and your cryptocurrency startup gives you a unique perspective into the reasons why it happened. Maybe there's a major new development around autonomous vehicle technology or sharing economy regulations and you can provide an insider's take on what it all means for the "road ahead." Or maybe there's simply an ongoing news cycle stemming from a political scandal or industry upheaval or legislative debate and your startup is uniquely positioned to inject itself into the story in a positive way.

The idea here is to play a smaller role in a bigger story. Even though your company may only garner a quick mention or you may only appear in a short quote in the story, these media hits can be equally valuable and can be easier to obtain, because they're stories that journalists are either already writing or are looking for a unique angle into. If you can provide that unique voice or perspective on the bigger picture, that will greatly bolster your public relations efforts, and earn goodwill with reporters that you may be able to cash in later.

Ola Doudin has been able to ride two powerful waves in generating earned media for BitOasis in the Middle East: fascination with cryptocurrencies and excitement about the growth of the startup ecosystem in the region. It's rare to read about Bitcoin in a Middle Eastern publication without seeing BitOasis's name and a quote from Ola. Serving as an exemplar for the transformative power of startups for the region has been nearly as important. "*Forbes Middle East*, for instance, covered us as part of a big piece that they did on entrepreneurship in the region, and that was an important piece for us," Ola says.

Of course, today's hot topic could be a distant memory tomorrow, so you have to be ready to pounce when relevant stories or trends surface. This is where a timely email pitch to a journalist can prove effective. Far less formal than a press release, an email pitch should grab a journalist's attention by quickly flagging the bigger news story or trend that you can give them a new or different perspective on.

Sometimes, this can be as simple as working that broader story into a press release headline, just as Valor Water did when they distributed a release in June 2016 carrying the header: "San Francisco Company Closes $1.6M Round to Deliver Water Loss Analytics *to Help Utilities Cope with the Drought*."[6] With those last seven words, suddenly it's not just technology or startup reporters who may be interested in reading the release and potentially covering the story; it's environmental or local beat writers, too. And for those who are on the former beats, the timely hook is enticing. A story that ran in TechCrunch the day after the release began: "Faced with droughts and an increasing environmental effort in America to conserve water, utility companies have struggled . . ."[7]

For issues that are less fleeting, you can take a longer-term approach to riding the wave of interest in a given topic by inserting yourself into events and forums about the issue that you expect media to attend and cover. In addition, you can either package up data that your startup has collected that might be interesting to a journalist or conduct separate market research that supports the message you would like to convey to the public and serve that up to the media.

Again, as a regulatory hacker, you should have an advantage on riding waves. Journalists love to cover public interest stories. As a regulatory hacker, your startup is all about the public interest. What you have to do is be creative in thinking about all the ways in which you can connect your regulated startup to the zeitgeist of the moment.

Another route is to write and pitch an opinion-editorial, or *op-ed*. Op-eds are columns written and contributed by a nonmember of the media sharing a subjective view on an issue or question of the day. Most often, they make an argument for or against something, although some merely comment on or pose new questions about an ongoing debate. In terms of credibility, op-eds fall somewhere between owned media and earned media; that is, because they are written by you and not an unbiased journalist, and because they appear as an opinion piece and not a pure editorial piece of reporting, they will be perceived as less credible than true earned media. Still, op-eds must be approved by a publication's editor to run in a newspaper or online, so there is some degree of third-party validation at play, as most editors won't run simply anything.

One additional key point about earned media: Don't limit your thinking to traditional news outlets and publications. Today, citizens get their news from and consume content from myriad sources. Most notably, blogs and so-cial media channels have become go-to sources for the latest news and develop-ments, and your public relations strategy should reflect those trends. Getting an influential blogger in your industry or a civic activist with five million fol-lowers to share your story can make just as much if not more of a public rela-tions impact as placing a more traditional piece in a more formal publication.

There's no better example here than HopSkipDrive, which has managed to secure profiles in national publications like *The New York Times*, the *Los Angeles Times*, and CNN Money to go along with feature stories in *Fortune* mag-azine and *Entrepreneur*. But because of the audience HopSkipDrive needs to reach, no less important to the company are the stories on the company pub-lished by the so-called mommy bloggers behind L.A. Parent, Romper, Mod-ernMom, The Family Savvy, and Macaroni Kid. Sure, those sites reach fewer readers than *The New York Times*, but they are reaching precisely the right audience.

There are other plusses to consider with bloggers, too. For instance, Hop-SkipDrive provided a custom discount code for a free first ride that was pub-lished by the author of the Macaroni Kid blog—a win-win-win for readers who got discount codes, the blogger who was able to give a value add to her readers, and HopSkipDrive which got a promotional placement in front of a target audience. Rarely would you see something like that included at the bottom of a traditional media story.[8]

Today, it matters less whether your story is being told in a 10,000-word profile or a 280-character tweet. What matters is that the story is interesting, the story is endearing, and the story is reaching the right audience.

Amplify Your Earned Media with Owned and Paid

Just because earned media should be your focus as a regulatory hacker, that doesn't mean you should ignore owned media and paid media. In fact, owned media and paid media are critical components to your public relations strategy.

Our experience at 1776 and now Union is a great example. Morgan Gress, our marketing guru, has built a powerful owned media channel, with almost fifty thousand people reading our email newsletter each week and nearly ninety thousand Twitter followers and a similar complement on Facebook. Our owned media channels reach precisely the audience that is important to us: startups, investors, institutions, and policymakers interested in innovative ways to solve challenges in complex markets. We actually have much greater reach to our audience than many earned media outlets do. But they have *credibility*. The magic formula, then, is to earn the article in the credible third-party publication, whether about us or a startup in our community, then amplify it through our owned channels.

We can do the same with paid media. We've developed detailed look-alike models for social media advertising so that we can very precisely promote stories on Facebook and Twitter to startups, investors, institutions, and policymakers by geography or industry. We can then earn a story in a credible publication, then share it on our Facebook page and spend a few hundred dollars to flood the story to exactly the audience we want to reach.

Where this really gets interesting is when your owned media channels begin to fuel or contribute to more earned media. Instead of taking the time to source a quote via a phone interview or even over email, an increasing number of journalists are content with pulling text directly from a company's blog post or simply embedding a tweet or Facebook post into their story, which then serves as the voice of the organization where a more traditional press release quote might have otherwise stood. You can create a virtuous circle where you earn some media and amplify it through your owned media channels, which then sparks more earned media. This is how you start to engineer the impression of buzz within your complex market.

As Stephanie puts it: "It's campaigning 101 to take a mainstream media story or editorial and put some paid dollars behind it. You get the best of both worlds: the independent credibility of an earned media piece with the targeted reach of ad dollars to expand its impact. Short attention spans in a 24/7 media world mean you can't take for granted that someone will read the newspaper or watch television on the specific date and time your story runs. But, if you put a small amount of paid behind it—whether it's on Facebook, search, LinkedIn, or wherever you think your targeted audience spends most of its time—you'll get more out of that story with very little effort."

The bottom line is that you can't think about these earned, owned, and paid media channels in a vacuum. A smart regulatory hacker looking to accrue influence, access, and credibility will devise a public relations strategy that considers all three options and how they can play off one another.

Chapter 13

GRASSROOTS

On a cloudy Monday morning in July 2015, a group of San Francisco home-owners and affordable housing activists walked into the city's elections office and submitted more than fifteen thousand signatures in favor of a new ballot initiative that would become known as Proposition F. One week later, the city verified the signatures and officially added the ballot for the upcoming city elections that November.[1]

For Airbnb, it was the moment to pull out all the stops.

Airbnb had been founded seven years ago In the same city to connect trav-elers to property owners offering short-term rentals. One of the darlings of the sharing economy, Airbnb had by that summer of 2015 raised nearly $800 mil-lion and had a valuation upwards of $20 billion.[2]

During its meteoric rise, the startup had skirmished with affordable hous-ing advocates, hotel lobbyists, and city officials who had attempted to tighten rental regulations to shield their cities from what some worried would be the ill effects of the company's entry into their markets. However, unlike Uber, Airbnb had until then been handling their regulatory fights fairly discreetly.

Not any longer. Now officially slated for a vote in four months' time, Prop F placed Airbnb's fate in the San Francisco area with voters. If approved, the ballot measure would considerably toughen regulations on short-term rentals of residential apartments and homes across the city. For instance, the measure called for limiting vacation rentals of entire units (as opposed to single rooms) to seventy-five days a year, down from ninety, ratcheting up potential enforcement and penalties, and creating windfall payouts for neighbors who success-fully sued violators.[3]

Although the rule would hurt other short-term rental platforms like VRBO and HomeAway, there was no mistaking that Airbnb was the primary target of Prop F's proponents. Their argument: Airbnb-style rentals were crippling the city's already limited housing supply, as they encouraged property owners to cater to short-term travelers rather than traditional, long-term tenants.

Over the next four months, those proponents formed a coalition known as Share Better SF, which was largely funded by a hotel association and Unite Here, a union representing hotel industry workers. Groups like the Affordable Housing Alliance, the San Francisco Apartment Association, the Housing Rights Committee of San Francisco, and the Coalition for San Francisco Neighborhoods were all helping sell Prop F to voters.[4] So, too, were a host of local influencers, including former San Francisco mayor turned U.S. senator Diane Feinstein.

"Prop F closes loopholes and provides effective enforcement that will truly protect housing and neighborhoods," Feinstein wrote in an op-ed in the *San Francisco Chronicle* a couple weeks before the vote. "Prop F is a San Francisco solution to a San Francisco problem: It's fair, reasonable and effective, and supported by one of the broadest and most diverse coalitions we've ever seen— as it should be."[5]

Prop F's supporters would spend more than $1.5 million encouraging vot-ers to support the measure, including ads detailing how Airbnb was hammer-ing the city's housing market.[6] One such ad concluded with the tagline: "Yes on Prop F: Keep San Francisco affordable for locals." It was a carefully coordi-nated political blitz.

Chris Lehane and the Airbnb team were prepared for the challenge.

Lehane—a former aide to President Clinton—had been consulting for Airbnb on political and regulatory matters at a national level for a couple years and, while on the way to coach a little league baseball game, received a call from Kim Ruby, then the head of communications for Airbnb. Kim, who had worked for Lehane in the Clinton White House, mentioned that the company was starting to brace for an emerging political battle in San Francisco and asked him to come in for, as Lehane recalls, "a quick chat."

Lehane showed up to Airbnb's headquarters in San Francisco—the aes-thetics of which Lehane likens to the Willy Wonka factory—and was ushered into a conference room that looked, he thought, exactly like the crisis room from *Dr. Strangelove* (it turned out that the room is, in fact, an exact replica). What had been described as a quick chat was actually a Situation Room–style battle planning session involving two dozen of the company's top officials, all of whom were looking to Lehane for advice on how to defeat Prop F. This wasn't a "quick chat," he realized. This was game on.

"We began to think about this election in a little bit of a different way," Lehane, who joined Airbnb as the head of global public policy, would say weeks later.

"Was there something we could do? We had this big base of support, and the lightbulb went off in our heads: Could we actually organize and activate this community and change what the voter pool in San Francisco was going to look like?"[7]

That's exactly what Airbnb did.

For starters, the company identified 138,000 city residents who had either stayed in Airbnb rentals or hosted Airbnb guests in the past year. For context, there were only about 446,000 registered voters in San Francisco in 2015, and only about half of them voted in the previous year's election. The first step, Lehane says, was to poll those hosts and guests to see exactly how they felt about Airbnb and whether they felt passionately enough to take up arms in the fight against the new regulations. The survey results showed promise, with around 80 percent of respondents expressing very positive views of the company and sympathy for Airbnb's position on the new regulations. This gave the Airbnb team the confidence to move forward with an aggressive, systematic campaign to turn those sympathizers into grassroots activists.

The company contacted every single one of them and urged them to vote against Prop F. Later, Airbnb started running "No on F" digital banner ads for anyone visiting their website from the San Francisco area, and it began including anti–Prop F language in booking confirmation emails to all San Francisco hosts.[8]

Soon, Airbnb's "No on F" campaign rallied more than 1,000 volunteers who joined company employees in knocking on 285,000 doors and engaging in 105,000 conversations with voters about the dangers of Prop F. Airbnb tapped eleven short-term renter advocates, one for each city district, to serve as a face of the "No on F" campaign in each district, and they fed those group leaders important data and talking points to ensure they were equipped with the tools they needed to advocate effectively, Lehane says. The team also gathered testimonials from more than 2,000 local small businesses, posting and promoting positive messages about Airbnb's impact on the local economy on their Facebook page.[9] In some cases, the most impassioned, evangelical hosts started creating their own video testimonials and posting them to their own social media channels, helping the company reach an even larger swath of voters. Others went and met with editorial boards for local news outlets, adding a media dimension to the grassroots effort.

Lehane notes that while the majority of the most active supporters were initially motivated to join the campaign for personal economic reasons, many seemed to eventually become as attracted to the social and interpersonal nature of the campaign, which allowed them to interact with and forge new relationships with fellow hosts across the city.

"Once people began doing it, it started to take on a life of its own," Lehane says.

None of it came cheap. Airbnb would wind up spending more than $8.5 million on the "No on F" campaign, flooding local television networks and newspapers with ads that painted a dark picture for San Francisco residents under Prop F rules. More than half of that—about $5.6 million—went toward Airbnb's efforts to organize and communicate with local guests and hosts,[10] such as Cathryn Blum.

"I've not been a politically involved person until now, but it's drawn me in quite substantially because I am one of the people who depends on the income," Blum, a San Francisco homeowner and Airbnb host who volunteered for the company and spoke to press in opposition to Prop F, told CNN. She also said she attended every possible meeting to defend Airbnb and speak out against the ballot measure.[11]

On November 3, 2015, San Francisco voters turned down Prop F by a comfortable margin, 55 percent to 45 percent, delivering Airbnb their most important regulatory victory to date and clearing what would have been a costly and embarrassing stumble in the company's own backyard.[12]

"Voters stood up for working families' right to share their homes and opposed an extreme, hotel-industry-backed measure," Airbnb spokesman Christopher Nulty said in a statement. Noting that Airbnb mobilized their local user base to go door to door, he added, "The effort showed that home sharing is both a community and a movement."[13]

The win emboldened Airbnb to replicate the successful "No on F" campaign in other cities. In fact, the morning after the vote in San Francisco, Lehane announced that Airbnb would invest in building one hundred community clubs in key cities around the world. The "grassroots" groups, as he described them, would receive support and funding from the company to help them fight regulations that restrict short-term rentals.[14]

After that initial support to get them off the ground, as *Wired* magazine reported at the time, Airbnb "expects hosts and guests to ultimately run them as the clubs proliferate in the same 'grassroots' manner that Airbnb itself has grown."

"We decided to replicate what we had in San Francisco, which is to put on the ground, in a global way, a mobilization effort," Lehane told *TIME* magazine.[15]

In October of 2016, less than one year removed from the Prop F fight, Airbnb celebrated the formation of their hundredth "Home Sharing Club" in Berlin. That number has since doubled to more than two hundred clubs, which the company now describes on its website as "independent, host-led local organizations that drive initiatives to better their neighborhoods."[16]

In an interview about the clubs with CNN, Lehane used the same word Nulty had in the company's statement following the Prop F victory in San Francisco: "movement."

"It is not unique or specific to San Francisco," Lehane said of the company's citizen-fueled Prop F victory. "It really is reflective of a larger global movement."[17]

Citizen Power

Lehane chose his words carefully in describing Airbnb's hack.

In the world of elections and advocacy, *the grassroots* refers to a collection of citizens that may be rallied or activated to advance an electoral or policy outcome. If you can get citizens to start engaging their fellow citizens in a way that grows virally, then you're taking it a step further by leveraging a grassroots *movement*. By definition, the grassroots consist of those at the bottom of the power pyramid, hence the term "roots." These are not influencers or government leaders or industry titans. These are everyday citizens who believe in what you're doing, believe it will improve their lives, and may even be willing to lend their voice, time, energy, and social network to your cause.

In Chapter 14: The Grasstops, you'll learn about hacks that involve mobilizing small groups of well-connected and powerful individuals, or *the grasstops*. In contrast, grassroots hacks are about mobilizing a relatively large group of average citizens, each of them with markedly less political clout than a grass-top. For the most part, the grassroots' power is almost entirely derived from their overwhelming numbers, coupled with passion for your cause.

You can leverage the grassroots for a range of powerful regulatory hacks. As you'll learn later in the chapter, when Sylvan Learning leveraged campaign tools to directly engage precisely targeted citizens, that was a grassroots hack. When Airbnb encouraged their hosts to share their stories online, or when Uber asked their riders and drivers to email their city councilmembers, those were grassroots hacks. Even the way we built our 1776 brand *as a movement* is a form of grassroots hack.

Grassroots Campaigns: From Activation to Movements

Before we get into how to apply grassroots hacks to building your startup, it's important to understand the range of activities contained within the broad idea of a grassroots campaign.

At the core, any grassroots campaign is about getting citizens to take an action that you want, when you want, generally known as grassroots activation. The most common example of grassroots activation is "get out the vote" campaigns, or GOTV, in an electoral context. It's great to convince a citizen to support you, but their support doesn't matter if you cannot get them to show up at the polls on the one day that matters. Other actions you might want a citizen to take at a particular moment include communicating with their representative, signing a petition, showing up to a town hall, or marching in a protest.

You might rally some citizens to do more than participate in your campaign, recruiting them to help you execute your grassroots campaign or become an activist. For example, you might want them to volunteer to go door to door on election day to remind people to vote as part of a GOTV campaign. Or perhaps you want them to help put mailers in envelopes to send to other citizens to remind them to call their representative about a particular policy issue. A small number of committed activists willing to give their time can power surprisingly effective grassroots campaigns.

This is the ideal scenario for a grassroots campaign, when activists are willing not only to give their time but actively recruit and organize their friends, causing it to cross a tipping point and magically go viral. In other words, it's when a *campaign* becomes a *movement*. Self-motivated grassroots activists who believe that they are part of something bigger than themselves can cause explosive change. There's a snowball effect with grassroots movements that you don't see with other regulatory hacking tools in this book. Sure, one earned media story might get picked up by another outlet or two. A good influencer should be able to introduce you to at least two or three more good influencers. But an inspired grassroots movement can truly fuel its own fire. When motivated, grassroots activists will not only make phone calls, send letters, knock on doors, organize rallies, and donate money, but they will contact their friends and distant relatives, email their entire contact lists, light up their social media channels, put up yard signs, and lend their voices in countless other ways. One activist can meaningfully advance your cause. But when that activist brings two friends and each of them bring their friends, and so on, drawing hundreds or thousands of activists to be part of a unified movement, the impact can be enormous.

How grassroots movements form also helps explain their potency. Some grassroots movements are genuinely spontaneous, starting from the ground up, forming organically as motivated citizens rally around a cause or objective. The quintessential organic grassroots movement starts in a neighborhood or community and slowly expands to the local, state, and even federal level through word of mouth or other informal methods of expansion. Many other grassroots movements, like Airbnb's response to Prop F, are neither organic nor unanticipated. They are seeded through explicit, thoughtful tactics and guided through central leadership. Yet the successful ones have the feeling and appearance of being a spontaneous movement by tapping into citizens' genuine passion about a perceived injustice, such as those Airbnb hosts in San Francisco earning an average of $11,000 per year in supplemental income[18] feeling like they would get screwed in favor of big corporate hotels. Movements have *authenticity*, which, coupled with their inherent vitality, can make them the ultimate tool for credibility and reach.

"There were two reasons our grassroots efforts worked," Lehane says. "One, you had a group of evangelical hosts whose economic well-being was highly dependent on the platform and needed Airbnb to help make ends meet, and two, you had guests who had traveled on the platform and generally thought it was a very good thing." He later adds that "those two groups combined were able to really create a movement, and what we had to do was just help organize and unleash that movement."

The First Piece of the Grassroots Puzzle: Belief

Grassroots hacks must start with answering the most basic question: Can you get a group of citizens to care enough about what you're doing to take an action?

Airbnb had to get their hosts to vote and organize against a straightforward threat to their economic well-being. In contrast, if your health startup's technology would make it easier for patients to affordably access the care they need, but you need to change an outdated regulation in order to bring your technology to market, can you rally those patients to help your cause? Will they even understand the issue? Or, maybe you want a municipal government to purchase and implement your solution. Can you convince enough residents that it would benefit their lives enough to demand it from officials?

Few people I know understand the nuances of getting people on board better than Teddy Goff. Teddy was the digital director for Obama's 2012 re-election campaign and is now Stephanie Cutter's partner at Precision Strategies, the marketing and advocacy consultancy they formed in 2013. Teddy's specialty is using digital tools to organize and support grassroots campaigns.

As Teddy puts it: "People want to make their lives better, and they are happy to spend a little bit of time to fight for things that make sense to them, that they believe in, especially if it's going to help them or help the world in some way."

The key idea here is *belief*. Unless you can get citizens to believe in what your startup can do for them and society, when push comes to shove, they're not going to take action to help your cause. They need to believe that your interests are aligned with theirs. But it's more than that. This belief needs to be visceral and emotional, flowing from citizens falling in love with the *why* behind your startup.

"There's a very simple underlying truth to all this, which is that the substance and reality and authenticity of your message dictates about 90 percent of the outcome, and the marketing is really only about 10 percent, maybe less," Teddy says. "Ultimately, it has to be real."

Because the best grassroots campaigns feel like they were built for and *by* the people and not for and *by* the powerful, the inception process can prove awfully delicate. Grassroots campaigns need the buy-in of lots of people who believe it's vitally important for them to add their voice to the cause. If your citizen army feels like they're a pawn in someone else's game, a movement will fizzle out before it ever truly starts—or worse, provoke a backlash.

The Second Piece of the Puzzle: Timing

The effectiveness of a grassroots campaign is not measured by the number of citizens who believe. Whether a grassroots hack helps your startup advance its agenda depends on getting enough citizens to take an action *and* whether you can get them to do it *at the right time.*

That second piece of the puzzle is easy to overlook, but make no mistake, coordination and timing are key when it comes to grassroots activation. Even if you've won the hearts and minds of a sizable group of citizens, if you can't get them to take up arms in a unified way when your moment arises, your movement will fail.

This is obvious for elections, which need voters to turn out in droves on election day. It's true, too, for advocacy campaigns, which may need to flood lawmakers' phone lines and social media feeds with timely messages when an important bill comes up for a vote.

It's just as true for regulatory hackers.

Getting a large group of citizens to believe in your cause is only half the battle. It's not even enough to build a big grassroots army that's willing to take action. For a grassroots hack to succeed, you must be constantly priming your army to be ready to take the right actions *at the right moment.* Otherwise, not only will you lose that particular policy fight, but your grassroots army will become discouraged, making it even harder to rally them for the next fight. Belief is easier with victories and victories depend on seizing a particular moment.

Let's dive into the art of how to do that.

The Grassroots Arms Race

Grassroots campaigns in the modern sense have existed since the beginning of mass electoral politics in America at the end of the eighteenth century. And for more than two hundred years, it's been a constant arms race to find better ways to activate citizens and harness grassroots movements.

Not long ago, when politicos and activists wanted to ignite a grassroots movement, they turned to activities like press relations, direct mail outreach, television and radio advertising, and on-the-ground field operations. Traditionally, the toolbox contained fairly blunt instruments. A campaign or advocacy group would develop or buy a physical mailing list of people potentially interested in their candidate or cause. They would send mailers or emails to that list with a "call to action," such as a request to donate money, volunteer, or call their elected representatives. Sometimes, television or radio advertising would serve as a complement, but those were even blunter instruments.

But over the last twenty years, political and advocacy campaigns have found ways to sharpen their instruments, becoming markedly more sophisticated and data-driven. Powered in large measure by the sheer volume of data that can now be obtained about citizens and the availability of powerful data processing software that can derive useful insights from that endless torrent of data, the process of creating, growing, and harnessing a grassroots movement has become less an art form and more a lab science since the turn of the century.

Award-winning political journalist Sasha Issenberg's book explored the beginning of this shift in *The Victory Lab: The Secret Science of Winning Campaigns*. The book describes highly-sophisticated regression equations used by the Bush campaign in 2004 to analyze polling data and identify names of Ohio labor union members who might be willing to vote for Bush over Kerry, based on the former's foreign policy stance, even if they disagreed with his stance on unions and other economic issues. This enabled the campaign to focus their grassroots activity on the ground in Ohio with precisely targeted messages.

With help from Chris Hughes, a cofounder of Facebook, Obama took those techniques to another level in his fights against Clinton and then McCain in 2008, with even more robust data analysis as well as emerging social media tools to truly turn his campaign into a movement. In 2012, with Teddy Goff at the helm of his digital team, and help from Harper Reed, the former CTO of Threadless, an online clothing company that pioneered crowdsourced design, Obama raised the bar again. For instance, his campaign staff conducted polling that showed that single women who leaned strongly Republican were nevertheless susceptible to "war on women" appeals and could potentially be swayed to vote for Obama based on that issue alone. The campaign segmented women in that group and targeted them with mailings, phone calls, in-person visits, and more, helping to engage them with emotional appeals that motivated them to take action and organize for Obama.

Then there's President Trump's stunning victory over a deep Republican primary field and then Hillary Clinton in the general election, which continues to be unpacked, analyzed, and debated by political minds the world over. There's no question that his team's data-driven grassroots activation initiatives played a big role in Trump's victory. One of the most interesting aspects of Trump's grassroots game is the extent to which his team appears to have ignored field operations in favor of entirely digital approaches.

As the political campaigns have increasingly looked to the world of digital startups for inspiration—whether in the use of data or ways to increase viral coefficients—the grassroots hacks that regulatory hackers are deploying today bring things full circle. D.C. is learning from the Valley and the Valley is in turn learning from D.C. David Plouffe, Obama's 2008 campaign manager who famously hired Chris Hughes to build their digital platform, later left the Obama White House to join Travis Kalanick at Uber as his SVP of policy and strategy.

Although your startup likely won't have access to nearly as much data about your audience or as powerful a set of tools as a presidential campaign, you also won't need to reach as many citizens as a presidential candidate does. What's important is to understand the tools that can help you build your own citizen army.

There are a variety of standard tools for data-driven grassroots campaigns, and many of them complement one another. These include tools like:

- Data profiling
- Microtargeting messages via digital or direct mail based on known user behaviors or attributes
- Hosting house meetings or parties (converting passionate users into brand ambassadors)
- Guerilla marketing, such as lawn signs and posters
- Going door to door, often with informational clipboards
- Gathering signatures for petitions
- Mobilizing letter writers, phone callers, and email senders

In many cases, simple tools are the best, particularly when optimized with sophisticated data behind them.

"At a very tactical level, everybody undervalues email," Teddy says. "Of course, you have to use it carefully and sparingly, and any advocacy work you need to do has to make sense and be aligned with your normal marketing cadence, but email can be a very, very powerful tool."

More recently, social networks such as Facebook, YouTube, and Vimeo have become outlets for creating and distributing viral "campaign ads" that inspire citizens to take up arms in your fight.

The most powerful use of these tools is often omnichannel; that is, they're most effective when they are working in unison and feeding off one another. In addition, you should be using these tactics to both influence your target citizens while also gathering data on and learning about them. The insights you'll gain might help you understand the issues or messages most likely to resonate with a group of citizens, the best way to reach them, or whether they react best to being asked to step into an activist role. Just like with influencers, you're not aiming for a onetime transaction. You're trying to establish a relationship that you can readily turn to in your startup's times of need.

As you explore ways to use grassroots hacks for your startup, you should think about three broad tiers of hacks that might be appropriate, each more comprehensive than the next.

Tier 1: Using Campaign Tools

The simplest grassroots hack is to use grassroots activation to market your product. Sylvan Learning, with their venerable after-school learning programs, used this to great effect after President Bush's No Child Left Behind Act became law in 2001. In the law, there was a little-noticed provision that provided tax credits for supplemental learning for low-income families who lived in school districts with failing schools. Sylvan knew this could help expand their market significantly, but parents in these districts were unaware of this tax credit and how to take advantage of it. Sylvan solved this problem by using data profiling to microtarget those households with kids in failing schools who would be most likely to qualify for the tax credit, then sending canvassers door to door to let parents know about this opportunity and sign them up for a special program on the spot.

Sylvan could have run Facebook ads to reach families who should qualify for the supplemental learning tax credit, or set up an inside-sales funnel, with sales executives sitting on the phone converting leads into customers, but Sylvan had the creativity to see their marketing challenge through the lens of a grassroots campaign and use data profiling and field operations to connect with potential customers at their front door.

The most important insight the Sylvan team had was the importance of an in-person connection. For many people, a conversation about their failing neighborhood school is intimate, the kind you're accustomed to having with a neighbor or a family member on your front porch, not with someone in a call center. Sending a field team to every door that might qualify, however, would have been a prohibitively expensive way to sell their service. So, as in an election campaign, Sylvan coupled field teams with sophisticated data analysis to make sure they were going to the doors of people with school-age kids who were likely to qualify for the tax credit, creating a powerful sales engine.

Tier 2: Building Your Brand as a Movement

A more involved grassroots hack is to transform your citizen users or beneficiaries into passionate brand advocates for your startup, thereby turning your startup into a movement and thinking of your marketing efforts as a campaign.

This was how we built the 1776 brand in our first few years. We worked hard to craft a narrative around an inspiring *why*, namely that anyone in the D.C. region could play a role in solving meaningful problems for everyday people, and that the D.C. region could rise up to become an epicenter for these kinds of startups. We drew a contrast between the old way of doing things in D.C. and the new way that 1776 startups represented. We used the tactics of a political campaign to build our brand as a movement, hosting large and small events open to anyone who wanted to join, giving away stickers and T-shirts, to help people identify as part of our movement. We made it easy for people to organize their own ways to engage people around the 1776 brand, such as hosting their own event or bringing through a tour. Of course, we were thoughtful about targeting our outreach to people who could be particularly helpful, such as those with political, social, or financial capital. Our message was inclusive, but our outreach was targeted.

We also created satisfying feedback loops so that our community could see the progress we were making through their support of 1776. If you opted in as a 1776 supporter, which eventually included hundreds of thousands of people across our email and social media channels, then we would regularly share our community's wins, such as a startup raising funding, closing a big deal, or challenging the regulatory status quo.

That feedback loop is vital in creating a genuine movement and cultivating loyal advocates. As Teddy puts it, political campaigns or cause-based groups often solicit an action from their networks of followers but fail to circle back with the impact that their action had. "You have to point back and show, 'because X number of you took that action, we were able to get this done or that accomplished,'" he says. "It makes it real."

Zac Bookman, whom you met in Chapter 5: Arbitrage, has built the OpenGov brand in a similar way.

"We have a vision for the world, and we think there's an open impact movement happening out there," Bookman says. "There's this old world of government where decisions are made in a smoky back room and there are dusty filing cabinets and staff spend all their time doing rote, manual tasks, and citizens are cut out of the process . . . and then there's a new world and an open impact movement that's about modern government and a modern budget process in which more money gets channeled toward things that work and less money to things that don't. It's a movement that's focused on performance and open platforms and flexibility and a collaborative process. I think people are getting excited about that movement."

Bookman has used the OpenGov-as-a-movement brand to encourage government leaders to lead the charge on their behalf. "You have to get the leaders to stand up and take the lead," Bookman emphasizes. "You've got to find the visionary, the evangelist, the one who wants to make a change and who can drive change through their organization and who can tell their neighbors. We love those people and we want to tell their stories and make heroes out of them. They are the ones who are innovating in very tough operating environments."

If you are going to craft your brand as a movement, though, then be prepared for the consequences that come with the terrain. It's important to remember that most change begets winners and losers, which means that if you're successful you will inevitably face a reaction.

Teddy makes this point well in contrasting Airbnb and Uber, and who the loser was in the change that each was driving toward. It's comparatively easy for the average citizen to support a disruptive startup that chips away at the market share of billionaire families like the Hiltons and the Marriotts. While taxi commissions may not warm many hearts, some citizens are less comfortable fighting for a company that dismantles the livelihood of, as Teddy puts it, "the hardworking immigrant cab driver who saved up for twenty years to buy a taxi medallion." Airbnb has never faced a major backlash against their brand, whereas Uber quickly morphed from scrappy underdog to evil empire, at least in part because the genuine losers in Uber's movement were everyday people themselves.

Alison Griswold made this contrast particularly well in a story she wrote in *Slate* about Prop F[19]:

> Uber long ago embraced its persona of the brash revolutionary. Aggressive campaigns from the company—like its "de Blasio mode" blitz in New York this summer—no longer shock us, and that's OK. The central promise of Uber is not a friendly, welcoming service but a reliable and competitively priced ride, something borne of ruthless efficiency. Airbnb, on the other hand, is in the business of hospitality and so has built its reputation on qualities that are quite different: being genial, responsible, a good corporate citizen. Even if you didn't think Airbnb really had the best interests of a city at heart, it was hard to make the case, because the company's branding was so consistently benign and neighborly. That's a valuable card to hold.

If you create your brand as a movement, then you need to understand that people will expect more of you than they might from other startups. After all, a great movement is *about them*, not your startup. We learned this over time at 1776. As we grew as a business, we made the inevitable choices that all businesses have to make, to focus on certain things and stop doing others. The response from our community could be intense, driven by the emotional connection we had built with them. Becoming a movement can be a double-edged sword, incredibly powerful, but hard to control. As Chris Lehane from Airbnb put it after the Prop F campaign, "A movement is a little like riding a tiger."

Tier 3: Changing Policies

The ultimate use of grassroots hacks isn't sales or marketing—it is activating citizens to achieve a desired policy outcome. Before Uber faced a backlash to their brand, they managed to use grassroots hacks to execute one of the most stunningly successful grassroots campaigns in business history, shattering entrenched iron triangles in cities around the world.

As I shared in Chapter 1: Regulatory Hacking, I had a front-row seat as Uber first tested their regulatory hacking strategy in D.C. For a Valley startup, Uber wrote an entirely new playbook. But when seen instead as an advocacy campaign, Uber's tactics were obvious. Travis personally sent passionate emails to Uber users asking us to save Uber and making it one-click easy to email their councilmember. Uber carefully stoked a sense of crisis, reinforcing that if *we didn't act right then*, the forces of evil would triumph and the fight would be over. The language and tactics were straight from a political campaign.

Invest in Your Grassroots

If your startup is improving the lives of citizens, you should be building connections with your community. Even if you don't need to mobilize an army of supporters right this moment, you might need to do so in the future, and at that point, it may be too late to start building your army.

Much of this basic investment relies on strategies you've already learned in this book, such as crafting your brand around the *why* for citizens. This is easier when you have a B2C or marketplace model, like Uber, Airbnb, or Sylvan Learning. Even with indirect business models, though, you should be treating the citizens who benefit as if they were a customer, if at all possible.

Direct or indirect, maintaining citizen relationships that you can activate when necessary means being *able* to directly communicate with them. As Teddy said, email may be boring, but it remains amazingly effective. Make sure you're gathering emails and more as part of your day-to-day operations.

Maintaining your relationships also means learning as much as you can about the citizens who support you. Email alone is better than nothing, but email plus data profiles is getting you somewhere. As you learn more about your citizens, you should segment them along dimensions such as on *how* they want to join your movement. A powerful few will want to feel like leaders, and these would-be activists are gold to you. Others will want to feel like they're part of something important, to derive a sense of meaning from supporting you. Still others may want something from you as simple as nuggets of insights they can share with their friends. Many will want nothing more than updates on how they can personally benefit from your product or service, and you may even offend them by engaging them beyond that. Developing these citizen segments, and learning how to activate them, is an investment you need to make early and maintain continuously, so you have the asset of an organized grassroots army when the time comes.

When you do need your citizen army to take an action, you shouldn't be afraid to adopt many of the tactics you've learned about in this chapter. Make the appeal *personal* and *emotional*. Be clear who the *enemy* is. Create urgency by building to a key moment. Let them know you need them, and even better, how they can help you engage others.

Whatever happens as a result of their action, win or lose, make sure to close the loop with your loyal supporters. Let them know the impact they have had. Thank them.

Grassroots Loop

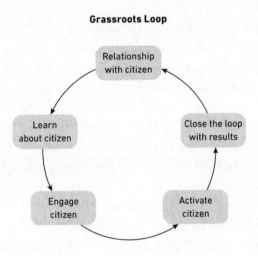

This grassroots loop should feel familiar. It's the grassroots equivalent of the get-keep-grow-refer flywheel that the Valley preaches to startups. In fact, you can apply many of the same data-driven tools you use for customer acquisition and success to building and nurturing your grassroots army.

A Formidable Constituency

If you can successfully execute grassroots hacks, particularly if you can inspire a movement, it will be one of the most powerful forces you could unleash for your startup. Chris Lehane put Airbnb's movement in perspective when he compared the millions of Airbnb hosts and guests to the membership of formidable grassroots organizations such as the National Rifle Association, the Sierra Club, the National Education Association, and the Human Rights Campaign: "The [Airbnb] voting bloc that is growing is a formidable constituency."[20]

Chapter 14

THE GRASSTOPS

It was December 2012, a few days before Christmas, and Hans Miller and Adam Tsao were sitting in the lobby of the Meridian Hotel in Rosslyn, Virginia, just across the Potomac River from Washington. At the time, Hans and Adam—who had both spent their careers in the airport and transportation sectors, including stints at the Transportation Security Administration (TSA)—were running a sputtering in-airport food delivery startup and were strapped for financial resources. Though still running their current venture, they had started to kick around new business ideas.

On that cold morning in December, Hans opened an email newsletter featuring an article about the U.S. Custom and Border Protection agency's mounting challenges with long customs lines at airports across the country. The article went on to detail how the agency was starting to more aggressively experiment with new technologies to help address the problem.

Hans—who was employee number eleven hired at the TSA in 2002 and who had been a key member of the team that designed the first mobile boarding passes a little less than a decade later—immediately thought: "We can solve this problem with an app." He handed the laptop to Adam before he even finished reading the story.

Adam did finish the story—and it's a good thing he did.

"Adam looked up at me and said, 'Wait, at the bottom of the story it says that CBP officials are presenting on this topic in Washington,'" Hans recalls. "'When?' I asked."

"Right now," Adam responded.

Hans and Adam sprinted out of the hotel and hailed a cab. On the roughly twenty-minute ride from Rosslyn to the Washington Convention Center, the two talked through the basic app design and business model that would later become Airside Mobile, the startup they founded to modernize and expedite the customs process for travelers.

"I know this almost never happens, but that little light bulb that popped into our heads that morning, and what we worked out in the back of that cab, it's actually ridiculously identical to what we ended up building," Hans says.

While the idea was hatched quickly, building the business was anything but a breeze.

At the conclusion of the conference that morning, the duo managed to catch a couple of CBP officials and asked for a meeting to discuss their ideas. "It helped that we were a known quantity from our time at TSA and from the food delivery app," Hans says.

At the resulting meeting, Hans and Adam pitched an app that they believed would vastly expedite the customs process for travelers and save time and money for the agency.

The response was positive but cautious, Hans says.

"After they had heard us out, they said, 'Well, that's great, but we really want to make sure the industry is behind this,'" Hans recalls. "They expressed interest in working with the industry groups and major players, like the airlines and airports, rather than with us directly."

Fortunately, Hans had developed strong relationships with key influencers throughout the air-travel industry during his tenure at TSA and while building his earlier startup. His first call was to the North America arm of the Airports Council International, a large and powerful trade group representing the owners and operators of commercial airports in the United States and Canada that fights for policies to help commercial airports better serve their passengers, customers and communities.

"It only took one phone call for them to get what we were trying to do, and they soon signed on as our partner and our official sponsor to the CBP," Hans says. "You have to take into account that the commercial airlines are a big economic engine, and it matters a lot to those airports how fast travelers are getting through customs and how much time they're spending in those lines."

He continued: "Getting that group on board and getting them to advocate for us was powerful. We're no longer just three guys with a slide deck. Suddenly, we have the voice of the industry on our side, we have LAX and Atlanta and Dulles on our side, and that goes a long way."

Like airports, airlines also benefit from a faster customs process.

"Long lines at customs are very expensive for the airlines, because travelers miss their flights," Hans explains. "It's quite expensive to rebook those people, and more broadly, it's not productive when you're trying to schedule banks of flights and you have to leave a long time between them to make time for travelers to go through customs. That's not ideal, either."

With that as leverage, Hans and Adam were also able to solicit the support of groups representing major airlines like United, American, and Delta. Coupled with support from the airport industry leaders, the doors started to open, and CPB brought Hans and Adam back to start working through the beginnings of a mobile customs app.

"Basically, that whole process and the support we received from our partners paved the way to a somewhat long and torturous process of laying out what the requirements were going to be with CPB in terms of security and privacy and operational readiness and everything else," Hans says. "Once we agreed on that, then we just had to build it." Which they did as members of 1776 in Virginia!

Airside Mobile's Mobile Passport app debuted for travelers at Atlanta's Hartsfield-Jackson International Airport in August 2014[1] and has since expanded to twenty-four airports and one cruise port across the county. The company currently earns its revenue through in-app display advertising, but Hans and Adam hope their service will eventually be purchased by airlines and incorporated as a feature in their respective mobile apps, giving customers a single-app travel experience.

Next time you travel through a U.S. international airport, look for Mobile Passport signs. Then think about the impact to the lives of the more than three million American and Canadian citizens who have downloaded Mobile Passport, all of which came from Hans's and Adam's connections in the airport and airline industries, and those connections' connections. And Hans and Adam have been able to parlay that into a scaling business as well, having completed a $6 million Series A in 2017.

Who You Know Matters, but Who They Know Matters Even More

If the grassroots are about engaging everyday citizens to help achieve your ends, then the grasstops are about engaging a smaller number of influencers to achieve those same ends. When someone talks about grasstops, they're talking about more directly reaching the power players and decision makers.

A simple example can help show the difference between the grassroots and grasstops.

A grassroots campaign is creating a groundswell of support for a policy among enough voters in a lawmaker's district that the sheer volume of phone calls, emails, and letters flooding into his office push him to vote in favor of the bill. It's Travis emailing all the Uber users and drivers in D.C. and asking them to email their councilmember.

A grasstops campaign is meeting with that same politician's chief of staff, then sitting down with his former cochairman from a local nonprofit board, then going to lunch with the CEO of a union that organized for his last campaign, and then following that up with a call to two of his biggest campaign donors, and persuading each of them to put a bug in the lawmaker's ear about the benefits of the policy the next chance they get. It's Rachel Holt, Uber's then leader in D.C., bringing an intimate group of leaders in the D.C. tech community together in person to ask us to make personal appeals to the mayor and councilmembers.

"Grassroots is about the quantity—having as many bodies and voices as possible," Ilisa Halpern Paul, who leads the lobbying shop at the law firm Drinker Biddle & Reath, explained in a 2012 interview with *The Washington Post*. "Grasstops is about a smaller group of people who are from those targeted areas developing close one-on-one relationships with officials."[2]

A Dividend from Your Investment in Influence

In Chapter 8: Data, you learned about systematically cultivating influence, where influence refers to a startup's network of relationships with powerful individuals, trade associations, unions, advocacy groups, think tanks, universities, lobbying firms, or major media outlets that are themselves connected to key decision makers and market leaders. Those individuals and organizations are influencers, as they have the access and credibility to help shape the complex market in which your startup operates.

Grasstops hacks are about getting a small but focused set of influential individuals and groups advocating on your behalf for a specific outcome. That is, identifying those who hold influence over the power players you need to sway and finding ways to persuade them to use that influence to your advantage.

In political circles, grasstops organizing has become just as common and no less potent than grassroots campaigning, often serving, as with Uber, as a discreet complement to more public grassroots campaigns. Grasstops campaigns have also become more sophisticated as more data becomes available. Ten years ago, the state of the art in a grasstops campaign in the United States was a "fly-in" of prominent people to influence a policymaker. Today, you can precisely map the most impactful influencers and microtarget your outreach to them.

Sara Fagen is one of America's leading political strategists and a serial entrepreneur herself. Sara served as White House political director to President George W. Bush and serving as a senior strategist to his 2004 reelection campaign, where the *Wall Street Journal* called her a "data whiz" who "helped perfect political micro-targeting." After the campaign, Sara founded a series of companies that integrated data and technology to help brands achieve policy outcomes. She now specializes in grasstops advocacy as a partner with DDC Advocacy, a public affairs shop.

"My experience is grasstops advocacy is the most effective way to influence key decision makers, more so than direct lobbying, advertising, or traditional public relations tactics. However, the mix of grasstops and grassroots can create a surround sound that will convince an office holder to not only support you, but to become a champion," Sara says.

What makes grasstops organizing appealing for political operatives and activists is the same thing that makes it useful to you. That is, it's helpful to engage with those individuals who can persuade the people who wield power over the complex market in which you operate. That's grasstops hacking in a nutshell.

Finding Your Grasstops

The reality of complex markets is that power is not distributed evenly. Some people and organizations have much greater ability to determine the fate of your startup than others. Which ones? Well, they tend to be within one degree of separation from the decisions or actions that impact your startup. They are either the decision maker or they have a direct line into the decision maker.

Depending on your power map, that decision maker could be in government, in an institution, in an association, or in a media organization. She might be a mayor, a cabinet secretary, the director of an agency, or the top official at a regulatory commission. Or, you may be looking at the president of a hospital or the head of innovation for an electric utility. You might even need to influence the head of an association, the editor of a media organization, or a prominent scholar at a university.

Your power map should show you whom you can realistically reach given your network of influencers. You may be able to go straight to the source, or you might need to take a two-step "bank shot" approach by engaging with someone whom you know who can access the power player. This may be someone in the key decision maker's "political family" or inner circle of influence.

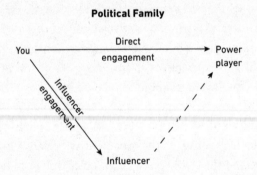

In either case, whether they're a step removed or not, the grasstops are likely to be able to either directly enact change that would help your startup, or indirectly influence the real decision makers through their trusted relationships.

"An element of grasstops organizing is common sense," Sara says. "We are all prone to be influenced by people we know and trust, whether or not we are voting, buying a product, or shopping for a new doctor. It makes sense that finding trusted friends and adviser to speak to office holders is often the most effective tactic in gaining support for an issue or cause."

Is a grasstops hack something you should use? The answer isn't all that different than the one from the previous chapter. If you need to persuade a person in power to do something, change something, or buy something, then the grasstops might be a lever you want to pull. Either as a complement—or an alternative—to grassroots organizing, going to the source of the power, or at least close to it, can prove beneficial to startups who need to induce some type of action by authority figures. Grasstops campaigns can also have the benefit of discretion, a contrast to more public grassroots campaigns.

As I mentioned above, Uber learned to skillfully weave together the grassroots and grasstops in a city for maximum impact in busting apart taxi iron triangles. They would often drive a strident message via the grassroots, while using the grasstops to discreetly signal how hard Uber was willing to fight certain provisions and where the potential for compromise might lie.

Grasstops hacks aren't necessarily easy; after all, we're talking about a person in power—or at least an influencer very close to power. Naturally, that means you aren't going to be the only one who would like to bend their ear, so getting access to them directly may be an uphill climb. The more power an individual has, the more they are likely to be able to assist you, sure, but also the more layers of protection and lines of handlers they probably have in place to insulate them from a daily barrage of meeting requests and event invitations. Those layers can be tough to claw your way through.

But grasstops hacks aren't impossible. While powerful individuals may be insulated from direct engagement, they have personal and professional networks just like anyone else. They have friends and peers, colleagues and former colleagues. You may not be able to get to the decision maker directly, but getting within one degree of separation can often be just as good. Understanding those social networks is key to working a grasstops hack, and oddly enough, this can actually be easier to do in a complex market.

The advantage that complex markets afford is that those personal and professional social networks are often publicly visible in a way that they may not be for a corporate executive or an important investor.

Getting to Your Hero Mayor

Let's look at a simple example. Suppose you need to engage with the mayor of a midsized American city. Maybe you think her town should purchase your software service, or perhaps you need her help to change a local ordinance or turn back a market threat. Whatever the reason, you have decided that you need to get in front of that mayor, and you need to do it quickly.

There's rarely any harm in trying once or twice to engage directly. Unlike many corporate executives, many mayors have their direct phone lines and email addresses listed on their city's websites. Your voicemail or email will almost assuredly go through a staff assistant or some other layer of vetting before ever having a shot at reaching its intended recipient, but it still can't hurt to try to go the direct route with a message or two before you move on to more indirect routes.

Now let's say those attempts have fallen on deaf ears, or perhaps you've started to get the runaround from her assistant. Where to next? What's your hack?

From publicly available data sources, you may be able to quickly determine who has made significant campaign contributions to that mayor. You can research what boards she served on and which organizations she worked for before running for mayor, and then you can find out who her peers or her fellow board members were during that period of her career.

Without much trouble, you can also find out which companies or organizations supported her as a candidate. You can see which individuals are influential within that mayor's political party, and you can see who her former staffers are and where they're working now.

You can determine what mayor-focused organizations she may belong to and who runs those organizations. In a way, the grasstops exercise is a lot like creating a power map, except for an individual rather than an entire market.

With little more than an online search engine, you can quickly figure out

Individual Power Map

the grasstops that have grown up around that particular mayor. That presents you with a path to either publicly or privately influence her, depending upon your objective.

Okay, so now you know who *could* help you at the grasstops level. But who *will* help you? The basic principles of power mapping come into play here, too, because what you really need to know is what will motivate an influential person to help you.

There are a few ways to approach this.

First, if you've nailed your narrative, the influencer may simply be inspired enough by your mission that they want to help you succeed. This is probably the best-case scenario, but let's face it, you're not going to turn every grasstops connection into a passionate brand ambassador.

Second, you might be able to make them into a hero. If your software solution can help that mayor solve a tough challenge for her constituents, that translates into a win for her. The same applies when working through an intermediary who has access to the mayor. If you can solve a problem for your hero mayor, then the intermediary who made the connection stands to gain some political capital with the mayor.

Third, there's always quid pro quo. Someone who has managed to ascend into the grasstops probably recognizes the value in stockpiling favors. They may help you in order to accrue a favor they can cash in some time in the future. You'll want to be sure you know if that's the case.

Fourth, and most simply, maybe it's just not that hard for them to make a change or make an introduction. Every day, decisions are made on a shoulder shrug and an "Eh, why not?" This will certainly happen more often for startups that have a good story to share, but it will also happen to founders who are polite, personable, and professional. Being endearing and earnest can go a long way.

It's also worth noting that grasstops hacks can often be scaled. Let's assume that you eventually succeed in reaching that hero mayor, and it turns out that mayors seem to be a perfect entry point for your startup to engage with municipalities. The Conference of Mayors, an enormous association of mayors from around the country, may be helpful in connecting you to many more mayors, and perhaps there's an opportunity for an informal or even formal partnership with the group.

Once you figure out a consistent pattern in one city or market, look for ways to test whether that pattern can be replicated elsewhere. Remember, it's a test. Don't just assume that what worked in one city will work in others. The learnings from these tests tend to produce the kinds of subtle "hacks" that separate successful startups in complex markets from promising ones that fizzle out.

Influence Is Your Investment in the Grasstops

The grasstops is an area where having nurtured networks into a sizable stockpile of influence can make all the difference. If you have quality relationships with influencers who are motivated to help you, you may find that grasstops engagement just happens organically. It's not even something you have to actively think about beyond questions like, "Okay, whom do I know who can get me a meeting with that city's mayor?"

On the other hand, if you don't have influence, the notion that you could even land on a power player's calendar—let alone solicit their help—may seem completely ridiculous. Much like building a community for grassroots activation, to successfully use grasstops hacks, you need to start building and nurturing your networks of influence long before you need to tap them for favors or introductions. When the need arises and you have to quickly get in front of a prominent government official or industry titan, you want that influence waiting in your back pocket.

Chapter 15

LOBBYING

Dan Yates was skeptical.

Dan, who had only just cofounded Opower with Alex Laskey, was walking out of a meeting with Brian Ward, the project lead on a green energy program run by the city of Palo Alto. The two founders had pitched Ward on their vision to reinvent the utility bill in ways that would encourage consumers to save energy. Ward had enthusiastically told the Opower founders that he would be their first customer if they ever actually built what they had pitched, and he promised to introduce them to other utility leaders in Northern California.

Alex, in his own words, walked out of the meeting "like I was in that scene in 'Singing in the Rain,' clicking my heels together in excitement, because I believed we now had proof that this was a viable business idea." Dan wasn't convinced—not yet.

"He looked at me like I was crazy," Alex said. "He basically said, 'I'm not starting a business based on one conversation with someone in Palo Alto. We need to go prove to ourselves that this isn't something that only people in hippy, liberal Northern California get excited about. We need to prove to ourselves that this can work anywhere.'"

Alex agreed.

"So we set out to prove it," he added. That meant finding a place that was as unlike hippy, liberal Northern California as possible. "And in our minds," he said, "that was Texas."

Through some quick grasstops hacking, Alex and Dan managed to secure meetings with two key players in the Lone Star State in the spring of 2007. The first was with William "Dub" Taylor, director of the State Energy Conservation Office, an appointee of Governor George W. Bush. The second was Tom "Smitty" Smith, head of the Texas office for Public Citizen, a D.C.-based liberal advocacy group largely focused on environmental issues.

Both Taylor and Smith expressed interest in Alex and Dan's pitch—though not as energetically as Ward had in Silicon Valley—and noted that his timing was impeccable. The Texas legislature, which only meets every two years, was in session at the moment and starting to debate House Bill 3693, which pertained to rules and incentives around energy efficiency for consumers and utilities. "They both encouraged us to come down to Texas and offered to help set up meetings with some of the important players in that world," Alex said. "We quickly mocked up some Texas-specific utility bills based on our vision, we called them the Lonestar Home Energy Reports, we printed them out, and we both hopped on a Southwest flight down to Texas."

Over the next several days, Alex and Dan pounded the pavement in and around Austin, meeting with Representative Joe Strauss, the lawmaker who had introduced the bill, and numerous members of his legislative staff. It didn't take long to realize that there was indeed an opportunity to fold language into the pending legislation that would encourage Texas utilities to use a platform like Alex and Dan envisioned. One of Strauss's top staffers told Alex, in the latter's paraphrased words, "Your idea sounds good to me, and if you want to write some proposed language, I'll include it in the bill."

There was a catch, though. "He told us that if anyone at all objected to the language, he would take it out," Alex said. "Basically, our idea made sense to him, and he was willing to try to do Dub and Smitty a favor, but he wasn't willing to fight for it or potentially lose votes over it."

So Alex and Dan pitched their language, essentially stating that Texas utilities could use a tool like Opower to meet the new energy conservation requirements outlined in the legislation. "The language would basically make us an approved option for utilities as they tried to meet new standards set by the proposed law," Alex explained.

He continued, "We then spent the next four days trying to convince everyone who would listen to us to either support our text—or at least not be opposed to it."

Rushing from office to office, Alex and Dan met with staffers working for the speaker of the Texas House and the Texas lieutenant governor, as well as key influencers in various corners of the state's energy landscape. Those included the chair of the Texas Public Utility Commission, Governor Rick Perry's energy adviser, key members of local environmental groups, and the state policy and government affairs representatives for many local utilities.

"With each person, we basically asked, 'Who else is going to weigh in on this? Who are the other players involved? Who might be supportive of this or who might object to it, and how do I get a meeting with those people?'" Laskey said. "It was five straight days of meetings."

The next week, before the vote on the bill, Alex and Dan returned to Austin to formally testify before the legislative committee in which the bill had been introduced—a first step before it could be moved out of committee and toward a full vote in the legislature.

Days later, the state legislature approved House Bill 3693—known as the Energy Efficiency Bill—with the Opower duo's desired text woven in. Shortly thereafter, it was signed into law by Governor Rick Perry.[1]

"That was enough for us to say, 'Okay, we really are onto something,'" Laskey said.

The Smoke-Filled Rooms

It's not an accident that lobbying is the last chapter in this book. It's a word that evokes images of shadowy figures and smoke-filled rooms, special interests, and secret deals. When most people in the Valley think about dealing with government, their default image is lobbying to change inconvenient rules. As you've learned throughout this book, though, regulatory hacking is much more than trying to change laws and regulations.

With that said, and as we've learned from Alex and Dan, for regulatory hackers, lobbying can be the ultimate hack in your toolkit.

Once upon a time, smoke-filled rooms and secret deals may very well have been the reality of lobbying. But today, smoking has been banned in D.C., even in the back rooms, and lobbying in practice bears little resemblance to its boys-club connotation. Relationships are important, as in any industry, but lobbying is now much more about doing your homework than calling in favors.

Defined broadly, lobbying means seeking to persuade a politician or public official to take one action over another. It's influence in action, and it's an art form that may be practiced by individuals, companies, nonprofits, law firms, trade associations, consumer groups, or specialty lobbying shops. Just like free speech, the right to petition the government is protected under the first amendment of the Constitution. Under this broad definition, hacking the media, the grassroots, and the grasstops could all fall under the umbrella of "lobbying," as they are common tools you might use as an indirect means of persuading policymakers to set rules and regulations in a favorable way for your startup.

This chapter, however, is about a narrower definition of lobbying, namely, the rare but important cases when you have to directly affect a specific piece of legislation or regulation—either to change something in your favor or to prevent something from being changed to your detriment. In this sense, lobbying is what you do when more subtle attempts to sway policymakers haven't worked.

Lobbying Laws and Practices

The first thing to understand about lobbying is that governments often define and regulate the practice, at least in formal settings. In the United States, there are specific rules at the federal level and a mishmash of different rules in statehouses and city halls across the country. These rules govern who can formally lobby, what steps one must take to register as a lobbyist, and what public reporting and disclosures you must follow. At the other extreme, there are few rules around lobbying in many emerging economies, where lobbying often has a considerably more "wild west" culture.

No less important than understanding the laws that govern lobbying is understanding the norms that govern the practice. What may be perfectly legal in one place may be completely taboo in another.

The point is, if you plan to lobby a government's officials, you should either take the time to understand the relevant laws and norms or hire someone who does and can help you play the game right. For many growing startups in the United States, that person is Heather Podesta, the founder and CEO of the powerhouse lobbying shop Invariant, with clients such as SpaceX, Uber, ZocDoc, FitBit, Kabbage, Ring, TaskRabbit, and Niantic (the creators of Pokémon GO).[2]

In person, Heather's disarming candor is a striking departure from the dissembling manner of many Washington lobbyists. At the 2008 Democratic National Convention, Heather wore a scarlet L to razz then Senator Obama for talking so much about curbing lobbying enthusiasm. *The Washington Post* once described her as the "It Girl" of Washington.[3] She in turn described herself to the *Post* as a geek: "There is this twelve-year-old geeky girl in me who just wants to read books and have nothing to do with anyone."

Invariant Technology Clients for 2017	
SpaceX	$320,000
Uber	$120,000
ZocDoc	$200,000
FitBit	$240,000
Kabbage	$320,000
Ring	$120,000
TaskRabbit	$320,000
Niantic	$320,000

Source: Center for Responsive Politics[4]

It's the geek in Heather that helped her see the collision between the Valley and the Hill before many others, at least on the Hill side of things. I remember having breakfast with Heather at the Four Seasons in Georgetown in 2012 to recruit her to join K Street Capital as an angel investor. She joined K Street, but most of the breakfast turned into Heather systematically extracting a tutorial on the world of startups and venture capital, and then explaining why startups would need assistance in Washington and the help of lobbyists. Five years later, she's the lobbyist with perhaps the best network in Silicon Valley, appearing on a16z and Vox podcasts to explain lobbying to the uninitiated on Sand Hill Road.

If lobbying is a hack you're going to need, you'll either need the background, determination, and time to figure out how the game works, like Alex and Dan, or hire someone like Heather to help solve your political problem, showcase your company, and create market opportunities.

Understanding Government

The next thing to understand about lobbying is that it can be a technically complex field where expertise matters. That is, most lobbyists come from a background in government and with an understanding of the details of the laws and regulations that govern the industries they represent. Heather, for example, is an attorney who worked as a congressional aide to members of Congress, including Senator Bill Bradley, before becoming a lobbyist.

Money and Politics

In the same way, many lobbyists are also active in politics and political fundraising, for example, serving as bundlers for candidates and causes. The intertwining of lobbying and fundraising makes sense for a couple of reasons. One, you have access to those already in power when you need to take action. Two, you can help support those policymakers who are already inclined to take your perspective into consideration.

Why Lobby?

So how effective is lobbying?

It turns out, incredibly so.

Numerous studies have shown that lobbying produces one of the greatest returns on investment of any activity for a major corporation.[5] This is obvious when you think about apocalyptic fights in the United States over recent federal policies such as Obamacare, Dodd-Frank, or the Tax Cuts and Jobs Act of 2017. Much of the returns from lobbying, however, come from influence over esoteric policy issues that never register on the radar of the average citizen. Minor tweaks over tax policy, for instance, can have enormous financial implications for a large company, and a favorable interpretation on an antitrust matter can be worth many billions of dollars.

Top U.S. Corporations by Lobbying Spend for 2017	
Blue Cross/Blue Shield	$24,330,306
Alphabet	$18,150,000
AT&T	$16,780,000
The Boeing Company	$16,740,000
Dow DuPont	$15,877,520
Comcast Corporation	$15,310,000
Lockheed Martin	$14,464,290
Amazon.com	$13,000,000
Southern Company	$12,970,000
Oracle Corporation	$12,385,000

Source: Center for Responsive Politics[6]

Now, effective does not mean fast. Lobbying at almost any level of government and in any country in the world tends to be a long game. Considerable lobbying effort is invested in maintaining a status quo, as that status quo is likely the result of years of lobbying by groups that wanted the rules set up that way. For incumbent firms, the status quo is an investment that they need to protect. What's more, these major corporations know the ins and outs of the system, the key decision makers, and how to play the game. Startups must learn the rules of the game, find their own guide, or risk being taken off the field before the game even begins.

Google and Amazon started small. In 2003, Google spent a total of $60,000 on federal lobbying. Today, they spend over $18 million with close to one hundred registered lobbyists engaged on issues as varied as STEM education, human trafficking, and data privacy issues. Amazon's story is similar. They started lobbying in 2000, spending less than $10,000. Now, federal lobbying costs top $13 million with fourteen external firms on retainer.

When you do need to change things, particularly big things, it can take a long time to overcome dual forces: the natural inertia in the system and the many powerful interests vested in the status quo. The result is enduring lobbying campaigns that move the needle inch by inch, with success or failure determined over the course of years, if not decades.

These points are all broadly true whether you're lobbying the U.S. federal government or the Colorado General Assembly, the European Union in Brussels or the Kenyan Parliament.

Even in small municipalities, you'll find professional lobbyists with a background in that government and an understanding of the minutiae of local ordinances. And those individuals can help provide significant returns on investment for local business interests, with common clients including local industry leaders in sectors like real estate, energy production, manufacturing, or taxis!

It's Never Too Early

When should you consider lobbying?

Sometimes, from day one.

While this may not be true for all of you, certain regulated startups can't start lobbying early enough. As you learned back in Chapter 4: Growth, Opower's business model depended on regulators nudging utilities to enact energy conservation initiatives. For Dan and Alex to know they had a big market in which to scale, they had to know they could work with legislatures and regulators to enact these kinds of policies. Getting a law changed in Texas was less a hack for growth than a test to prove that they had product-market fit.

Of course, it helps that prior to founding Opower, Alex had spent much of his career in politics and policy, serving as a campaign manager and polling analyst for various progressive candidates. While the Texas legislature wasn't exactly progressive Northern California, Alex didn't feel out of place having policy conversations with lawmakers. Alex didn't have to retain a lobbyist to validate the Opower business model because he already had the raw skills.

Some regulated startups do retain lobbyists early on. As soon as they realized they needed to be ready for a fight, Uber famously retained Bradley Tusk, a former adviser to politicians such as Michael Bloomberg, Rod Blagojevich, and Chuck Schumer. Of course, this ended up being a win-win for both as Tusk agreed to accept shares in Uber in lieu of his $25,000 per month fee. Those shares are thought to be worth more than $100 million today.[7] Tusk has taken this win and turned it into a new model with Tusk Ventures, where he blends lobbying services with venture investments. If you're not an Alex Laskey, it helps to find a Bradley Tusk.

Heather noted that startups most commonly retain a lobbyist when they start to scale fast and a regulator suddenly starts asking questions about their business model or when a competitor starts drawing attention to the startup's operations, either through the press or by pressuring the politicians with whom they're friendly.

"When that feeling of being attacked begins, and they don't feel like they have another option to protect themselves, that's when we get called in," she says.

In Chapter 8: Influence, I explored 23andMe, who had this experience when they received the letter from the FDA. After that, 23andMe was able to successfully build relationships with scientists and other influencers in the regulatory community—and in fact directly lobby—to start providing guidance on health risks based on their genetic tests. It took several years, however, and when they relaunched, it was with a dramatically scaled-back product.

If you've avoided regulatory scrutiny and competitors' attention, then you'll typically look to someone like Heather after your Series B or C. With startups in complex markets, venture capitalists want to know that you have an engagement strategy and plan for Washington or statehouses. An essential part of a regulatory hacker's pitch deck with later-stage investors is how you plan to deal with legislative and regulatory risk.

Most obviously, you'll tend to wait until you've raised later-stage capital because lobbying is traditionally an expensive endeavor. If you've attempted other hacks, but are still stuck, then the outcome you're trying to achieve is probably a thorny one. You may need to spend serious money to bring in the right lobbyist to help. Or look at creative equity agreements like the Uber and Bradley Tusk setup.

For startups, hiring a lobbyist can be similar to hiring a public relations firm. Instead of pitching stories and profiles to TechCrunch and Recode while tailoring your message to the next funding round, a lobbyist frames your story to key decision makers and the inside-the-Beltway publications like POLITICO and Axios.

It's Never Too Late

Of course, there's another time when you should consider hiring a lobbyist: as a last resort.

If you've tried everything else, a great lobbyist may be your best friend. "We can find solutions even when you think there are none left," Heather explains.

Heading into 2016, Carolyn and the rest of the HopSkipDrive team were feeling frustrated. They had expanded their coverage area to include the Bay Area, Los Angeles, and Orange County, but they couldn't seem to create more public-private partnerships with government agencies that they were convinced made sense for everyone involved.

During a luncheon that summer with some of the company's investors, Carolyn had the opportunity to hear Heather speak about lobbying as it pertains to technology startups.

She was struck by one sentence.

"I remember Heather saying, 'You bring us in when you are so stuck that nothing else can be done,'" she recalls. "We were at that point, and that's when I picked up the phone."

Heather knows how to play the long game and is often willing to serve as a fairy godmother of sorts to earlier-stage startups in HopSkipDrive's position, talking through ideas, strategies, and providing strategic counsel on how and when to engage in Washington, whom to hire, and how to think through next steps.

Lobbying to Create Your Market

While Heather notes that most startups first approach lobbying to provide defense or protection—in other words, shielding the company from policy outcomes that would threaten its business model and its very survival—some smart and effective startups deploy lobbying as an offensive strategy to help create, sustain, or grow a market. This is what Alex and Dan were doing with Opower, but they're not the only ones.

Take Guillermo Pepe and Mamotest, for example.

"When I started doing the research in the beginning, I realized there was no legislation in our country to encourage women to get a mammogram every year," says Pepe, founder of the Argentine telemedicine startup. In fact, women risked getting docked up to 20 percent of their salary if they skipped a day of work to get tested, he found. Of course, Pepe's company makes money when more women get tested, so that presented a major barrier to growth.

"Women we interviewed would tell us, 'No, I'm not going to have my yearly mammogram because I don't have the time to do it,'" he says.

It was a completely different setup in other countries, his research showed.

"I found out in Europe, in certain countries, they basically tell the women, 'You have to go get your mammogram, and if you don't do it, you may lose your health program,'" he said. "So, women do it."

However, Pepe knew a penalty-based system that threatened to strip women of their healthcare could never fly in Latin America, not when government leaders are focused on getting more citizens into the healthcare system, not booting them out.

So Pepe started devising a plan to do the opposite.

"Instead of penalizing women for not getting a mammogram, we wanted to find a way to encourage them," he said. "We knew one thing they would value would be a day off of work, so they could get the mammogram in the morning and then have the rest of the day off."

Pepe approached the leader of the government in the province of Corrientes with his idea: a government-mandated day off from work without penalty for every woman in the province to get an annual mammogram. Corrientes was home to his company's first outpost and the governor had become a staunch supporter of Pepe's mission.

"We told him about the idea, and he thought it would make him very popular if he put this rule in place and that he would get support from the people because he was helping take care of the women in the province," Pepe says. "So he said yes, and we got the rule approved."

Once he had one success, it became easy to scale his lobbying efforts.

"Once that first province said yes, we went to the others and said, 'Look what they are doing in Corrientes, why don't you create the same law in this province?'" Pepe says. "We replicated that exact strategy in three other provinces, and they all accepted it."

Lobbying on Behalf of Your Customers

Lobbying can also provide an avenue to build deeper relationships with your customers, a strategy that is part policy positioning and part grassroots activation.

In Twiga's case, founder Grant Brooke took it upon his company to fill an advocacy vacuum for local farmers and produce vendors, as there was no formal trade group or union speaking with government leaders on behalf of those informal industries. One obvious policy that both groups wanted to see changed was the steep taxes on produce sellers and buyers who wanted to use government-operated wholesale markets.

"We've started meeting with governors around the country and telling them that there was a correlation between the counties where they charged the highest tax and the elected officials who were removed from office during the most recent round of elections," Grant says. "Now, we're seeing the counties that we're active in eliminate those taxes, and it looks like they will soon be lifted throughout the country."

In that way, Grant says, "Twiga has started to represent our customers in the government."

How Startups Lobby

Let's say you've decided, like Dan and Alex, that lobbying is something you need to pursue, even before you have oodles of cash in the bank. Given the challenges I've outlined in this chapter, how do you survive, much less win, in this environment? How do you, as a startup with limited runway, last long enough to even move the needle, much less effect real policy change? How do you afford to wage a sustained lobbying campaign?

What you may notice about Opower, HopSkipDrive, Mamotest, and Twiga (as well as Uber, for that matter) is that they were all primarily lobbying at the local or state level. Not that you can't be effective with persuading federal legislators and regulators, but as I've argued before, your ability to shape policy tends to be greater the closer you are to the direct interests of citizens—for example, with cities, rather than at federal government levels. This will be true whether you're serving as your own lobbyist or hiring a lobbyist, like HopSkip-Drive did.

Your impact is also likely to be greater in more esoteric areas rather than in major policy fights. If, for example, all you need is a minor tweak to the definition of a small business in your city, you might be able to do that in a few weeks with an introduction or two and a few phone calls. We faced exactly this issue early on at 1776, when we learned that the D.C. Department of Small and Local Business Development required startups to have their own physical office in D.C. to qualify for favorable city procurement opportunities, and incubators and coworking spaces didn't count as offices. It took a few phone calls to change that minor but important rule on behalf of our community.

Beyond focusing on the right issues, success often comes back to your power map and the following question: Do you share a policy objective with another influencer who's already lobbying to enact the same change or protect the same rule that you need to change or protect?

"Who else can you bring to the table?" Heather asks. "Can you join another group's efforts? Is there a consumer group or trade association that wants the same thing you do? Or a think tank? Or an environmental or consumer group?"

If so, look for ways to insert your startup into the fight that the influencer is already waging. Do you have an endearing story that the group can use to bolster its arguments? Do you have any data that could prove helpful in their attempts to persuade lawmakers or regulators? Often, startup founders can put a more charming face behind a lobbying campaign than, for instance, a large corporation that's pursuing the very same goals.

"Successful lobbyists find ways to make any issue about something much bigger than their one client, and a lot of that comes down to storytelling,"

Heather says. "You need to be able to clearly and quickly show the chairman of a committee or the top regulator at an agency why they should care about your company before you can make them care about your issue. In other words, if you are lobbying at the federal level, how do you connect your objective to the direct interests or a congressman or senator's constituents?"

The Limits of Lobbying

Even if you do everything right, hiring a lobbyist by itself is no silver bullet.

Mark DeSantis, the RoadBotics founder from Pittsburgh who previously worked as a lobbyist for Texas Instruments to the European Union, says, "One of the mistakes entrepreneurs make in this area is saying, 'Boy, this is just a complicated mess, and I'm just going to hire a lobbyist to solve it for me.' They expect to be able to just step aside and let someone with the right connections fix the problem for them. In reality, those people need as much guidance as possible, and they don't know your startup and your story like you do. Don't overdepend on an outside lobbyist. They can be helpful, but only to a point—you're going to need to be involved."

Heather agrees with DeSantis. "A good lobbyist takes the time to learn your business model, your power map, and your culture," she says. "It's also important to hire someone who understands and speaks tech, and can translate that message into one the Hill can understand."

The Ultimate Hack

You have to be smart about when to play the lobbying game, and if you decide to enter the fray, you should know the rules and play to your startup's strengths. You should do your homework. You should have your narrative singing and know your data backward and forward. You should have invested into building quality relationships with influencers and should be strategically looking to turn them into allies in your fight.

And even if you do all that right, you should be prepared for a knock-down, drag-out fight.

ELON MUSK:
THE ULTIMATE REGULATORY HACKER

He launched a company that changed the way we purchase goods and services and share money with friends and family. Three years later, he launched another to design and build spacecraft that will soon ferry passengers to and from the International Space Station and may someday shuttle a colony of humans to Mars. Not two years after that, he helped found an electric car company that has been credited with fundamentally changing the automotive industry and the way we think about the future of sustainability and transportation.[1]

Later, he unveiled designs for a tube-based, vacuum-sealed transportation system that many believe will change the way we move people and products from one place to another. His electric car company has morphed into a solar energy startup and has built some of the most revolutionary manufacturing plants on earth and developed battery systems that can power entire homes and businesses. And his latest venture is pioneering implantable technology that will let our brains seamlessly and subconsciously communicate with computers.

And yet, for all of Elon Musk's mind-bending breakthroughs over the past two decades, his most impressive and most important invention may be Elon Musk.

Not the person, that is, but the persona. Not the man, but the myth and mystique that surrounds him. When we hear his name, we don't just think billionaire business tycoon, South African genius, or Silicon Valley inventor . . . we think world saver, superhero, Iron Man. His most meaningful invention is that unique image that we have of Elon Musk, the narrative thread weaving through his entire career and stitching together each of his business ventures, because it's the foundation that has made all of the others possible.

And it didn't happen by accident.

Over the course of several decades, Musk has deliberately and audaciously cultivated the narrative that has now come to define him—that of a superhumanly genius inventor who's using his hard-earned fortune to invent a future torn from the pages of science fiction books, a future that will be vastly better for individual citizens and for civilization as a whole.

He has built Elon Musk the character through years of carefully orchestrated media interviews and public appearances. In these settings, he consistently presents a vision for human civilization, beyond even our world, that's even more provocatively futuristic than the last time he graced the pages of a tech magazine or took the stage at an industry event. His mystique grows with every new proclamation about the high speed at which we will one day travel through his Hyperloop transit system[2] or the ever-shrinking number of years between present day and a manned shuttle landing on Mars.[3]

"I think we'll be able to do short flights [of his Mars spaceship], up and down flights, some time in the first half of [2019]," Musk told an audience at the South by Southwest (SXSW) festival in Austin, Texas in March 2018.

He consistently talks less about the financial aims of his ventures than about the societal challenges they seek to solve. In other words, Musk has mastered selling the "why" behind his companies. When he talks about colonizing Mars with his space exploration company, SpaceX, he does so in the context of prolonging the history of our species. "The most important thing is to create a self-sustaining city on Mars. That's the critical thing for maximizing the life of humanity [and] how long our civilization will last."[4]

Even on the occasions when he does publicly speak about the financial imperatives driving his businesses, he still connects it all back to the "why." In an interview a few years ago, he said, "Not being motivated by money is not the same as saying that SpaceX should not make money. In fact, it's very important that SpaceX is profitable or we will not be able to earn the money necessary to continue future developments."

What may set Musk apart, from a storytelling standpoint, is his uncanny ability to render far-fetched ideas in a way that's totally plausible. In part, he does this by talking about the notion of, say, building an entire civilization as though it's a simple math problem that needs to be worked out. As soon as we can hammer out the numbers, we can pack our bags: "In order to have a self-sustaining city on Mars—there would need to be millions of tons of equipment and probably millions of people. So how many launches is that? Well, if you send up one hundred people at a time, which is a lot to go on such a long journey, you would need to do ten thousand flights to get to a million people. So ten thousand flights, but over what period of time? Given that you can only really depart for Mars once every two years, that means you would need like forty or fifty years."[5]

Suddenly, we're not talking about *whether* we're going to Mars. We have moved beyond that. We're talking about how long it will take to get there. Through the way he frames the narrative, he has moved us from *if* to *when*.

"His greatest asset is his ability to take this big, big dream and make other people believe that it's true," Max Chafkin, a technology and business reporter who has profiled Musk on multiple occasions, said in an interview with Bloomberg a few years ago.[6]

Musk has also curated an almost robotic persona in interviews about subjects unrelated to his business ventures. Asked about his greatest fears as a child, he once said: "When I was a little kid, I was really afraid of the dark. But then I came to understand that the dark just means the absence of photons in the visible wavelength, four hundred to seven hundred nanometers. So then I wasn't afraid of the dark anymore."[7] He has also been quoted as saying: "If there was a way that I could not eat, so I could work more, I would not eat. I wish there was a way to get nutrients without sitting down for a meal."[8] He has in several media interviews openly questioned whether our world and our lives are merely playing out within another civilization's video game.[9]

Over time, through these and so many other comments, the Elon Musk that emerges in our minds is a man that is simply wired differently. Then again, for someone looking to establish a personal brand as someone who may very well be able to save mankind from itself, being seen as a little other-worldly isn't such a bad thing.

The result is a carefully-crafted, painstakingly-maintained narrative around Elon Musk that's best summed up by author Ashlee Vance in her 2015 biography, *Elon Musk: Inventing the Future*. In it, she writes: "Musk is the possessed genius on the grandest quest anyone has ever concocted. He's less a CEO chasing riches than a general marshaling troops to secure victory. Where

Mark Zuckerberg wants to help you share baby photos, Musk wants to . . . well . . . save the human race from self-imposed or accidental annihilation."[10]

Why is that so important for Musk from a business standpoint?

Because Musk is the ultimate regulatory hacker.

His companies—from PayPal to Tesla and SolarCity to SpaceX and Neuralink—operate in extraordinarily complex, regulated markets. Whether you're trying to change the way money is exchanged or blast humans into the stars, you are going to have complex regulatory questions to answer. When you're aiming to change the way we move about the world or developing new ways to power our daily lives or seeking to embed computer-connected chips into our brains, the public interest courses through every move you make, and with that, you're going to have to work with—not around—governments. There's no way to avoid it.

It helps when every public official you encounter in every city around the world knows who you are when you come calling. It makes it even easier when every one of those officials believes that you're genuinely trying to make life better for their citizens, and even, as Vance put it, save the human race. It becomes a devastating weapon, though, when you couple it with a track record of consistently delivering success in the face of soul-crushing odds and a cacophony of naysayers. That's why the legend Musk is so unmistakably important to his success across all his business ventures. It's all about his brand, and Musk has managed to transform his personal brand from that of a scrawny bookworm from South Africa to become the inspiration for Iron Man,[11] *Fortune* magazine's Business Person of the Year, and—as he was described in a bestselling biography—"a deity in Silicon Valley."[12]

"Brand is just a perception, and perception will match reality over time," Musk once said in an interview. "Sometimes it will be ahead, other times it will be behind. But brand is simply a collective impression some have about a product."[13]

Musk's mastery of his personal narrative and the narrative surrounding his many companies stands out as an obvious regulatory hack, but the billionaire entrepreneur has actually used nearly all of the regulatory hacks outlined in this book. His strategic use of the media, for instance, extends well beyond his knack for building his own brand. He has become a master at leveraging the media to generate positive attention around each of his companies and pique the interest of investors, customers, and other key stakeholders.

At this point, we can imagine the scene in our minds. An enormous white curtain stretches from the stage to the ceiling. Suddenly, blue and orange strobe lights begin to flash as an ominous voice begins to count down. "Ten. Nine. Eight." Dramatic music starts softly but begins to build, a dance beat thumping through speakers. "Three. Two. One." The curtain falls and flutters out of sight as a foggy mist billows out onto the stage. The crowd goes wild as the colored light display gives way to a flurry of flash bulbs.

Standing centerstage? Not a rock star and his band.

Musk and his rocket ship.

That's the scene that unfolded inside the cavernous rocket factory of SpaceX in what was once a Northrop Grumman facility just south of Los Angeles in May 2014. Musk had gathered hundreds of reporters to join investors and other Valley VIPs to witness the unveiling of SpaceX's new Dragon 2 spacecraft, a capsule designed to ferry human passengers into space, including trips to and from the International Space Station. One reporter on hand would later describe it as "an event worthy of a Hollywood premiere."[14]

Over the top? Maybe. But that same reporter, writing for Space.com, concluded his story as follows: "For those of us old enough to remember the space race, there is a remarkable sense of potential at SpaceX, and it's impossible to spend time there without an almost forgotten sense of optimism about human spaceflight to take over. It was a night few in attendance will soon forget."

The press coming out of the event was a major victory. "The debut of this upgraded spacecraft is a very good sign for U.S space travel and couldn't have come at a better time," Vox concluded in a story about Dragon 2's debut.[15] *Smithsonian Magazine*'s headline declared: "SpaceX Will Soon Be Able to Send People to Space (Take That, Russia.)."[16] Dozens of media outlets followed suit with similarly glowing headlines.

Nearly every new product or new development coming out of Musk's companies over the last couple of years has been immediately met with a deluge of media coverage—effortlessly catching waves on topics like space and automobiles, but bolstered by smart public relations tactics that create positive stories about the companies at every turn.

Musk's mastery of earned media has even allowed him to save money on paid media, according to some experts. "Tesla doesn't really have to use traditional advertising because it is unique and the brand perception is so strong," Robert Klara, *Ad Week* senior editor, said in an interview with *Platform Magazine*. "Tesla doesn't need to take out a national TV ad because its market is people who already know about Tesla."[17]

Taking this truth to an almost absurd extreme, Musk held the media—tens of millions of people around the world—spellbound when he launched his personal Tesla Roadster into space on his staggeringly powerful Falcon Heavy Rocket, which has to rank as perhaps the coolest earned media hack of all time! It doesn't always require a glamorous event to generate coverage and build product awareness, either. Using data to seed an evidence-based story, SolarCity published a blog post in May 2016 using its own data to generate a list of the ten most "contagious" solar cities in the country, where the largest share of SolarCity's installations resulted from word-of-mouth referrals.[18] The company circulated the blog post to reporters, generating press pickup in publications like Vox and TreeHugger.com.

And even on the occasions where a piece of media coverage hasn't gone his way, Musk has managed to use his owned media channels as a weapon. When *The New York Times* journalist John Broder penned a brutal review of the Tesla Model S,[19] Musk and team investigated and discovered that many of the author's claims about his experience with the car were either false or misleading.

"Most people said, 'It doesn't matter if you're right or wrong, you don't go to battle with *The New York Times*,'" he said in an interview later. "I said, 'To hell with that.'"[20]

Musk published a data-rich article on Tesla's blog titled "A Most Peculiar Test Drive," in which he presented the facts and asked *The New York Times* to investigate.[21] The *Times*'s public editor did just that and later acknowledged in a column "problems with precision and judgment" in the original article.[22]

To recap: Develop a narrative? Check. Generate earned and owned media? Check. Use data? Check. Now, let's run through some of the additional regulatory hacks Musk has used to help him build a market for and scale company after company in complex industry after complex industry.

As I outlined in Chapter 5: Arbitrage, regulatory hackers benefit from being able to identify and take advantage of arbitrage opportunities—and even getting governments to compete for them. One illustrative example is Tesla's quest to find the right home for a massive new "gigafactory."

As Peter Elkind wrote in *Fortune* magazine, "Musk took a process that typically plays out behind the scenes and made it public. He played an Oz-like role as master orchestrator, sending signals through earnings calls and blog postings while keeping the states in the dark and playing on their fears of losing out. The combination of his strategy, the electric Musk factor, and the lure of 6,500 jobs inspired excited bidding among seven states and staggering leaps of faith."[23]

Musk ultimately secured a reported $1.4 billion in tax breaks, free land, and other benefits from Governor Brian Sandoval and the Nevada Legislature to build the factory near Reno. In the days that followed, Musk used his media prowess to defend the package in the press. "The $1.3 billion or so is the maximum tax incentive that Tesla could get over twenty years, so an average of, like, $50 or $60 million a year, is a tiny fraction of what this factory's output will be," he said in one interview. "It is not material to the economics of the factory."[24]

Musk's hack proved so effective that Jeff Bezos has stolen the script with "HQ2," the very public competition among North American cities to be home to Amazon's second headquarters. Another tool in Musk's regulatory hacking toolkit: grassroots activation. In 2014, Musk hired Jon Carson, a former campaign strategist for President Obama, to spearhead a multiyear grassroots campaign to place solar panels on every roof in the country. As *The Washington Post* reported at the time, "the idea is to use the tactics of a grassroots political campaign to influence consumers' energy decisions."[25]

Carson would go on to lead SolarCity's so-called ambassadors program, through which customers received a $250 credit when they referred a friend to sign up the company's service. Because as Carson pointed out in a separate interview with Yale, "The number-one thing we can do to convince people that solar is right for them is to have their friends, family members, and co-workers explain why it was right for them. The ambassador program gives people those conversation starters, and helps them understand the movement they're part of."[26]

He added, referencing *movements:* "If you're one of our solar ambassadors, and you help ten families in your neighborhood switch to clean power, that is real and impactful. And at the same time, you feel part of the movement. You feel that you're part of these thousands of people moving in the same direction."[27]

Naturally, Musk and his team at SpaceX have also mastered selling to governments—currently, the only buyers on the market for trips to the International Space Station. To date, NASA has awarded twenty space station cargo-supply missions to SpaceX, with the agency representing the overwhelming majority of the company's revenue over the past decade.[28] And it will surprise no one that companies run by Musk embrace the importance of gathering data to validate their products and services as they go through a mandatory gauntlet of third-party rigor when it comes time to test, say, introduce a new Tesla model or test SpaceX's latest rockets.

Musk's empire has also become deeply familiar with lobbying. Over the eighteen-month period starting in January 2016, Tesla spent more than $100,000 on lobbying around issues related to electric vehicles and more than $450,000 overall shaping policies with the U.S. federal government, according to lobbying disclosure records. Tesla's lobbying efforts included "discussions regarding electric vehicle manufacturing and sales policies and regulation," as well as "discussions regarding issues impacting [electric vehicle] manufacturers regarding autonomous drive vehicles," the documents show.[29]

Over at SpaceX, a recent report published by the Sunlight Foundation, a group that tracks government spending, found that SpaceX has spent $4 million on lobbying Congress since Musk launched the company in 2002 and has dished out more than $800,000 in political contributions to congressional leaders on both sides of the aisle.[30]

"SpaceX's campaign to win political support has been systematic and sophisticated," Sunlight wrote, noting that Musk has personally donated about $725,000 to various campaigns over that same period. If you want to change the world, you need influence.

Elon Musk is a deity in Silicon Valley because he chose to commit himself utterly to improving our lives as citizens during an era when much of the Valley was chasing more trivial problems. Today, as the Regulatory Era dawns, there is perhaps no better role model for entrepreneurs around the world. He is sophisticated in his pursuit of the public interest and he isn't afraid to do things his own way.

"I think people can choose to not be ordinary," Musk said in an interview. "I think it's possible for ordinary people to choose to be extraordinary."[31]

Acknowledgments

This book could not exist without the contributions and support of many people, but none more than one in particular. Kaushik Viswanath at Portfolio/Penguin heard a podcast that I had done with a16z on regulatory hacking and reached out to me suggesting it should be a book. This is the first book that he has owned from start to finish as an editor, and he has guided me every step of the way with his patient confidence.

Kaushik introduced me to my agent, Rafe Sagalyn, who helped me understand the business and creative process of creating a book and provided invaluable counsel on this journey.

J.D. Harrison and I have known each other since early in his career at *The Washington Post*. Our relationship continued when he moved over to the U.S. Chamber of Commerce, and he was the first and best choice to collaborate with me on this book. Neither of us knew what we were doing going in, but it has been a joy to figure it out together. J.D. is a much better storyteller than I could ever be, and this book is much stronger for his contributions.

Donna Harris was the best cofounder I could imagine during our journey together with 1776. Our discussions about our 1776 investment portfolio continue to be high points of my week. The experiences that Donna brought to 1776 as a serial entrepreneur and public affairs expert formed the basis for what has evolved into regulatory hacking. If there is one person without whom *Regulatory Hacking* would not exist, it is Donna.

Donna and I could not have created 1776 without Brittany Heyd and Brandon Pollak. Brittany was the "getting shit done" force behind 1776. Brandon brought his political network to help our startups overcome obstacle after obstacle.

Morgan Gress Johnson was twenty-two years old when she became one of our first and most important hires at 1776. It has been a privilege to watch her grow into a powerhouse for 1776 and now an indispensable adviser to Union and to me personally. Her patience in helping me shape this book has been deeply appreciated.

Penny Lee was one of the first people I met when we started thinking about K Street Capital, before 1776 was even an idea. Her credibility and connections have always been powerful, but they are nothing compared with the grace and patience she has shown in working with me over the years.

Regulatory hacking is the synthesis of many important ideas, most of which came through conversations and debates with members of the 1776 and Union teams. Thank you to Rusty, Zipper, Christian, Margaret, Dominique, Vero, Veronica, Garrett, Ashley, Yuri, Meagan, Dolan, Kate, Shahier, Rachel, Camille, Rianna, Ned, Tarek, Jude, Steve, Fred, Fabio, Pedro, David, Margarida, Brandon, and so many others who contributed to the 1776 journey.

1776 and Union exist because of the support of a small band of board members and investors who have stood by us through thick and thin. Thank you to Ron Klain, Tim Peterson, Mike Culhane, Mitchell Shear, David Hall, Sapna Mehta, and Ankur Shah for your tireless support, particularly at moments when it would have been easy to throw in the towel.

Joshua Baer of Capital Factory was an inspiration to us when we were thinking about what 1776 could be. He is a partner and board member with Union today. In between he has supported me, challenged me, and been a great friend through more late-night phone calls than I can count.

It is hard to hand over the reins of something that I care about as much as 1776, but handing them to Jennifer and Anthony Maher made it much easier. They believe in the power of startup ecosystems as much as Donna and I do, and they remain wonderful collaborators as we continue to grow the 1776 community.

Before 1776, my experiences leading Synteractive taught me important lessons about how governments work, up close and personal. Synteractive wouldn't have been possible without my wonderful colleagues and supporters. Thank you to Robert Groat, Shirin Rahimi, Diane Johnson, Nina Ward, Joe Gerczak, Teresa Carlson, Chris Dorobek, and so many more.

Adam Sharp has been a friend for years. When I needed someone to read early drafts of this book, he jumped in and provided me brutally direct feedback. The book is much stronger today for it.

Tony Fratto, Heather Podesta, Steve Rochlin, Teddy Goff, Stephanie Cutter, and Sara Fagen have all been friends and supporters over the years. I am appreciative of the time that each spent explaining the details of their specialties with me and reviewing drafts of this book.

Noah Raford is one of my favorite thinkers about the world. The story that I tell in the book about meeting him for the first time is the literal truth.

Cristina Pompo Rivera was one of the first people I reached out to when I was looking for regulatory hackers in Latin America. Her work with the Inter-American Development Bank is important and it is a privilege to partner with her.

Peter Cherukuri and Roy Schwartz have been friends since way before 1776. Our adventures at the 2012 Republican and Democratic conventions remain indelible. They were my Sherpas into the world of politics and public affairs.

This book would also not exist without Christopher Schroeder, the author of *Startup Rising*. He arranged the a16z podcast that started the journey to this book. I will always be grateful for his willingness to extend the support of his network from Silicon Valley to Singapore.

Steve and Jean Case did more than anyone else to inspire the creation of 1776. Steve's ideas on the Rise of the Rest and in *The Third Wave* are woven through this book, as is Jean's leadership on impact investing. Their leadership within the Washington, D.C., community, across America, and around the world motivates me every day.

I could only hope to live up to the example that Katherine and David Bradley have set as leaders in the community. They were the first limited partners in our venture fund, when everyone else thought we were nuts. They have always been generous with their time and wisdom. More than anything, though, their grace, warmth, and humility guide me every day.

Thanks to Margot Stamas, Taylor Edwards, Tess Espinoza, Christina Caruccio, Laura Corless, and the rest of the team at Portfolio/Penguin for getting this book out into the world.

And finally, I could not possibly conclude these acknowledgments without profound thanks to my family. Vera is my best friend and the greatest partner in life I could imagine, mostly because she never goes easy on me. This book is no exception. When other people were willing to let me slide with a faint "looks good," Vera would tell me the brutal truth and send me back to work.

Rusty and Matthew put more time into reading early drafts and providing me feedback than anyone outside of Vera, Kaushik, or J.D. You guys are the greatest brothers I could have. Thank you for always having my back when I need it.

I am the son of lobbyists who dedicated their careers to the public interest. Until I sat down to write this book, I don't think I realized what an impact my father and stepmother's dinner table stories of legislative maneuvering had on me. Dad and Diane, I hope I got it right.

To Mom and Chris, thank you for picking up the slack when I had to go deep into writing, and for cheering me on in everything I do.

To Endeavour and Lymond Daneel, you are my hostages to the future, driving me to do everything I can to make sure you grow up in a *Star Trek* future, rather than a *Mad Max* one. I hope you'll read this someday and know that everything I do, I do for you.

—Evan

Thank you, first and foremost, to Evan. I remain humbled and profoundly grateful that you invited me to collaborate on this important and rewarding endeavor. A big thanks, too, to our editor, Kaushik Viswanath, who deftly and calmly guided us through the entire process.

I owe a special thank you to two incredible teachers who sparked my love affair with writing, Estelle Clark and Jeff Lang. I owe another to four brilliant editors who pushed me to be a better reporter and storyteller: Justin Catanoso, Sandy Padwe, J. "Josh" Jennings Moss, and Dan Beyers. And I owe a third to Tom Collamore, Mia Walton, and Blair Holmes, who supported me throughout this project and who have provided invaluable mentorship since I arrived at the U.S. Chamber of Commerce.

I want to thank my loving parents, Jan and Kevin, who have always encouraged me to run toward challenges like this one and who provided encouragement at every step in the journey. I also want to thank my two extraordinary siblings, Clark and Sarah, who inspire me every day with their talents, drive, and creativity.

Finally, I offer my deepest gratitude to the entrepreneurs who took time away from saving the world to share their stories and their wisdom with us. So many of you gave so richly of your time, and it was a joy and a privilege to help bring your remarkable stories to life in the pages of this book.

—J.D.

Notes

Except where otherwise noted, all quotes from startup founders and experts are based on interviews conducted by the authors between May 2017 and February 2018.

INTRODUCTION: THE REGULATORY ERA

1. Richard Florida, "The Global Cities Where Tech Venture Capital Is Concentrated," *The Atlantic*, January 26, 2016, https://www.theatlantic.com/technology/archive/2016/01/global-startup-cities-venture-capital/429255/.
2. Tomasz Tunguz, "How Developed Is Global Venture Capital Market?" Tomasz Tunguz (blog), July 23, 2017, http://tomtunguz.com/global-venture-snapshot/.
3. Anita Balakrishnan, "Facebook should be regulated like a cigarette company, says Salesforce CEO," CNBC.com, January 23, 2018, https://www.cnbc.com/2018/01/23/salesforce-ceo-marc-benioff-says-regulate-facebook-like-tobacco.html.
4. Business and Sustainable Development Commission, "Better Business Better World Report," January 2017, http://report.businesscommission.org/report.
5. Brian O'Keefe, "The Red Tape Conundrum," *Fortune*, October 20, 2016, http://fortune.com/red-tape-business-regulations/.

CHAPTER 1: REGULATORY HACKING

1. Mike Debonis, "Uber car impounded, driver ticketed in city sting," *The Washington Post*, January 13, 2012, https://www.washingtonpost.com/blogs/mike-debonis/post/uber-car-impounded-driver-ticketed-in-city-sting/2012/01/13/gIQA4Py3vP_blog.html.
2. "Uber funding rounds," Crunchbase, accessed February 9, 2018, https://www.crunchbase.com/organization/uber/funding_rounds/funding_rounds_list.
3. Polina Marinova, "Early Uber Investor Says SoftBank Tender Offer Is a 'Low Blow,'" *Fortune*, December 4, 2017, http://fortune.com/2017/12/04/tusk-ventures-softbank-uber/.
4. Seth Fiegerman, "Uber for failure: How on-demand startups crash and burn," Mashable, April 20, 2016, http://mashable.com/2016/04/20/uber-for-failure/.
5. Ibid.
6. Ibid.

CHAPTER 2: POWER

1. "Walter Kidde," accessed February 9, 2018, http://www.kidde.com/home-safety/en/us/about/walter-kidde/.

2. "Carbon Monoxide Detector Requirements, Laws and Regulations," National Conference of State Legislatures, accessed February 8, 2018, http://www.ncsl.org/research/environment -and-natural-resources/carbon-monoxide-detectors-state-statutes.aspx.
3. Benjamin Freed, "Metro Has Lost So Many Customers It's Dragging Down National Ridership Figures," *Washingtonian*, March 10, 2017, https://www.washingtonian.com/2017/03 /10/metros-ridership-fell-so-much-in-2016-it-dragged-down-all-us-subway-ridership/.

CHAPTER 3: BUSINESS MODELS

1. TroopSwap.com, screenshot of website, accessed February 2013.
2. ID.me support, "Using your ID.me credentials to claim discounts," accessed February 8, 2018, https://help.id.me/hc/en-us/articles/201967984-Using-your-ID-me-credentials-to-claim -discounts?mobile_site=true.
3. Tesla support, "Vehicle Incentives," accessed February 8, 2018, https://www.tesla.com/sup port/incentives.

CHAPTER 4: GROWTH

1. "Percentage of Household Income Spent on Electricity by State," Electric Choice, November 28, 2016, https://www.electricchoice.com/blog/percentage-income-electricity/.
2. Katie Fehrenbacher, "Opower hires CFO, considering IPO down the road," GigaOm, November 16, 2011, https://gigaom.com/2011/11/16/opower-hires-cfo-considering-ipo-down-the-road/.
3. Paul Graham, "Startup=Growth," Paul Graham (blog), September 2012, http://www.paulgra ham.com/growth.html.
4. Anne Wojcicki, "An Update Regarding The FDA's Letter to 23andMe," 23andMe Blog, November 26, 2013, https://blog.23andme.com/news/an-update-regarding-the-fdas-letter -to-23andme/.

CHAPTER 5: ARBITRAGE

1. Department for Transport and The Rt Hon John Hayes CBE MP, "Government invests over £2.5 million in new technologies and ideas to futureproof UK's transport sector," Gov.UK, December 6, 2016, https://www.gov.uk/government/news/government-invests-over-25 -million-in-new-technologies-and-ideas-to-futureproof-uks-transport-sector.
2. Paul Graham, "Ramen Profitable," Paul Graham (blog), July 2009, http://www.paulgraham .com/ramenprofitable.html.
3. Ibid.
4. "Our Roads," Transurban, accessed February 9, 2018, https://www.transurban.com/our -operations/our-roads.
5. "Boston Scientific Receives CE Mark for Vercise™ Gevia™ Deep Brain Stimulation System Industry's First MR-Conditional Directional DBS System with Stimulation Visualization," *Boston Scientific*, June 6, 2017, http://news.bostonscientific.com/2017-06-06-Boston-Scientific-Receives-CE-Mark-for-Vercise-TM-Gevia-TM-Deep-Brain-Stimulation-System.
6. Dana Mattioli and William Boston, "Daimler Expands into Ride Sharing," *Wall Street Journal*, September 3, 2014, https://www.wsj.com/articles/daimler-moves-into-ride-sharing -economy-1409750844.
7. Issac John, "Dubai is world's 5th fastest growing city economy: Report," *Khaleej Times*, August 20, 2015, https://www.khaleejtimes.com/nation/dubai-worlds-5th-fastest-growing-city -economy-report. 5th
8. Armin Rosen, "Inside Dubai's Bid to Become the Middle East's Tech Hub," *Fast Company*, September 26, 2017, https://www.fastcompany.com/40472785/inside-dubais-bid-to-become -the-middle-easts-tech-hub.

9. Ibid.

10. Michael del Castillo, "Dubai Wants All Government Documents on Blockchain by 2020," Coindesk, October 5, 2016, https://www.coindesk.com/dubai-government-documents -blockchain-strategy-2020/.

11. "Dubai Land Department becomes world's first government entity to conduct all transactions through Blockchain network," Government of Dubai Media Office, October 7, 2017, http:// mediaoffice.ae/en/media-center/news/7/10/2017/dubai-land-department.aspx.

12. Tyler Woods, "Here's CTO Miguel Gamiño Jr.'s vision for New York's tech future," Technically, December 13, 2017, https://technical.ly/brooklyn/2017/12/13/cto-miguel-gamino -j-new-york-tech-future/.

13. "De Blasio Administration Launches NYCx to Stimulate Economic Growth, Create Jobs and Solve Big Challenges Through New Technologies," City of New York, October 19, 2017, http:// www1.nyc.gov/office-of-the-mayor/news/665-17/de-blasio-administration-launches -nycx-stimulate-economic-growth-create-jobs-solve-big.

14. "About SBIR," SBIR.gov, accessed February 9, 2018, https://www.sbir.gov/about.

CHAPTER 6: NARRATIVE

1. "Safety," HopSkipDrive, accessed February 9, 2018, https://www.hopskipdrive.com/safety/.

2. "HopSkipDrive: Created By Moms. Driven With Love," Lioness, April 17, 2015, https://lion essmagazine.com/hopskipdrive-created-by-moms-driven-with-love/#.WlefFpM-cU0.

3. Emma Johnson, "Joanna McFarland, HopSkipDrive: Frees moms from kid-schlepping" (podcast), December 26, 2016, http://emmajohnson.libsyn.com/joanna-mcfarland-hopskipdrive -frees-moms-from-kid-schlepping.

4. Alison Griswold, "The Year in Uber," Slate, December 30, 2014, http://www.slate.com /articles/business/moneybox/2014/12/uber_spent_2014_expanding_aggressively_and _pissing_off_just_about_everyone.html.

5. Jason Clampet, "Airbnb's New Logo and Website Want You to Feel Belonging," Skift, July 16, 2014, https://skift.com/2014/07/16/airbnbs-new-logo-and-website-want-you-to-feel -belonging/.

6. Simon Sinek, "How Great Leaders Inspire Action" (TED Talk), accessed February 9, 2018, https://www.ted.com/talks/simon_sinek_how_great_leaders_inspire_action.

CHAPTER 7: DATA

1. Anastasia Christman and Christine Riordan, "State Infrastructure Banks: Old Idea Yields New Opportunities for Job Creation," National Employment Law Project, briefing paper, December 2011, http://www.nelp.org/content/uploads/2015/03/State_Infrastructure _Banks.pdf.

2. Geoffrey A. Moore, Crossing the Chasm, 3rd ed. (New York: HarperCollins, 2014).

3. "Clinical Data," iSleepSound, accessed February 9, 2018, http://isleepsound.com/clinical -data/.

4. Dr. Nancy Markley, "Due diligence is a responsibility for investors, an opportunity for startups," TechCrunch, October 4, 2016, https://techcrunch.com/2016/10/04/due-diligence -is-a-responsibility-for-investors-an-opportunity-for-startups/.

5. "Clinical Data," iSleepSound, accessed February 9, 2018, http://isleepsound.com/clinical -data/.

6. Vadim Polikov, "New Research Proves Game-Based Learning Works—Here's Why That Matters," EdSurge, March 6, 2017, https://www.edsurge.com/news/2017-03-06-new-research -proves-game-based-learning-works-here-s-why-that-matters.

7. Ibid.

8. Sarah Gantz, "Legends of Learning raises $9 million for expansion," *Baltimore Sun*, April 20, 2017, http://www.baltimoresun.com/business/bs-bz-legends-of-learning-20170419 -story.html.

9. "The world's most valuable resource is no longer oil, but data," *The Economist*, May 6, 2017, https://www.economist.com/news/leaders/21721656-data-economy-demands-new -approach-antitrust-rules-worlds-most-valuable-resource.

CHAPTER 8: INFLUENCE

1. Katie Benner, "23andMe wants to change the face of health care," *Fortune*, December 12, 2012, http://fortune.com/2012/12/12/23andme-wants-to-change-the-face-of-health-care/.

2. Elizabeth Murphy, "Inside 23andMe founder Anne Wojcicki's $99 DNA Revolution," *Fast Company*, October 14, 2013, https://www.fastcompany.com/3018598/for-99-this-ceo-can-tell-you -what-might-kill-you-inside-23andme-founder-anne-wojcickis-dna-r.

3. Kara Swisher, interview with Anne Wojcicki, "Anne Wojcicki of 23andMe Talks," *Wall Street Journal*, January 11, 2013, http://www.wsj.com/video/anne-wojcicki-of-23andme-talks /319BCD6F-2DF2-4797-AF17-13D0D52F1331.html.

4. Sarah McBride, "Russian billionaire invests in U.S. genetics company 23andMe," Reuters, December 11, 2012, https://www.reuters.com/article/us-venture-genetics-billionaire/rus sian-billionaire-invests-in-u-s-genetics-company-23andme-idUSBRE8BA1EP20121212.

5. U.S. Food and Drug Administration, "Warning letter" to Anne Wojcicki, November 22, 2013, https://www.fda.gov/ICECI/EnforcementActions/WarningLetters/ucm376296.htm.

6. Matthew Herper, "23andStupid: Is 23andMe Self-Destructing?," *Forbes*, November 25, 2013, https://www.forbes.com/sites/matthewherper/2013/11/25/23andstupid-is-23andme -self-destructing/.

7. Jason Sanchez, "23andMe: FDA ruling had huge impact" (video), CNNTech, March 17, 2014, http://money.cnn.com/video/technology/2014/03/17/t-23andme-anne-wojcicki-fda. cnnmoney/index.html.

8. Carolyn Y. Johnson, "23andMe gets FDA approval to report breast cancer risk without a doctor," *The Washington Post*, March 6, 2018.

CHAPTER 9: SELLING TO GOVERNMENT

1. "GSA Schedule FAQ," accessed February 9, 2018, http://gsa.federalschedules.com/gsa -schedule/gsa-schedule-faq/.

2. Brent Adamson, Matthew Dixon, Pat Spenner, and Nick Toman, *The Challenger Customer* (New York: Portfolio/Penguin, 2016).

CHAPTER 10: SELLING TO CITIZENS AND PRIVATE INSTITUTIONS

1. "About Us," Arlington Transportation Partners, accessed February 9, 2018, https://arlington-transportationpartners.com/about-us/.

2. "Obama Administration Pushes Electric Vehicles," Institute for Energy Research, March 10, 2011, https://www.instituteforenergyresearch.org/analysis/obama-administration-pushes -electric-vehicles/.

3. Jerry Hirsch, "Elon Musk's growing empire is fueled by $4.9 billion in government subsidies," *Los Angeles Times*, May 30, 2015, http://www.latimes.com/business/la-fi-hy-musk-subsidies -20150531-story.html.

4. Josh Harkinson, "Taxpayer Subsidies Helped Tesla Motors, So Why Does Elon Musk Slam Them?," *Mother Jones*, September/October 2013, https://www.motherjones.com/politics /2013/10/tesla-motors-free-ride-elon-musk-government-subsidies/.

5. "Fact Sheet—Small Unmanned Aircraft Regulations (Part 107)," Federal Aviation Administration, June 21, 2016, https://www.faa.gov/news/fact_sheets/news_story.cfm?newsId=20516.

CHAPTER 11: SELLING WITH SOCIAL IMPACT

1. Guest lecture by Tom Davidson at "Startups that Matter" speaker series, Startup Hoyas, Georgetown University McDonough School of Business, November 2015.
2. Wayne Visser, "Exposing the CSR Pretenders," CSRWire, October 27, 2011, http://www.csrwire.com/blog/posts/188-exposing-the-csr-pretenders.
3. Business and Sustainable Development Commission, "Better Business Better World Report," January 2017, http://report.businesscommission.org/report.
4. Malcolm Johnson, "Digital Solutions to achieve the SDGs," Global e-Sustainability Initiative, May 18, 2016. http://gesi.org/blog/detail/digital-solutions-to-achieve-the-sdgs.
5. "The Circular Economy Could Unlock $4.5 trillion of Economic Growth, Finds New Book by Accenture," Accenture, September 28, 2015, https://newsroom.accenture.com/news/the-circular-economy-could-unlock-4-5-trillion-of-economic-growth-finds-new-book-by-accenture.htm.

CHAPTER 12: THE MEDIA

1. "Civic engagement platform brings the town meeting online," Springwise, September 8, 2015, https://www.springwise.com/civic-engagement-platform-brings-town-meeting-online/.
2. "HopSkipDrive Releases Inaugural Survey on State of Back to School Transportation in America," Cision, August 16, 2016, http://www.prweb.com/releases/2016/08/prweb13616644.htm.
3. Melissa Willets, "Parents Say Driving Their Kids Everywhere Is More Stressful Than This?!," *Parents*, accessed February 9, 2018, https://www.parents.com/toddlers-preschoolers/everything-kids/parents-say-driving-their-kids-everywhere-is-more-stressful/.
4. Maricar Santos, "The Time We Spend Shuttling Our Kids to School Equals a Part-Time Job," *Working Mother*, September 27, 2017, https://www.workingmother.com/time-we-spend-shuttling-our-kids-to-school-equals-part-time-job.
5. Lea Lane, "Airbnb Predicts 2018's Most Popular Travel Destinations & Adventures," *Forbes*, December 19, 2017, https://www.forbes.com/sites/lealane/2017/12/19/airbnb-predicts-2018s-most-popular-travel-destinations-adventures/.
6. "San Francisco Company Closes $1.6M Round to Deliver Water Loss Analytics to Help Utilities Cope with the Drought," Valor Water Analytics, June 9, 2016, https://www.valorwater.com/news/2016/6/10/san-francisco-company-closes-16m-round-to-deliver-water-loss-analytics-to-help-utilities-cope-with-the-drought.
7. Sam O'Keefe, "Where are they now? Startup Battlefield participant Valor Water raises $1.6M," TechCrunch, June 14, 2016, https://techcrunch.com/2016/06/14/where-are-they-now-startup-battlefield-participant-valor-water-raises-1-6m/.
8. Faith Mellinger, "My Child's Ride with HopSkipDrive," Macaroni Kid, June 4, 2015, https://pasadena.macaronikid.com/articles/58264b0c24d8f4da3aac103f/my-childs-ride-with-hopskipdrive.

CHAPTER 13: GRASSROOTS

1. "City of San Francisco Initiative to Restrict Short-Term Rentals, Proposition F (November 2015)," Ballotpedia, November 2015, https://ballotpedia.org/City_of_San_Francisco_Initiative_to_Restrict_Short-Term_Rentals,_Proposition_F_(November_2015).

2. "Airbnb > Funding Rounds," Crunchbase, accessed February 9, 2018, https://www.crunch base.com/organization/airbnb/funding_rounds/funding_rounds_list.

3. Tracey Lien, "Everything you need to know about San Francisco's Airbnb ballot measure," *Los Angeles Times*, October 30, 2015, http://www.latimes.com/business/technology/la-fi-tn -airbnb-prop-f-san-francisco-20151029-htmlstory.html.

4. Ibid.

5. Dianne Feinstein, "Don't Hand San Francisco over to Airbnb," *SFGate*, October 20, 2014, http://www.sfgate.com/opinion/openforum/article/Don-t-hand-San-Francisco-over-to -Airbnb-5835325.php.

6. Alison Griswold, "After Offending All of San Francisco, Airbnb Still Trounced the Hotel Industry on Election Day," *Slate*, November 4, 2015, http://www.slate.com/blogs/moneybox /2015/11/04/airbnb_defeats_prop_f_in_san_francisco_despite_its_tactless_ad_campaign. html.

7. Davey Alba, "After Victory, Airbnb Compares Its Influence to the NRA's," *Wired*, November 14, 2015, https://www.wired.com/2015/11/after-victory-airbnb-compares-its-influence-to -the-nras/.

8. Ibid.

9. Heather Kelly, "Airbnb wants to turn hosts into 'grassroots' activists," CNN, November 4, 2015, http://money.cnn.com/2015/11/04/technology/airbnb-after-prop-f/index.html.

10. Ibid.

11. Ibid.

12. Carolyn Said, "Prop. F: S.F. Voters Reject Measure to Restrict Airbnb Rentals," *SFGate*, November 4, 2015, http://www.sfgate.com/bayarea/article/Prop-F-Measure-to-restrict-Airbnb -rentals-6609176.php.

13. Ibid.

14. Alba, "After Victory."

15. Katy Steinmetz, "Inside Airbnb's Plan to Build a Grassroots Political Movement," *Time*, July 21, 2016, http://time.com/4416136/airbnb-politics-sharing-economy-regulations -housing/.

16. "Home Sharing Clubs," Airbnb, accessed February 9, 2018, https://community.withairbnb .com/t5/Home-Sharing-Clubs/ct-p/en_clubs.

17. Kelly, "Airbnb wants to turn hosts."

18. Ken Yeung, "How Airbnb bought San Francisco's vote with $8M—and how it'll defend itself nationwide," November 4, 2015, https://venturebeat.com/2015/11/04/how-airbnb -bought-san-franciscos-vote-with-8m-and-how-itll-defend-itself-nationwide/.

19. Alison Griswold, "Airbnb Just Threw Away Its Most Valuable Card in the Sharing Economy," *Slate*, October 22, 2015, http://www.slate.com/blogs/moneybox/2015/10/22/airbnb_s_tax _ads_in_san_francisco_lost_it_the_nice_guy_edge_in_the_sharing.html.

20. Alba, "After Victory."

CHAPTER 14: THE GRASSTOPS

1. Kelly Yamanouchi, "Technology Reducing Wait Times at Customs," *Atlanta Journal-Constitution*, June 12, 2015, http://www.ajc.com/travel/technology-reducing-wait-times -customs/pYb7PNkL8WivIONXe2rFWI/.

2. Catherine Ho, "Drinker Biddle & Reath cultivates the 'grass tops' over grass roots," *The Washington Post*, November 18, 2012, https://www.washingtonpost.com/business/capitalbusiness /drinker-biddle-and-reath-cultivates-the-grass-tops-over-grass-roots/2012/11/16 /f1825f08-2dc2-11e2-89d4-040c9330702a_story.html?utm_term=.9a74d0003c55.

CHAPTER 15: LOBBYING

1. "H.B. No. 3693," Texas Legislature Online, May 23, 2007, http://www.capitol.state.tx.us/tlodocs/80R/billtext/doc/HB03693F.doc.
2. "Invariant LLC: Summary," OpenSecrets, January 24, 2018, https://www.opensecrets.org/lobby/firmsum.php?id=D000034396.
3. Manuel Roig-Franzia, "Heather Podesta, a Storm in the Summer of the Lobbyist," *The Washington Post*, August 24, 2009, http://www.washingtonpost.com/wp-dyn/content/article/2009/08/23/AR2009082302381.html.
4. "Groups That Have Retained Invariant LLC," Center for Responsive Politics, February 28, 2018, https://www.opensecrets.org/lobby/firmsum.php?id=D000034396.
5. Nick Bernabe, "Corporations Lobbying Government Reap 76,000% Return on Investment," March 18, 2015, http://www.mintpressnews.com/corporations-lobbying-government-reap-76000-return-on-investment/203447/.
6. "Top Spenders," Center for Responsive Politics, January 24, 2018, https://www.opensecrets.org/lobby/top.php?showYear=2017&indexType=s.
7. Matthew Flamm, "Bradley Tusk made $100 million helping Uber conquer New York, and he's not apologizing," *Crain's Chicago Business,* September 13, 2017, http://www.chicagobusiness.com/article/20170913/NEWS02/170919947/bradley-tusk-made-100-million-helping-uber-conquer-new-york-and-hes-not-apologizing.

CONCLUSION: ELON MUSK: THE ULTIMATE REGULATORY HACKER

1. Andrew J. Hawkins, "How Tesla changed the auto industry forever," The Verge, July 28, 2017, https://www.theverge.com/2017/7/28/16059954/tesla-model-3-2017-auto-industry-influence-elon-musk.
2. Danielle Muoio, "Everything we know about Elon Musk's ambitious Hyperloop plan," *Business Insider*, August 17, 2017, http://www.businessinsider.com/elon-musk-hyperloop-plan-boring-company-2017-8.
3. Mike Wall, "Elon Musk Tweaks His Audacious Plan to Put People on Mars," NBC News, September 29, 2017, https://www.nbcnews.com/mach/science/elon-musk-tweaks-his-audacious-plan-put-people-mars-ncna805891.
4. Collins Eban, "To maximize the life of humanity, we must create a self sustaining city on Mars—Elon Musk," Technicollit, September 26, 2016, http://technicollit.com/elon-musk-wants-to-create-a-self-sustaining-city-on-mars-to-save-humanity/.
5. Ashlee Vance, *Elon Musk: Tesla, SpaceX, and the Quest for a Fantastic Future* (New York: Ecco, 2015).
6. Bloomberg, "Elon Musk: How I Became the Real 'Iron Man,'" YouTube, June 10, 2014, video, 44:59, https://www.youtube.com/watch?v=mh45igK4Esw.
7. Ibid.
8. Vance, *Elon Musk.*
9. Ezra Klein, "Elon Musk believes we are probably characters in some advanced civilization's video game," Vox, June 2, 2016, https://www.vox.com/2016/6/2/11837608/elon-musk-simulation-argument.
10. Vance, *Elon Musk.*
11. Daven Hiskey, "Robert Downey Jr. Modeled His Portrayal of Tony Stark after Elon Musk, One of the Founders of Zip2, PayPal, Tesla Motors, Solar City, and SpaceX," Today I Found Out, August 5, 2011, http://www.todayifoundout.com/index.php/2011/08/robert-downey-jr-modeled-his-portrayal-of-tony-stark-after-elon-musk-one-of-the-founders-of-zip2-paypal-tesla-motors-and-spacex/.

12. Amanda Schaffer, "Tech's Enduring Great-Man Myth," *MIT Technology Review*, August 4, 2015, https://www.technologyreview.com/s/539861/techs-enduring-great-man-myth/.

13. Ananya Bhattacharya, "5 Great Elon Musk Quotes on Innovation," *Inc.*, March 20, 2015, https://www.inc.com/ananya-bhattacharya/5-elon-musk-quotes-about-innovation.html.

14. Rod Pyle, "Glitz, Glam and SpaceX: Inside Elon Musk's Dragon V2 Spaceship (Video)," Space, May 30, 2014, https://www.space.com/26068-elon-musk-spacex-dragon-v2-glam-reveal.html.

15. Joseph Stromberg, "SpaceX's new Dragon capsule could be the future of space travel," Vox, May 30, 2014, https://www.vox.com/2014/5/30/5764124/spacexs-new-dragon-capsule-could-be-the-future-of-space-travel.

16. Colin Schultz, "SpaceX Will Soon Be Able to Send People to Space. (Take That, Russia.)," May 30, 2014, *Smithsonian Magazine*, https://www.smithsonianmag.com/smart-news/spacex-will-soon-be-able-send-people-space-take-russia-180951618/.

17. Josh Downey, "Tesla Advertising: It's All About PR," *Platform*, March 10, 2017, http://platformmagazine.org/2017/03/10/tesla-advertising-its-all-about-pr/.

18. Barry Fischer, "The Remarkable Reason that Solar is Going Viral in These 10 American Cities," Solar City, May 4, 2016, http://blog.solarcity.com/most-contagious-solar-cities/.

19. John M. Broder, "Stalled Out on Tesla's Electric Highway," *The New York Times*, February 8, 2013, http://www.nytimes.com/2013/02/10/automobiles/stalled-on-the-ev-highway.html.

20. Bloomberg, "Elon Musk: How I Became the Real 'Iron Man.'"

21. Elon Musk, "A Most Peculiar Test Drive," Tesla, February 13, 2013, https://www.tesla.com/blog/MOST-PECULIAR-TEST-DRIVE.

22. Margaret Sullivan, "Problems With Precision and Judgment, but Not Integrity, in Tesla Test," *The New York Times*, February 18, 2013, https://publiceditor.blogs.nytimes.com/2013/02/18/problems-with-precision-and-judgment-but-not-integrity-in-tesla-test/.

23. Peter Elkind, "Inside Elon Musk's $1.4 Billion Score," *Fortune*, November 14, 2014, http://fortune.com/inside-elon-musks-billion-dollar-gigafactory/.

24. Benjamin Spillman, "Elon Musk talks about Tesla's Nevada tax breaks," July 27, 2016, http://www.rgj.com/story/money/business/2016/07/27/elon-musk-talks-teslas-nevada-tax-breaks/87635566/.

25. Matt McFarland, "SolarCity hires former Obama strategist to ignite a grass-roots movement for solar energy," *The Washington Post*, December 17, 2014, https://www.washingtonpost.com/news/innovations/wp/2014/12/17/solarcity-hires-former-obama-strategist-to-ignite-a-grassroots-movement-for-solar-energy/.

26. "SolarCity's Jon Carson on Building a Solar Movement," Yale School of Management, November 4, 2015, https://som.yale.edu/news/2015/11/solarcitys-jon-carson-building-solar-movement.

27. Ibid.

28. Peter B. de Selding, "SpaceX wins 5 new space station cargo missions in NASA contract estimated at $700 million," Space News, February 24, 2016, http://spacenews.com/spacex-wins-5-new-space-station-cargo-missions-in-nasa-contract-estimated-at-700-million/.

29. Susan Crabtree, "Tesla Inc. Spent $565K Lobbying for Fed Subsidies Musk Says He Doesn't Need," *Washington Free Beacon*, June 5, 2017, http://freebeacon.com/issues/tesla-inc-spent-565k-lobbying-fed-subsides-musk-says-doesnt-need/.

30. Ryan Grim and Jason Cherkis, "Elon Musk, SpaceX Founder, Battles Entrenched Rivals Over NASA Contracts," Huffington Post, February 28, 2013, https://www.huffingtonpost.com/2013/02/20/elon-musk-spacex_n_2727312.html.

31. MulliganBrothers, "Elon Musk Incredible Speech-Motivational Video 2017," YouTube, October 29, 2017, video, 23:42, https://www.youtube.com/watch?v=wD3pflBggMQ.

Index